Barns

12

# Mobile Homes
and the Law

AUSTRALIA AND NEW ZEALAND
The Law Book Company Ltd.
Sydney: Melbourne: Perth

CANADA AND U.S.A.
The Carswell Company Ltd.
Agincourt, Ontario

INDIA
N.M. Tripathi Private Ltd.
Bombay
*and*
Eastern Law House Private Ltd.
Calcutta and Delhi
M.P.P. House
Bangalore

ISRAEL
Steimatzky's Agency Ltd.
Jerusalem: Tel Aviv: Haifa

MALAYSIA: SINGAPORE: BRUNEI
Malayan Law Journal (Pte.) Ltd.
Singapore and Kuala Lumpur

PAKISTAN
Pakistan Law House
Karachi

# Mobile Homes and the Law

by

## C. M. Brand, LL.B.

*Solicitor*
*Lecturer in Law*
*at the University of Liverpool*

LONDON
SWEET & MAXWELL
1986

Published in 1986 by
Sweet & Maxwell Limited
11 New Fetter Lane, London
Computerset by
Promenade Graphics Limited
Cheltenham, Gloucestershire
Printed in Scotland

**British Library Cataloguing in Publication Data**

Brand, Clive
Mobile homes and the law.
1. Mobile homes—Law and legislation—
England
I. Title
344.2064'3      KD1154.M6

ISBN 0-421-33470-3

# Preface

The law relating to mobile homes derives its substance from a number of different fields of law as well as being documented in three principal Acts of Parliament which are directly relevant to the subject. While the Caravan Sites and Control of Development Act 1960, the Caravan Sites Act 1968, and the Mobile Homes Act 1983 provide the main statutory contribution, the subject extends well beyond their scope into town and country planning law, as well as aspects of housing, landlord and tenant, highways, public health, and rating law. An examination of these topics reveals an intricate and complex web of law, the growth of which has obscured the historical roots which lie, principally, in public health law. The rapid evolution of the mobile home, from the comparatively humble static caravan to one which is highly sophisticated and which compares favourably with bricks-and-mortar housing, has produced a steady flow of case law. While judicial activity has been largely concerned with statutory interpretation, some of the desicion-making has been conducted against the background that a mobile home is not necessarily to be regarded as a mere chattel placed on land. It has now become clear that a mobile home is, in some instances, to be treated as a house or bungalow, thereby making applicable legislation which may originally have been drafted without mobile homes in mind, for example the Rent Act 1977.

*Mobile Homes and the Law* is presented in the hope that it will be a practical guide for all those who have cause to inquire into the legal aspects of mobile homes, whether they be professional advisors, central or local government officers, commercial caravan site operators, or residents. With a view to enabling non-lawyers to develop an understanding of the principles of the relevant law, I have endeavoured to avoid using a writing style which only lawyers can be expected to decipher. At the same time I have not been deterred from giving appropriate space to the more demanding aspects of the subject, thus furthering an attempt to be reasonably comprehensive. In trying to maintain a balance between these twin objectives I trust I have not provided ammunition for those who regard them as incompatible.

Although I must bear the responsibility for any errors, I have a number of people to thank for their generous help in the course of preparation of the text. I am particularly grateful to Joe Finn, Executive Administrator of the National Federation of Site Operators (the industry's representative body), who provided access to data compiled by the Federation on a number of matters, and whose enthusiasm for the project helped overcome the occasional bout of flagging spirits. My thanks are also extended to Eric Stocker, of Messrs. Tozers, solicitors, who as legal advisor to the National Federation of Site Operators was kind enough to read the first draft of some of the chapters and to make some helpful suggestions for their development. Miss K. Thomas of the Directorate of Rural Affairs, Department of the Environment, was also particularly helpful among the civil servants I consulted. Last, but certainly not least, I extend my thanks to the secretarial staff of the Faculty of Law, Liverpool University, for their rapid and accurate transformation of my handwriting into an attractive typescript.

I have attempted to describe the law as it stood on February 26, 1986. I have, however, anticipated the coming into force of the Local Government Act 1985 and the Housing Act 1985, both of which are effective from April 1, 1986.

C. M. Brand
Liverpool.

February, 1986.

# Contents

## Chapters

## Appendices

# Table of Cases

# Table of Statutes

# Table of Statutory Instruments

# 1. Introduction to the Mobile Homes Legislation

The use of mobile homes, as the larger type of residential caravans are now popularly known, for permanent accommodation is very much a post-war innovation in housing provision. The modern type of mobile home, particularly of the "twin-unit" variety, offers quite spacious living facilities which can be favourably compared to a small flat. Yet it was not many years ago that caravan life was commonly thought of as the lot of those who could not afford bricks and mortar homes and who had to make do with such accommodation as they could find. A comparison of two major government investigations into the use of mobile homes reveals the changes that took place in the space of less than twenty years. It is noticeable that the first of these, the report of Sir Arton Wilson entitled *Caravans as Homes* Cmnd. 872 (1959) does not even use the term "mobile home," while the second investigation, the result of a study carried out within the Department of the Environment entitled *Report of the Mobile Homes Review* (1977) only occasionally uses the word "caravan." In the case of the latter report it is explained that "the term 'mobile home' seems to have been devised to distinguish residential homes from the touring and static holiday caravans from which they have evolved." Although support was given to the use of the term "mobile home" the report's authors warned that "It may . . . help to promote the unfortunate and to a large extent outdated image of the mobile home as an impermanent and unsatisfactory form of accommodation": para. 1.1.2.

The report of Sir Arton Wilson, (hereafter referred to as "the Wilson Report") although admirably drafted, makes cheerless reading. In a thorough examination of the then comparatively new phenomenon of caravan life on a large scale, the report speaks well of caravan occupants but identifies a common intent amongst them to give up caravan life if a conventional house were to become available to them. A notable exception to the general view was, however, clearly discernible amongst middle-aged and elderly people, for whom a caravan offers an easily managed, self-contained home and the opportunity to realise capital on the sale of their former house. The commonest sources of difficulty encountered by those who wished to abandon caravan living were attributable to poor caravan designs, lack of security of tenure, inadequate regulation of the environment and management of caravan sites, and difficulty in finding suitable sites on which the caravan could be stationed.

At the time of the Wilson report, about 60,000 caravans in England and Wales were being used as permanent homes by about 150,000 people on approximately 13,000 sites. The figures which appear in the *Mobile Homes*

*Review* are 67,000, 147,000 and 9,000 respectively. Thus while the number of sites dropped considerably, the use of mobile homes—to adopt the latter report's term—increased slightly, and these were situated on larger and better-equipped sites, developed mainly from those which had previously existed. Figures kindly supplied to the author by the National Federation of Caravan Site Operators Ltd. indicate that in 1984 there were still fewer sites but a further increase in the number of mobile homes in permanent residential use. Use of these sites has been seen to change from the predominantly young couples observed by Sir Arton Wilson, in that the majority of users are now aged forty or over, although all age groups are represented. These persons were found by the 1977 *Review* to be generally well contented with their homes and site conditions and about 90 per cent. were owner-occupiers.

These changes in the attitudes of mobile home dwellers can be attributed to a number of factors. Improved designs—mobile homes must now conform to British Standard 3632 of 1970, although not yet to the Building Regulations standards applicable to conventional housing—have noticeably raised the quality of life. Credit must, however, be given in particular to parliamentary intervention. The Wilson report led directly to the Caravan Sites and Control of Development Act 1960, which greatly increased the powers of local authorities to regulate conditions on caravan sites of all kinds; that Act was later supplemented by security of tenure provisions contained in the Caravan Sites Act 1968 and the Mobile Homes Act 1975. Although the 1975 Act was only a qualified success, a discussion of the reasons for which occupies a significant part of the 1977 *Mobile Homes Review*, it was replaced with the much-improved though not entirely flawless Mobile Homes Act 1983.

Although this book is mainly concerned with the legal aspects of mobile homes used as permanent accommodation, it also deals with the rights and obligations of other types of caravan user. Thus holiday caravans, touring caravans, and gypsy caravans all come within the scope of the text. That this is the case is due not only to the desire to give as broad an account as possible within the space available, but in particular to the fact that the law uses a definition of a "caravan" which embraces both the mobile home as well as other forms of caravan. Before this point can be investigated further, however, it is necessary to undertake a brief survey of the development of legal provision for caravans and caravan sites.

## Legal provision for caravans prior to 1960

In the same way that modern, spacious mobile homes have been developed from touring and static caravans, so, also, were caravans developed from very unsophisticated structures which the law simply termed a "van." In using this word the law treated a "van" in exactly the same way as a tent, perhaps reflecting that such shelters were commonly used by the economically disadvantaged, often as a matter of necessity, rather than choice.

Bearing this point in mind it is apparent that the early development of legal provision for caravan sites shows two significant characteristics (i) the assimilation of caravans with tents, and (ii) that the law has its roots in the Public Health Acts. While the first of these characteristics ceased to apply in 1960 when the Caravan Sites and Control of Development Act 1960 was enacted, the latter is still relevant, albeit with much reduced significance.

It is necessary to go back a century to find any reference in an Act of Parliament to what we now recognise as a caravan. The first such reference is to be found in section 9(1) of the Housing of the Working Classes Act 1885 which applied the nuisance control provisions of section 91 of the Public Health Act 1875 to a "tent, van, shed or similar structure used for human habitation which is in such a state as to be a nuisance or injurious to health . . . ." Section 9(2) of the 1885 Act went on to provide for the making of byelaws by local authorities "for promoting cleanliness in and the habitable condition of tents, vans, sheds and similar structures used for human habitation . . . ." Although these provisions were repealed by the Public Health Act 1936 they were substantially re-enacted with amendments in section 268 of that Act, a section which still remains in force. (See further, Chapter 9.) Of particular significance, however, was the recognition by the Public Health Act 1936 that tents and caravans were not necessarily always to be thought of as inferior shelters to be treated with disdain and caution. This arose from greater mobility from access to private transport which, in turn, led to the phenomenon of holiday use of caravans mainly by persons enjoying above-average incomes. That the Public Health Act 1936 recognised this change in caravan use is clear from section 269 of the Act, which introduced a system of licensing of caravan and tent sites, structures which were collectively described as "moveable dwellings." In broad terms, the section required a licence to be obtained from the local authority if an occupier of land wished to use it for camping purposes for more than 42 consecutive days or more than 60 days in any period of twelve months, and it became an offence to contravene the section by permitting camping in excess of the stated periods without a licence, or by failure to comply with any conditions subject to which the licence was issued.

While section 269 of the 1936 Act still applies to tent sites, caravan sites were removed from its scope when the Caravan Sites and Control of Development Act 1960 came into force on August 29, 1960. Thus section 30 of the 1960 Act expressly provides that section 269 of the Public Health Act 1936 "shall cease to have effect in relation to caravans." This marked a radical change in the law since the 1960 Act arose from the need to make more extensive provision for public health and amenity matters affecting caravan sites, over which the licensing system of the 1936 Act had given inadequate powers, particularly in relation to sites on which caravans were permanently situated. The enactment of the Caravan Sites and Control of Development Act 1960 thus brought into being a new site licensing régime applicable only to caravan sites used for human habitation (though not necessarily on a permanent basis).

One further matter must be mentioned at this stage. On July 1, 1948, the modern town and country planning system came into existence under the Town and Country Planning Act 1947. This Act imposed a general control over development of land and thereby required planning permission to be obtained before a new caravan or tent site could be established, thus safeguarding land from the possible detrimental effect on amenity which the establishment of such sites can involve. This was especially relevant to caravans since the need for accommodation in the immediate post-war period led to a very rapid growth in the number of sites, the amenity aspects

3

of which section 269 of the Public Health Act 1936 was powerless to safeguard, a view which was confirmed by the Divisional Court in *Pilling* v. *Abergele U.D.C.* (1950). In this case, Lord Goddard C.J. decided that section 269 was concerned only with matters relating to public health and sanitary conditions, and that questions of amenity were the province of the town and country planning legislation.

It might appear from the foregoing that the provisions of the Public Health Act 1936 and the Town and Country Planning Act 1947, operating together, made adequate provision for regulation of caravan sites. This did not prove to be the case, however, and problems arising from use of land as a caravan site became the commonest source of litigation under the 1947 Act. This was due in part to the enforcement provisions proving excessively cumbersome, to the inadequate scope of section 269 of the Public Health Act 1936, and to abuses by site operators who unscrupulously took advantage of exemptions under both the planning and public health legislation which were originally designed to enable temporary sites to be formed without excessive local government control. Where site operators filled a site with persons needing permanent pitches for their caravans, the local authorities were effectively saddled with the problem of re-siting the residents if they chose to clear sites which had been in existence longer than the permitted temporary periods. The Wilson report disclosed that some 3,000 caravan sites were operating without planning permission, and (as has been mentioned) it was in response to this report that the Caravan Sites and Control of Development Act 1960 was enacted. This Act not only amended the system of enforcement of planning control but also enacted a special scheme of control over caravan sites which operates in addition to the normal town and country planning system and which has a direct connection with it. In general terms, the planning legislation continues to determine where sites can be situated, but leaves the internal management of them to the conditions attached to the site licence which must be obtained under the 1960 Act. The link between two schemes is that no site licence can be obtained unless a prior grant of planning permission for the site has also been obtained.

## Contemporary law

The law relating to caravans (and mobile homes) continues to be based on statutory provisions. The main statutes are the Caravan Sites and Control of Development Act 1960, the Caravan Sites Act 1968, and the Mobile Homes Act 1983. These statutes control two main features of caravan occupation, namely the regulation of conditions to be found on caravan sites, and security of tenure for persons who occupy caravans belonging to the site operator following the grant of a licence or tenancy agreement by him. The Mobile Homes Act 1983 is applicable to owner-occupiers of mobile homes, and confers (as a general observation) indefinite security of tenure on owner-occupiers in circumstances where their caravans are placed on site "pitches" under licences or tenancy agreements granted by the site operator.

To these main statutes must be added a variety of other provisions. Of particular relevance are some features of the Rent Act 1977, the Highways Act 1980 (dealing with caravans situated on the verges of highways), the

Public Health Act 1936, and the Rating (Caravan Sites) Act 1976. Of fundamental importance, however, is the Town and Country Planning Act 1971, together with the many subsequent amendments which have been made to that Act.

All of the relevant statutes are explained at appropriate points in this book, together with many of the leading cases to which their interpretation has given rise, but an initial statement must here be made of the significance of the Town and Country Planning Act 1971. This Act, like the earlier statutes it replaced dating from the Town and Country Planning Act 1947, is concerned with the regulation of the control of development of land. The stationing of a caravan or group of caravans on land is frequently to be treated under the Town and Country Planning Act 1971 as an act of "development," for which planning permission is required; this is obtainable from, usually, the relevant district council or London borough council in whose area the development takes place. It may not be apparent at first sight that this part of the legislation is that to which initial reference must often be made, for without a grant of planning permission for a caravan site the legislation dealing with site conditions and security of tenure takes on a lesser significance.

The regulation of grants of planning permission is the function of local planning authorities—the district councils and London boroughs mentioned above—which have discretionary powers to determine where sites for caravans shall be permitted to be established. Only after a successful application for planning permission has been made can a site licence be issued under the Caravan Sites and Control of Development Act 1960. As will be seen, a caravan site which lacks a grant of planning permission (and hence a site licence) is potentially the subject of enforcement proceedings on the part of the local planning authority involving severe financial penalties for non-compliance. Although the penalties which can be imposed for failure to comply with the site licencing provisions of the 1960 Act are also monetary, only enforcement proceedings taken by the local planning authority can secure the removal of caravans and restoration of the previous conditions prevailing on the land. The requirements of the 1960 Act are therefore especially relevant when planning permission has been granted but the stipulations of the site licence have not been observed by the site operator. While both the 1960 and 1971 Acts have features in common, *e.g.* the objective of control of amenity, the 1960 Act has the advantage of involving a less cumbersome enforcement procedure.

## Definitions of "caravan" and "mobile home"

The definition of a "caravan" appears in section 29(1) of the Caravan Sites and Control of Development Act 1960. This section provides that a caravan is:

> "any structure designed or adapted for human habitation which is capable of being moved from one place to another (whether by being towed, or by being transported on a motor vehicle or trailer) and any motor vehicle so designed or adapted, but does not include
> (a) any railway rolling stock which is for the time being on rails forming part of the railway system, or
> (b) any tent."

5

The growing popularity in the 1960's of the larger types of caravan, usually referred to as "twin-unit caravans," generated some doubt as to whether such caravans came within the definition given by the 1960 Act. To avoid difficulty, the definition was expanded by the Caravan Sites Act 1968. Section 13 of that Act provides that a caravan composed of not more than two sections which does not, when assembled, exceed 60 feet in length (exclusive of any tow bar), 20 feet in width, and 10 feet overall height of living accommodation (measured internally), is to be treated as a caravan falling within the definition given by section 29(1) of the 1960 Act. These dimensions are capable of being altered by a statutory instrument made by the Secretary of State for the Environment, though to date the dimensions stated continue to apply.

It should be appreciated that the scope of the definition, as amended, is a broad one. Included within it are dormobiles and touring caravanettes and even railway carriages taken off the railway system which have been adapted for human habitation. It also includes a houseboat, though the fact that river craft are not normally stationed upon land excludes a houseboat from most of the provisions relating to caravan sites: *Roy Crimble Ltd.* v. *Edgecombe* (1981). The limitations of the definition of a caravan were fully exposed, however, by the decision in *Backer* v. *Secretary of State for the Environment* (1983). In this case a local planning authority served an enforcement notice under the Town and Country Planning Act 1971 requiring the removal of caravans from the land in question. One such "caravan" comprised an old Commer van, into the rear of which had been placed a bed, valor stoves, cupboards, filing cabinets and clothing. The defendant appealed against the enforcement notice to the Secretary of State for the Environment who upheld the notice in favour of the local planning authority. A further appeal was made to the High Court contending that the Commer van was not a "caravan" within the meaning of section 29(1) of the 1960 Act, the same definition being equally applicable to proceedings under the Town and Country Planning Act 1971. The High Court upheld the appeal and decided that the words "designed or adapted" in section 29(1) were inapplicable to the present structure, since the Commer van was clearly not designed for human habitation; nor was it "adapted" since no physical alteration of it had taken place. The mere fact that it was equipped by the defendant for living in was not enough to render it a "caravan." Accommodation in this form is therefore outside the scope of the legislation.

Although the enforcement action failed in respect of the van in the *Backer* case, the strict approach to the interpretation of the word "caravan" can be equally disadvantageous to a person who does not comply exactly with a grant of planning permission to station a caravan on land for residential purposes. In an appeal decision given by the Secretary of State reported at [1982] J.P.L. 265, planning permission for a "residential caravan" was held to have been exceeded when a structure on wheels and supported by jacks, having dimensions of 45 feet long and 20 feet wide was brought onto the site. The structure looked like a permanent pitched roof bungalow and contained a living room, dining room, kitchen, bathroom and four bedrooms. While none of these features prevented the structure constituting a "caravan," it was found to be composed of more than two separately constructed parts and assembled on the site. In this respect, therefore, the structure exceeded the provisions of section 13 of the Caravan Sites Act 1968 and hence the limits of the planning permission granted.

The term "mobile home" is not defined separately from the word "caravan." Thus, the Mobile Homes Act 1983 equates them by providing in section 5(1) that "mobile home" has the same meaning as "caravan" in the Caravan Sites and Control of Development Act 1960. These terms are therefore interchangeable, though the use of the expression "mobile home" is commonly used to suggest a structure of substantial size, often of the twin-unit variety. In this book, "caravan" has been used more frequently than "mobile home," perhaps because the former appears more often in the relevant legislation and judicial decisions, though it should be clear to the reader that no special inference is to be drawn from this. It may also be borne in mind that, as Lord Denning M.R. pointed out in *Taylor* v. *Calvert* (1978), the term "mobile home" is virtually a misnomer for, once placed on a site, it is not often that such a structure is moved from one place to another.

### Development control and the meaning of "development"

Opportunity has already been taken in this Chapter to emphasise the importance of the Town and Country Planning Act 1971. Chapters 2 and 3 explain in some detail the circumstances in which planning permission is needed for stationing a caravan, or group of caravans, and the enforcement powers of the local planning authority if a breach of development control occurs. Those Chapters assume a working understanding of the development control system and so the basic principles of the relevant law, are explained here.

The entire system of development control revolves around the definition of "development" in section 22(1) of the 1971 Act, which is:

> "the carrying out of building, engineering, mining or other operations in, on, over or under land, or the making of any material change in the use of any buildings or other land."

The importance of this definition is emphasised by section 23 which provides that "planning permission is required for the carrying out of any development of land."

Examination of the definition contained in section 22(1) shows it to be in two parts. The first part is concerned with building and engineering activities on the land and includes mining and "other operations." Most acts of development falling within this part of the definition are constructional, involving the building of new structures on the land. The scope of the definition is, however, very great, as illustrated by the well-known case of *Barvis* v. *Secretary of State for the Environment* (1971). A crane eighty-nine feet high ran on tracks but was often dismantled and loaned on hire for construction work. When not so hired, it was used by the owners of the crane on the land concerned. The court held that the crane constituted "development" of the land despite the periodic absence of the structure from the site. A model village was held in *Buckinghamshire County Council* v. *Callingham* (1952) to be a "structure or erection" and hence "development" because the word "building," in section 22(1), is further defined in s.290(1) of the 1971 Act to include any structure or erection. The scope of this part of the definition is also further illustrated by *Scholes* v. *Minister of Housing and Local Govern-*

7

ment (1966) in which it was held that the replacement of a hedge by a fence constituted development requiring planning permission.

The second part of the definition deals with the making of any material change in the use of any buildings or other land. The word "material" is particularly important, for an act of development does not automatically follow from making a change of use in the building or land concerned: it must be a *material* change before planning permission is required. It is not possible to give a precise account of when a change of use is "material" since neither the 1971 Act nor the cases give a complete answer to the question. The view taken by the Secretary of State for the Environment is that there must be a substantial difference between the new use and the old use to qualify as "material." Whether a change of use is a material change is one of fact and degree mixed with law. The approach to be adopted was explained by Lord Parker C.J. in *Devonshire County Council* v. *Allens Caravans (Estates) Ltd.* (1962) who pointed out that "the materiality to be considered is a materiality from a planning point of view and in particular the question of amenities." The case itself involved a change of use of a holiday tent site to a holiday caravan site in use for the summer months only. The Divisional Court refused to disturb the Secretary of State's view that no material change of use had taken place.

In considering a possible material change of use, regard must always be had to the planning unit. This will normally be the whole of the land involved rather than the specific portion of it which is the subject of the change of use. Lord Widgery C.J. pointed out in *Johnston* v. *Secretary of State for the Environment* (1974) that "prima facie the planning unit is the area occupied as a single holding by a single occupier." Thus, where several garages had been let and one of them was the subject of a purported material change of use, the planning unit was the single garage in question rather than the whole of the garages which had been let in the block.

Many "material change of use" problems are solved by reference to the Town and Country Planning (Use Classes) Order 1972 (S.I. 1972 No. 1385). This Order was made by the Secretary of State under a power conferred by section 22(2)(f) of the 1971 Act. The effect of the Order is to specify a number of different classes of use (18 in all), so that a change of use from a use specified in a use class to a new use in the same use class is deemed not to involve development. The various classes of use cover, *e.g.* shops, offices, and various industrial processes. Despite the great importance of the Order—due to its wide scope—it is unlikely to require consideration in the context of caravans, but is nevertheless mentioned here in the interests of completeness.

### "Permitted development"

Not all acts of development require an express grant of planning permission. This is because planning permission is deemed to be granted for a large number of relatively minor acts of development in accordance with an Order made by the Secretary of State for the Environment pursuant to a power conferred by section 24 of the 1971 Act. The Town and Country Planning General Development Order 1977 (S.I. 1977 No. 289), as amended by the Town and Country Planning General Development (Amendment) Orders 1981 and 1985 (S.I.s 1981 No. 245, 1985 No. 1101 and 1985 No. 1981) is usually referred to simply as "the GDO." This sets out 30 classes of development for which planning permission is automatically granted; the classes of so-called "permitted development" are detailed in Schedule 1 to the GDO. It will be seen in Chapter 2 that Class XXII is relevant to caravan developments as this confers planning permission for numerous temporary caravan sites and confers special exemptions on members of exempted organisations.

### Applying for planning permission

When planning permission is not automatically granted by the GDO, the proposed development in question will require an express grant of planning permission. An application for planning permission is required to be made in writing in accordance with article 5 of the GDO and accompanied by a plan sufficient to identify the land to which it relates together with plans and drawings to describe the development proposed. No prescribed form of application is used but each local planning authority (usually the district council or London borough) issues forms for use in making an application. Up to three further copies of the application form and the plans and drawings must also be submitted before the application will be considered. It must be accompanied by a fee as specified in the Town and Country Planning (Fees for Applications and Deemed Applications) Regulations 1983 (S.I. 1983 No. 1674), as amended by the Town and Country Planning (Fees for Applications and Deemed Applications) (Amendment) Regulations 1985 (S.I. 1985 No. 1182), made by the Secretary of State, pursuant to section 87 of the Local Government, Planning and Land Act 1980.

Anyone can apply for planning permission so there is no need to acquire any interest in the land beforehand. The applicant must, however, certify whether or not he is the owner of the land and, if not, whether he has notified those having an interest in the land affected by the application. Sometimes the applicant will not know the identity of these persons, or may have identified only some of them. In both cases, he must certify accordingly that he has taken reasonable steps to identify the persons concerned, including local newspaper advertisements. Once the relevant notifications have been made, at least 21 days must elapse before the application is determined: section 27. Special provision is also made by section 27 to protect agricultural tenants: these parties must be notified since the grant of planning permission may prejudice their security of tenure under the Agricultural Holdings Acts 1948–84.

Notification of persons who have interests in neighbouring land is not, in general, required in respect of applications for planning permission. Some provision for notifying neighbours exists, however, pursuant to section 26 of the 1971 Act and article 8 of the GDO. These provisions list a number of types of development generally referred to as "bad neighbour" development, which include the construction of buildings for use as public conveniences. Although the use of land as a caravan site is not expressly included, the Secretary of State took the view in the planning appeal decision reported at [1983] J.P.L. 138, that a planning application for a caravan site should be subjected to the requirements of section 26 if it is inherent in the development proposed that there will be a need to provide toilet facilities on the site. The requirements are that a site notice must be placed on the land in a conspicious position for at least seven days in the month preceding the making of the application and a newspaper notification must also be made. If such measures are not taken the local planning authority is unable to entertain the application: section 26(2).

On receipt of an application, plus the supporting documents and fee, the local planning authority must give written acknowledgment of receipt and enter a copy of the application in part I of a register maintained pursuant to section 34 of the 1971 Act. This part of the register (commonly referred to as "the planning register") records all applications for planning permission on which a decision is pending. A period of up to eight weeks is permitted by article 7(6) of the GDO for the making of a decision on the application, unless a longer period is agreed in writing with the local planning authority. In reaching their decision, the local planning authority are directed by section 29 of the Act to "have regard to the provisions of the development plan and to any other material considerations," and may then reach one of three possible decisions. These are (a) to grant planning permission unconditionally, or (b) to grant planning permission subject to such conditions as they think fit, or (c) to refuse planning permission. If the local planning authority fail to reach a decision within eight weeks, or any longer period previously agreed, the application is deemed to be refused, pursuant to section 37 of the 1971 Act. The decision is recorded in part II of the planning register.

The matters referred to in section 29, the "development plan" and "other material considerations" require a brief explanation. The point of the development plan is that it provides the essential context within which the decision will be made and contains the details of the planning policies of the authority which made the plan. The development plan consists outside London and metropolitan areas, of the structure plan and any local plans which are applicable to the area. The former is an obligatory plan prepared by each county council setting out the general proposals and policies of the county council in relation to the development and other use of land in the area of the plan (including measures for improvement of the physical environment and the management of traffic). The plan is prepared in accordance with sections 6–10 of the 1971 Act and the Town and Country Planning (Structure Plans and Local Plans) Regulations 1982 (S.I. 1982 No. 555), and consists of a memorandum and written statement (but not a map). Local plans take the policies and proposals of the structure plan a step further and show how the structure plan is to be implemented in the area covered by the local plan. Whereas structure plan preparation is carried out by county councils pursuant to a statutory duty, the preparation of local plans is primarily a discretionary power conferred on district councils; it follows, therefore, that there will not always be a local plan for the area in question. It must be appreciated, however, that more than one local plan can exist having relevance to the same land. Thus there may be a district plan (one dealing with the consideration of the totality of matters affecting the development of the relevant area), or a subject plan (one which deals with a particular type of development, e.g. caravan sites), or an action area plan (relevant only to action areas identified in the structure plan as requiring specific attention). Preparation of these plans is regulated by sections 11–20 of the 1971 Act, together with the Town and Country Planning (Structure Plans and Local Plans) Regulations 1982.

A variation on the general scheme of development plans described above is applicable in London and in metropolitan areas. In these areas a scheme for the making of unitary development plans applies, pursuant to section 4 of and Schedule 1 to the Local Government Act 1985. These areas are presently subject to the structure and local plans made pursuant to the Town and Country Planning Act 1971, but which will be superseded when the unitary plans are made.

The importance of the development plan is apparent not only from section 29 of the 1971 Act but also from the requirements of section 86(3) of the Local Government, Planning and Land Act 1980. This provision imposes a duty on the local planning authority in determining applications for planning permission to seek the achievement of the general objectives of the structure plan. The extent to which this provision binds the local planning authority is not clear, but it is still relevant to bear in mind a previous comment of Melford Stevenson J. who stated in *Enfield London Borough Council* v. *Secretary of State for the Environment* (1975) that the local planning authority "need not adhere slavishly to the development plan." All development plans are available for public inspection at the offices of district councils and county councils without charge. For these purposes the Regulations of 1982 provide for a register of development plans to be maintained, giving brief particulars of any structure or local plan which has been made available for public inspection.

Matters termed "other material considerations" are often the subject of litigation to determine whether a particular issue was correctly taken into account by the local planning authority in reaching a decision. A guide was given by the Court of Appeal in *Clyde & Co.* v. *Secretary of State for the Environment* (1977) to the effect that in order to be "material" the consideration has to be relevant to the application and must be a planning consideration. The types of matters which have been held to be material considerations include the need to avoid a planning precedent: *Collis Radio Ltd.* v. *Secretary of State for the Environment* (1975); the effect of the application upon neighbouring private interests: *Stringer* v. *Minister of Housing and Local Government* (1970), and the desirability of retaining the existing use of the property in question: *Clyde & Co.* v. *Secretary of State for the Environment.*

## Conditional grant of planning permission

As section 29 of the 1971 Act enables the local planning authority to grant planning permission "subject to such conditions as they think fit" as an alternative to a straightforward acceptance or rejection of the application, it is clear that the local planning authority enjoys a wide discretion. The exercise of this discretionary power is, however, circumscribed by legal principles which prevent the local planning authority attaching conditions which are not directly relevant to the development proposed or which are unreasonable. If conditions are attached which exceed the powers of the local planning authority, they are *ultra vires* and illegal and can have the effect of rendering the entire grant of planning permission void. The principles which are to be applied were stated by the House of Lords in *Newbury District Council* v. *Secretary of State for the Environment* (1980). A condition will be *ultra vires* and therefore illegal unless it (i) fairly and reasonably relates to the permitted development; and (ii) fairly and reasonably

11

relates to the planning consent, and (iii) is not unreasonable in the sense that no reasonable local planning authority exercising their power to attach conditions would impose it. Examples of conditions found to be *ultra vires* by the High Court include an instance where the local planning authority sought to require a housing developer to accommodate local authority tenants: *R.* v. *Hillingdon London Borough Council, ex p. Royco Homes Ltd.* (1974) and another where a condition required the developer to lay out an estate road at his own expense and give access to the public: *Hall & Co.* v. *Shoreham-by-Sea Urban District Council* (1964).

When a condition is found to be *ultra vires* the effect on the whole grant of planning permission depends on the relationship of the condition to the planning permission. In the *Hall* case (above), Willmer L.J. said that trivial conditions can be removed leaving the rest of the permission standing. Most conditions are, however, likely to be treated as fundamental to the planning permission thus rendering the whole grant invalid. As planning conditions are commonly attached to a grant of planning permission for a caravan site, *e.g.* regulating numbers of caravans on the site or the colour of caravans, it is important to be aware of this possibility. In the latter case a condition will often require the colour of the caravans to be only those contained in the British Standards Institute Document PD 6491: 1980, entitled "Preferred Exterior Colours for Static Caravans." Conditions relating to numbers and the permitted colours are usually within the tests stated in the *Newbury* case and are not normally to be regarded as invalid. Where any doubt exists, the applicant for planning permission can make a further application to the High Court for a declaration as to the validity of the condition(s) in question.

Extensive advice to local planning authorities on the use of conditions when granting planning permission is contained in Department of the Environment Circular 1/85 entitled "The Use of Conditions in Planning Permissions." Paragraphs 86 and 87 of the Annex to this Circular provide specific advice on the attachment of conditions to grants of planning permission for caravan sites for temporary or holiday use.

### Right of appeal to the Secretary of State

If an application for planning permission is unsuccessful or is granted subject to conditions, the applicant has a right to appeal to the Secretary of State under section 36 of the 1971 Act. A similar right of appeal is available under section 37 in the case of an application which is deemed to be refused due to the failure of the local planning authority to reach a decision on it within the eight week period. The right of appeal is capable of being exercised by the applicant during the period of six months from the decision of the local planning authority by notice in writing to the Secretary of State.

In dealing with the appeal, the Secretary of State is obliged to give each party the opportunity of appearing before and being heard by a person appointed by him for the purpose: section 36(4). Where either party requires this facility, a public local inquiry will be convened at which the merits of the application will be considered. The decision on the appeal will often be taken by the inspector who chairs the inquiry, as most planning appeal decisions fall within the scope of the Town and Country Planning (Determination of Appeals by Appointed Persons) (Prescribed Classes) Regulations 1981 (S.I. 1981 No. 804). Those not falling within the scope of these regulations will be decided by the Secretary of State, to whom the inquiry inspector will report.

The majority of planning appeals do not involve the convening of a public local inquiry. This is because the parties may jointly opt for disposing of the appeal by making written representations to the Secretary of State. This procedure is followed in accordance with Department of the Environment Circular 38/81 and has the advantage of being much cheaper and usually considerably quicker than public inquiry procedure.

When an appeal is made to the Secretary of State, the applicant thereby places the whole planning application in issue. The Secretary of State is thus empowered to decide the matter as if the application had been made to him in the first place. He can therefore allow the appeal unconditionally and grant planning permission accordingly, or he may grant planning permission subject to such conditions as he thinks fit, or he may reject the appeal. It should be appreciated that an appeal to the Secretary of State against conditions attached to a grant of planning permission can result in the loss of the planning permission altogether.

After the Secretary of State has reached a decision on the appeal, section 242(1) of the 1971 Act applies. This section seeks to prevent further challenge by providing that the Secretary of State's decision "shall not be challenged in any legal proceeding whatsoever." The Act does, however, provide a right of appeal to the High Court under section 245, exerciseable within six weeks of the decision, on specified grounds. These are that the Secretary of State has acted *ultra vires* or that any requirement of the Act has not been complied with and that the appellant's interests have been substantially prejudiced by the failure. If the appeal to the High Court is successful, the decision of the Secretary of State will be quashed.

# 2. Caravans and Planning Control

It was observed in Chapter 1 that the town and country planning legislation is a primary code for consideration when the legality of the stationing of a caravan or a group of caravans on any land is brought into question. In this Chapter the nature and extent of planning control in its application to caravans is given further examination. The legal considerations which apply vary according to the circumstances in which the caravan is encountered, and an important distinction is to be drawn between the town and country planning requirements for a caravan which is kept at home and stationed in the curtilage of a dwelling-house, and those requirements which are applicable to one which is stationed otherwise than in such circumstances, *e.g.* on agricultural land, or with others on a permanent caravan site, or for temporary or occasional purposes. Although this broad distinction will form the initial basis for the discussion which is to follow, it is important to emphasise that it is one which is broad and general and is not to be treated as rigid. This is because although the caravan parked in the drive at home does not normally give rise to a situation which requires the householder to apply for planning permission, the use made of the caravan, and even its size, may attract the attention of the local planning authority, whereupon the need for planning permission may be placed in issue.

### The caravan in the curtilage of a dwelling-house

A leading provision of the Town and Country Planning Act 1971, s.22(2)(d), deals with the use which is made of the land which constitutes the curtilage of a dwelling-house. It is a most important provision in that it is not limited to the specific instance of the parking of a caravan in such circumstances, but covers many other types of use of the land as well. The relevant parts of the subsection are as follows:

> "The following operations or uses of land shall not be taken for the purposes of this Act to involve development of the land, that is to say . . .
>> (d) the use of any buildings or other land within the curtilage of a dwelling-house for any purpose incidental to the enjoyment of the dwelling-house as such."

To obtain the benefit of this provision—exemption from the need to obtain planning permission—three conditions must therefore be fulfilled:

(1) the presence of the caravan must constitute a "use" of the land and not an "operation" on the land;

(2) the caravan must be stationed on land which constitutes part of the curtilage of the dwelling-house;

(3) the use of the land for the parking of the caravan must be for a purpose

incidental to the enjoyment of the dwelling-house *as a dwelling-house.*

These three factors are now examined in turn, but it is the last matter which, in practice, gives rise to the most difficulty.

## (1) *"Use" or "operation" on the land?*

The parking of a caravan on the land will normally be treated as a use of the land rather than an operation on it. This is because an "operation" on land connotes some form of physical work carried out on land, while for a "use" of land to occur, such activity is not necessary. In *Guildford R.D.C.* v. *Penny* (1959) Lord Evershed M.R. expressed the view that parking of a caravan on land did not give rise to an operation on the land and that the use of the word "operation" was not appropriate since a caravan is a chattel placed on the land and does not form part of the land itself. This view has been echoed several times by the Secretary of State in deciding planning appeals; see for example [1967] J.P.L. 110, [1974] J.P.L. 498, [1975] J.P.L. 55, [1982] J.P.L. 267. In the last of these, the Secretary of State said:

> "The correct allegation for the unauthorised stationing of a caravan should refer to a material change of use of the land and not to 'operations'."

This view has also been confirmed by Forbes J. in *Borough of Restormel* v. *Secretary of State for the Environment* (1982). Despite the foregoing, it is possible that a caravan can be regarded as a building on the curtilage if the caravan is not readily movable. In such a case, section 22(2)(*d*) would not apply. To determine whether a caravan is properly to be regarded as a building it is necessary to apply the guidelines stated by Lord Parker C.J. in *Cheshire County Council* v. *Woodward* (1962). In this case the important factors were considered to be (a) whether the operation in question had changed the physical characteristics of the land; (b) whether the object could be regarded as part of the realty; and (c) the degree of permanency. In the specific context of a caravan, the matter would be determined by reference to the means of stabilisation, the presence or absence of wheels, and whether any provision has been made for the supply of mains services. The dimensions of the caravan are also relevant for, in one enforcement notice appeal reported at [1976] J.P.L. 330, involving a caravan which on account of its size would normally be referred to as a "mobile home," the Secretary of State decided that planning permission was necessary because the caravan was so large that its placement in the drive of a dwelling-house was equivalent in planning terms to the construction of another house on the site.

Where the correct conclusion is that the caravan is to be treated as a building and therefore within the "operations" part of the definition of "development" contained in section 22(1) of the Town and Country Planning Act 1971, a further question arises whether the caravan can come within any of the classes of "permitted development" specified in article 3 of and Schedule 1 to the Town and Country Planning General Development Order 1977 (the GDO). This order automatically confers planning permission for the types of development specified in numerous Classes in the Schedule. Of possible relevance is Class 1.3 which confers planning permission for:

> "The erection, construction or placing, and the maintenance, improvement or

other alteration within the curtilage of a dwelling-house, of any building or enclosure (other than a dwelling, stable or loose-box) required for a purpose incidental to the enjoyment of the dwelling-house as such. . . . "

If Class 1.3 of the Schedule to the GDO is to apply, a number of limitations on its application must be observed. These are:

(a) that no part of the caravan shall project beyond the forwardmost wall of the original dwelling-house which fronts on a highway: Sched.1, Class 1.3(a);

(b) the height of the caravan must not exceed three metres, unless constructed with a ridged roof whereupon the maximum height is four metres: Sched 1, Class 1.3(c);

(c) the area of ground which is covered by the caravan and any other buildings in the curtilage must not exceed 50 per cent. of the total area of the curtilage excluding the ground area of the original dwelling-house: Sched.1, Class 1.3(d).

While it will not be very often that the application of Schedule 1 to the GDO will be in question, as a caravan is not normally to be regarded as a building, this possibility must nevertheless be borne in mind. If the caravan is left unoccupied or not put to any use there should be no further difficulty from the planning point of view, but in the case of the occupied caravan, the view could be taken by the local planning authority that "incidental" in this context is to be construed narrowly to involve some activity which is not normally carried on within a dwelling-house but is incidental to activities which are so carried on, for example social life, leisure, sleeping, cooking and eating. Thus sleeping in the caravan would not be permitted. As yet there is no authoritative judicial ruling on the point, though the author submits that "incidental" is not to be construed widely. It is also unclear whether the exclusion of a "dwelling" from Class 1.3 would prevent a caravan from falling within the Class.

(2) *Within the curtilage of the dwelling-house?*

The words "curtilage" and "dwelling-house" are not defined in the Town and Country Planning Act 1971. The courts have, however, considered the meaning of these words and it is therefore to judicial opinion that reference must be made. The word "curtilage" was interpreted by Lord Mackintosh in *Sinclair-Lockhart's Trustees* v. *Central Land Board* (1951) who said that:

"ground which is used for the comfortable enjoyment of a house or other building may be regarded in law as being within the curtilage of that house or building and thereby as an integral part of the same, although it has not been marked off or enclosed in any way. It is enough if it serves the purposes of the house or building in some necessary or reasonably useful way."

Other statements of judicial opinion on the extent of "curtilage" appear in *Re St. John's Church, Bishop Hatfield* (1966), in which it was said by Chancellor G.H. Newson, Q.C. that "a curtilage must be near a house and must 'belong' . . . or go together with the house in a physical sense," and also in *Methuen-Cambell* v. *Walters* (1979) in which Buckley L.J. placed reliance upon the "intimate association" of the land alleged to form part of the curtilage with the building with which it is associated.

In most domestic situations it will be obvious what land constitutes the curtilage as this will normally include all the land which passes to a purchaser on a sale of the property. In other circumstances it will be less obvious, for example when a piece of agricultural land has been incorporated into the garden of a dwelling-house. In such a case there is probably a material change of use before the land can properly be regarded as part of the curtilage of the dwelling-house: *Sampson's Executors* v. *Nottinghamshire County Council* (1949) in which Lord Goddard C.J. expressed the *obiter* opinion that this was the correct approach. It has also been accepted by the Minister that the curtilage of a dwelling-house can extend to land which is physically separated from the house by a drive or highway (see [1958] J.P.L. 62 and [1969] J.P.L. 413). It is, however, essentially a question of fact whether or not land on which the caravan is situated forms part of the curtilage.

As the word "dwelling-house" is not the subject of a definition provided by the town and country planning legislation, reference must also be made to judicial views on the scope of this word. Although it was once defined in *Lewin* v. *End* (1906) as a house in which people live or which is physically capable of being lived in, it was more recently defined by McCullough J. in *Gravesham Borough Council* v. *Secretary of State for the Environment and O'Brien* (1982). In this case, the learned judge considered that to constitute a dwelling-house it was necessary that the building in question be capable of providing the facilities required for "daily private domestic existence." In determining whether a building falls within this definition he stated that it was not essential that the owner or occupier of the house should have the intention to use it throughout the year, nor that it could be so used lawfully, nor that the owner or occupier should be able to live in it permanently if he so wished. Thus an empty building is still capable of constituting a dwelling-house, but it must nevertheless be fit for permanent use. If it is not fit for such use the Secretary of State would probably decide that it does not qualify: see [1963] J.P.L. 273. Similarly he has refused to accept the site of a demolished dwelling-house as satisfying the term: see [1966] J.P.L. 491. In *Scurlock* v. *Secretary of State for Wales* (1976) a house was in partial use for office purposes by an estate agent, but it was held that it did not constitute a dwelling-house. The Secretary of State had earlier held in another decision that a café with a flat above did not come within the term: [1974] J.P.L. 241. It was stated there that "dwelling-house" means "a single private dwelling-house used for occupation by one family only and does not include a house or bungalow used exclusively for letting to holidaymakers throughout the year." Thus where land within the curtilage was used for parking a caravan used for accommodating paying guests when the adjacent house was full, the Secretary of State concluded that the use of the caravan was an integral part of the commercial use of the house which by virtue of that commercial use was not within the scope of section 22(2)(d). In *Prosser* v. *Sharpe* (1985) the view was expressed (*obiter*) that a renovated wooden building, comprising two rooms, to which mains services had been connected, was not a "dwelling-house" as it was not lived in, nor did anyone sleep in it.

Some difficulties may arise when the caravan is situated on land surrounding a block of flats. Although the Town and Country Planning Act 1971 treats a flat as a separate dwelling-house in section 22(3)(a), it may be difficult to determine which part or parts (if any) of the surrounding land constitutes the curtilage relative to an individual flat. But where a specific parcel of surrounding land is specifically allocated for the use and enjoyment of the owner or occupier of a particular flat, it is submitted that that land can constitute the "curtilage" and the flat a "dwelling-house" for the purposes of the provision.

### (3) Use incidental to the enjoyment of the dwelling-house as such

Where a caravan is simply parked on land forming part of the curtilage of a dwelling-house planning permission is not normally required; the mere parking of the caravan on the land is usually indistinguishable from the parking of a private car. Regard must be had, however, to the enforcement notice appeal decision referred to above and noted at [1976] J.P.L. 330, which concerned a large caravan of the "mobile home" type, the sheer size of which caused the Secretary of State to treat it as a building on the land requiring planning permission.

Difficulties arise when the caravan is occupied, however, as this state of affairs can constitute a material change in the use of the land which cannot be regarded as incidental to the use of the dwelling-house within section 22(2)(d). The rationale of this distinction between occupied and unoccupied caravans is simply that occupation invites the conclusion that a new unit of accommodation has come into existence separate from that afforded by the dwelling-house. If this has occurred, the stationing of the occupied caravan on the curtilage is no longer incidental to the use of the dwelling-house as a dwelling-house. There are a number of planning and enforcement appeal decisions which illustrate the approach of the Secretary of State to this situation but it appears that the matter has not yet been considered judicially.

Where a caravan is used for the purpose of providing additional sleeping accommodation for persons who otherwise live in the dwelling-house the view is normally taken by the Secretary of State that this use qualifies as 'incidental'; see, for example, the appeal decisions noted at [1970] J.P.L. 223, [1976] J.P.L. 586 and at [1979] J.P.L. 124, which are also consistent with other earlier decisions. In another instance it was accepted that even two caravans on the curtilage can be within the scope of section 22(2)(d) (then s.12(2) of the 1947 Act); see [1959] J.P.L. 809. It is clear, however, that the Secretary of State normally takes a narrow view of the scope of section 22(2)(d) in this context, for in the decision noted at [1976] J.P.L. 586, an instance where the sole use of the caravan was as an extra bedroom, the Secretary of State issued a pertinent warning to the effect that if the caravan was used in the future for preparation and taking of meals and otherwise used as a separate dwelling, the use of the curtilage for the stationing of the caravan would cease to be treated as incidental. It is clear from the decision noted at [1970] J.P.L. 223 that in reaching a conclusion on an appeal that the Secretary of State will take into account the facilities available to the occupant(s) within the caravan. If the caravan is a sophisticated model it is less likely that the occupier(s) will need to rely on the facilities available within the dwelling-house and hence its use is less likely to be seen as "incidental." In one planning appeal noted at [1971] J.P.L. 187, the argument was advanced that the facilities in the caravan were available to the occupants of the dwelling-house as well as vice-versa. The Secretary of State dismissed this argument on the basis that availability of the accommodation and facilities was secondary to the main issue of the actual use to which the caravan was put. A second argument based on the fact that the occupants of the caravan and of the dwelling-house were all members of the one family also failed, the Secretary of State ruling that this fact did not prevent a finding that the occupation of the caravan amounted to a second household.

Having regard to the Secretary of State's view of the meaning of the word "dwelling-house" (see above) as limited to "a single private dwelling-house used for occupation by one family only . . . " it is unlikely that a caravan used for occupation by paying guests would be treated as incidental. In the appeal noted at [1974] J.P.L. 241, the Secretary of State refused the appeal because both the dwelling-house and caravan were in commercial use and the use of the caravan could not be regarded as "incidental to the personal enjoyment or domestic needs of a private occupier." The Secretary of State subsequently ruled in another appeal decision that the use of a caravan for accommodating a lodger was not incidental to the use of the dwelling-house as such and therefore required planning permission: [1975] J.P.L. 433.

## Caravans not within the curtilage of a dwelling-house

To determine whether planning permission is required when a caravan is situated on land which does not form part of the curtilage of a dwelling-house, it is necessary to apply basic principles of planning law. The question to be determined in almost all instances is whether a material change of use of the land within the meaning of section 22(1) of the Town and Country Planning Act 1971 is involved. Although the definition of "development" contained within section 22(1) is in two parts, the first part (dealing with building, etc., or other operations on land) has already been shown to be normally inapplicable to the stationing of a caravan (see p.15 above). Usually, therefore, an evaluation falls to be made of the application of the second part of the development definition. The significant question is whether a material change of use can occur through the mere act of stationing a caravan on land, or whether it is necessary to inquire into the actual use to which the caravan is being put.

Since amenity is a primary concern of town and country planning law it may be thought that the only important issue in assessing the materiality of a change of use of land by stationing a caravan upon it is the effect on the visual aspect. Thus, as Lord Parker C.J. said in *Devonshire County Council v. Allens Caravans (Estates) Ltd* (1962), "The materiality to be considered is a materiality from a planning point of view and in particular the question of amenities." Since the visual effect is determined by the mere presence of the caravan and not by the use to which it is put, it should not be relevant to have regard to the actual use of the caravan, if indeed it is put to any use at all. This was the approach adopted by Stephen Brown J. in *Woodspring District Council v. Secretary of State for the Environment* (1982) but it was rejected by Forbes J. in *Borough of Restormel v. Secretary of State for the Environment and Rabey* (1982).

In the *Woodspring* case, the owner of some farmland placed three caravans on the land for use by farm workers. No planning permission was obtained from the local planning authority and an enforcement notice was issued and served under section 87 of the Town and Country Planning Act 1971. This notice alleged that a material change of use had occurred from use as farmland to use for the purposes of stationing three caravans. After a public local inquiry (by which time only one caravan remained on the land) the planning inspector issued a decision on behalf of the Secretary of State stating that "the allegation in the (enforcement) notice was too wide in referring only to the stationing of caravans" and quashed the enforcement notice on the basis that it was too uncertain. The council appealed to the High Court against this decision, whereupon Stephen Brown J. held that the enforcement notice was valid. His judgment did not, however, deal with the main issue but proceeded on the basis that the enforcement notice might require amendment, having regard to whatever facts had been adduced at the inquiry; he therefore remitted the matter to the Secretary of State for further consideration. In the *Restormel* case a single caravan was situated in the curtilage of an hotel and was used solely for the purpose of providing sleeping accommodation for two waitresses employed by the hotel during the holiday season. In the absence of a grant of planning permission the local planning authority served an enforcement notice alleging that a breach of planning control had taken place in that a material change in the use of the land had been made "to use for the purpose of stationing a caravan thereon." On appeal against the notice, the inspector held that the notice was too wide as it failed to specify the purpose for which the caravan was being used, and quashed the notice. On appeal to the High Court, Forbes J. said that he did not find the *Woodspring* case of much assistance since it did not deal with the central issue of whether it was a "planning heresy" that the mere stationing of a caravan could involve a material change of use without regard to the use to which it is put. In analysing the problem, the proper way of looking at the matter was to ask the question "What was, in planning terms, the effect on the planning unit? It was not, looked at in that way, sufficient to stop at the stationing of the caravan. You had to look further and say: for which purpose was the caravan stationed?" The effect of this approach is to give greater latitude to the owner or occupier of the land, since, as the *Restormel* case itself illustrates, there may be no breach of planning control when the matter is considered in the whole context of the planning unit. Thus the inspector had been right to conclude that the use of the caravan was ancillary to the main use of the premises as an hotel and it was thus not a development requiring planning permission. Forbes J. also stated that "the proper way of drawing these enforcement notices ought to be that somebody has made a material change of use by stationing the caravan . . . for the purpose of whatever it was" and concluded by saying "It was inappropriate when a caravan was stationed on land for a particular purpose to look at the stationing of the caravan separately and say that that was something which was development requiring planning permission because it made a material change of use." Consistent with normal planning law principles it is therefore a matter of fact and degree whether the *stationing and use* of a caravan is a material change of use of the land: *Marshall* v. *Nottingham Corporation* (1960). Ultimately this is a matter for the Secretary of State to decide should an appeal be made to him from refusal of planning permission or from the service of an enforcement notice by the local planning authority. Guidance in determining whether a material change of use has occurred and in considering the relevant planning issues can be derived from the following examples of reported appeal decisions issued by the Secretary of State:

**Stationing of residential caravan on site of former bungalow.** A caravan was placed on land forming the site of a demolished bungalow where existing bungalows were situated on either side of the land within an attractive semi-rural setting. The owner appealed against the service of an enforcement notice claiming that no breach of planning control had occurred. The inspector held that "the introduction of a caravan created as a matter of fact and degree a material change of use from no-use to a use for the stationing of a caravan." He refused to grant planning permission for the caravan, having considered "the determining issue to be whether the caravan . . . so detracts from the residential amenities of the surrounding area as to be unacceptable." To permit a residential caravan to be permanently stationed was inappropriate since it was visible from adjoining dwellings and detracted from their visual amenities. It was also relevant that if it were permitted to remain permanently it would encourage applications for similar developments elsewhere: [1979] J.P.L. 45.

**Stationing of caravan used for purposes incidental to premises used as café.** A caravan was sited adjacent to a café, ostensibly as a rest room for staff. The café was one of a number of structures, situated near a river estuary, which gave the landscape what the inspector described as a "patchy appearance." In declining to grant planning permission for the retention of the caravan, the inspector accepted that the caravan was not used residentially but decided that it was "a unit designed for residential accommodation and it appears as such in the local scene. By its nature and colouring it is conspicuous and it forms an additional item in the mixed collection of structures in this area adjacent to the coastline." He thus held it was "wrong to grant planning permission for it to remain in this position indefinitely adding to the generally unco-ordinated appearance of the land": [1980] J.P.L. 130.

**Stationing of caravan used for purposes incidental to premises with dual use as restaurant and for residential purposes.** A building listed as being of special architectural or historic interest was in use as a wine bar and bistro with living accommodation above. In the curtilage of the building a caravan was situated for purposes which the inspector accepted as "recreational purposes and for occasional sleeping of personal guests." On appeal against the service of an enforcement notice the inspector held that a material change of use had occurred but refused to grant planning permission for its retention. He regarded the main issue as "whether or not the stationing of the caravan . . . is acceptable bearing in mind planning policy for the area and the listed status of the building." He found that the caravan was prominently situated and clearly visible to passers-by from the highway and that "the utilitarian lines of the caravan clash starkly with the serene and mature appearance of the thatched . . . listed building to which it is in juxtaposition." Since the policy of the council was to enhance the natural beauty of the area and to exercise development control with particular care, special attention being given to siting and appearance, planning permission was not granted: [1981] J.P.L. 441.

**Stationing of caravan on nursery land: whether development involved.** A caravan was stationed on nursery land and was used as an office, for storage, and as a canteen. An enforcement notice was quashed on appeal as the inspector considered that the use of the land for stationing the caravan was ancillary to the use of the land as a nursery. He advised the appellant, however, that "The position would, of course, be entirely different if you should choose to use the caravan for residential purposes": [1983] J.P.L. 274.

In most instances, therefore, a material change of use will be found to have occurred. The question is then whether the planning merits in a particular instance will nevertheless permit the retention of the caravan on the site. The factors mentioned in the appeal decisions outlined above are all relevant, as are indications of ministerial policy evidenced in the form of Department of the Environment Circulars and Development Control Policy Notes.

Development Control Policy Note No.8 entitled "Caravan Sites" (set out in Appendix III) is particularly relevant. While this document is mainly directed to policy matters concerning sites for groups of caravans, it advises that caravans cannot normally be sited in green belts or in open country but should be close to existing development. The Policy Note states (para.3) that " . . . the best place will usually be on the edge of a residential area within reach of the necessary services but not far out in the country." This advice was specifically applied in an instance involving a single caravan, reported at [1971] J.P.L. 469. Planning permission for continued stationing for residential purposes was refused by the local planning authority on the grounds that the caravan detracted from the appearance of the rural locality, and that it would constitute a permanent isolated residential unit contrary to the authority's policy, which was broadly in line with Development Control Policy Note No.8. The planning inspector commented in his report that "A residential caravan would not normally, therefore, be permitted in this comparatively isolated position." He nevertheless allowed the appeal following medical evidence supporting the occupant's claim to need to live in a quiet, isolated location. The permission granted, however, was limited so as to be for the personal benefit of the appellant only.

Discussion has so far been limited to single caravans. More difficult problems occur when the number of caravans on a site is subject to an increase, a process known as "intensification" of the use of the land. Whether this process involves a material change of use is the subject of a number of judicial and ministerial decisions and it is to this problem that attention is now directed.

### Intensification of use as a material change of use

Is the increase in the number of caravans stationed on a particular site an act of development requiring planning permission? To constitute an act of development intensification of the use must, in accordance with normal principles, amount to a material change of use. Whether intensification has occurred, however, is a question of fact which therefore is a matter for the Secretary of State to decide and does not lie within the province of the courts. Thus in the leading case of *Guildford R.D.C.* v. *Penny* (1959) the Court of Appeal decided that an increase in the number of caravans on a site from 8 to 27 did not involve a question of law and the court would not interfere with the finding of the justices (who until 1962 had appellate jurisdiction in enforcement notice appeals) that no development was involved by such an increase. Lord Evershed M.R. said, *obiter*:

"[counsel] contended that the mere intensity of user or occupation could never be relevant. As a general proposition I am not prepared to accept that argument. . . . Mere intensity of user may (as it seems to me; but I must not be taken as deciding this point) affect a definable character of the land and of its use—or one of them"

Lord Evershed M.R.'s view has since been seen as affirming that mere intensification can be an act of development requiring planning permission. Thus in *James* v. *Secretary of State for Wales* (1966) Lord Denning M.R. considered that an increase in number of caravans from one to four could amount to a material change of use, and in *Esdell Caravan Parks Ltd* v. *Hemel Hempstead R.D.C. (1965)* Lord Denning M.R. stated:

"I doubt very much whether the occupier [of a site] could increase from 24 to 78 without permission. An increase in intensity of that order may well amount to a material change of use. . . . "

It is also worthy of note that in the earlier case of *Taylor* v. *Eton R.D.C.* (1957) the Divisional Court accepted without argument that an increase in the number of caravans on a site from 3 to 20 was an act of development requiring planning permission.

The view taken by the Secretary of State on this issue is illustrated by the following three appeal decisions:

**Increase in number of caravans on existing site from eleven to sixteen.** Planning permission was refused for the stationing of five additional caravans on a one-acre site in a green belt area on which there were eleven existing caravans; all of these were for use for holiday purposes only. One of the appellant's arguments was that the increase did not require planning permission as it did not amount to a material change of use. The decision letter contained the following passage:

"It is noted that the area of the site is not being extended and it is considered that the proposal to station a further five recreational caravans . . . would not therefore affect the character of the use of the site as a whole and would not involve development requiring planning permission.": [1967] J.P.L. 421.

**Stationing of second caravan on land already occupied by one caravan.** The increase in the number of caravans on a site adjacent to a café was from one to two; in response to this the local planning authority served an enforcement notice. The inspector stated that "the result of bringing a second caravan onto the land had been to create a new unit of residential accommodation . . . occupied throughout part of the year . . . and that this constituted a material change in the use of this small site." This view was not accepted, however, by the Secretary of State. He said:

"The first caravan was brought on to the site in 1964 and the second in 1965. Whilst there would appear to have been a material change of use of the appeal site when it was first used for the purpose of the stationing of a caravan for the purposes of human habitation, in view of the fact that both caravans are used exclusively by [the appellant] and his family in connection with his management of the café, it is not considered that the intensification resulting from the bringing of a second caravan onto the site has so changed the nature of the use of the land as to amount to a further material change of use. The view is taken, therefore, that what is alleged in the enforcement notice does not amount to development. . . . ": [1971] J.P.L. 405.

**Storage of caravans on agricultural land.** An enforcement notice had been served arising from an increase in the number of caravans kept in a farmyard from 2 to 12. The caravans were unoccupied, merely being stored there by their owners who were prevented by restrictive covenants from keeping the caravans on their own properties. The relevant planning unit for the purposes of determining whether there had been a material change of use was determined to be the whole farmyard. The inspector stated that in his view

> "the fact that the land set aside for storing caravans did not increase is not considered to be relevant. It is concluded that the important point is that some time after the beginning of 1964 the number of caravans stored on the appeal site rose above two and it is considered that as a matter of fact and degree this use became a substantial use of the site. The introduction of this independent although minor use created a dual use of the farmyard, namely both for agricultural purposes and for the stationing and storing of caravans. It is considered that this dual use was a material change of use of the planning unit constituting development for which planning permission was required but not obtained. . . .": [1982] J.P.L. 268.

It is to be noted that neither the judiciary nor the Secretary of State have resorted to percentage figures for expressing a view on whether development by intensification has occurred. Although this would be one way of looking at the problem it would disguise the real issue, which is whether as a matter of fact and degree, having regard to the use of the land comprising the planning unit, a material change of use has or has not taken place.

Intensification of use of land by the bringing on of additional caravans does not in every case raise problems. The local planning authority in granting planning permission for the stationing and use of caravans may limit the number of caravans to be stationed on the land. This is achieved by attaching a condition to a grant of planning permission pursuant to the power conferred by section 29(1) of the Town and Country Planning Act 1971 to grant permission "subject to such conditions as they think fit." Failure to comply with the condition is an automatic breach of planning control. Only where there is no such condition might the intensification problem arise, unless, however, the land was being used as a caravan site immediately prior to July 1, 1948 (the date on which the 1947 Act came into force). In the latter case the lawful use of the land will have been determined by the number of caravans in situ on that day (though an increase over that number will not automatically result in a breach of planning control). A further means of control over the number of caravans is available under section 5(1)(a) of the Caravan Sites and Control of Development Act 1960 where the caravans are used for residential purposes. This provision empowers the district council to attach conditions to a site licence in such cases and in so doing may limit the number of caravans on the site. A breach of this condition is an offence under section 9(1) of the 1960 Act.

## Temporary and occasional uses of land

Provision is made by the town and country planning legislation specifically to deal with the situation where land is used on a non-permanent basis for the stationing of a caravan, or in some cases, groups of caravans. The legislation designates certain temporary or occasional uses as "permitted development," i.e. planning permission is deemed to be granted. The relevant provision is article 3 and Schedule 1, Class XXII of the Town and Country Planning General Development Order 1977 ("the GDO"), which, makes reference to paragraphs 2 to 10 of Schedule 1 to the Caravan Sites and Control of Development Act 1960. These paragraphs may be summarised as follows:

2. Use of land as a caravan site for not more than two nights by a person travelling with a caravan provided that (a) no other caravan is stationed for the purpose of human habitation on the land at the same time and (b) the land has not been used for the purpose of stationing a caravan for human habitation on more than 28 days in the preceding 12 months.

3. Use of undeveloped land as a caravan site comprising not less than five acres provided that (a) the land has not been used for the purpose of stationing a caravan for human habitation on more than 28 days in the preceding 12 months and (b) during that time no more than three caravans were so stationed at any one time.

4. Use of land as a caravan site by members of an exempted organisation for the purposes of recreation and whilst supervised by the organisation.

5. Use of land as a caravan site by an exempted organisation provided (a) a certificate has been issued to the occupier of the land by the organisation stating that the land has been approved by the exempted organisation for use by its members for the purposes of recreation and (b) not more than five caravans are stationed on the land at any one time.

6. Use of land as a caravan site by an exempted organisation for a meeting of members supervised by the organisation and lasting not more than five days.

7. Use of agricultural land as a caravan site for seasonal use by agricultural workers employed on land in the same occupation. In *North* v. *Brown* (1974) it was held that this provision does not permit the permanent stationing of a caravan even if only occupied seasonally by agricultural employees.

8. Use of forestry land (including afforestation) as a caravan site for seasonal use by agricultural workers employed on land in the same occupation.

9. Use of land as a caravan site forming part of or adjoining land on which building or engineering operations are being carried out pursuant to a grant of planning permission, where required, provided that the use is for the accommodation of persons employed in those operations. In the appeal decision noted at [1982] J.P.L. 724, the Secretary of State held that this included self-help or do-it-yourself operations.

10. Use of land as a caravan site by a travelling showman who is a member of a certificated organisation of travelling showmen and who is travelling for the purpose of his business. Most showmen are members of the Showmen's Guild of Great Britain.

All of the above uses of land refer to use as a "caravan site." This term is defined by article 2(1) of the GDO to mean "land on which a caravan is stationed for the purpose of human habitation and land which is used in connection with land on which a caravan is so stationed." The references in paragraphs 4, 5 and 6 to an "exempted organisation" are explained in paragraph 12 of the Schedule, which empowers the Secretary of State to grant a certificate of exemption to any organisation if he is satisfied that its objects include the encouragement or promotion of recreational activities. Some of these organisations are named in DoE Circular 17/65, and include the Boy Scouts Association and Girl Guides Association. The current Department of the Environment list contains the names of 198 organisations; most of these are private caravan clubs having local membership. A further 14 certificates have been issued by the Secretary of State for Wales. In practice only the largest clubs, *e.g.* the Caravan Club, use their certificate of exemption otherwise than for the purpose of holding rallies under paragraph 6 of the Schedule.

Two further matters meriting note arise from Class XXII of Schedule 1 to the GDO. First, paragraph 13 of Schedule 1 to the 1960 Act empowers the Secretary of State, on the application of any district council, to make an order negating the effect of any or all of paragraphs 2–10 on a specified piece of land within that authority's area. Secondly, Class XXII imposes a condition to the effect that if any of the paragraphs should cease to apply due to exceeding the limits imposed, then all the caravans on the site must be removed.

### Caravans on agricultural land

No special planning law issues are raised by the permanent stationing of a caravan on agricultural land; the law which applies is outlined on pp. 19–24 above. This form of development merits further attention, however, for two reasons: the first is for comment on the possible application of a particular provision applicable to development on agricultural land contained in Class VI of Schedule 1 to the GDO, and the second is for discussion of planning policies applicable to the use of land for stationing a caravan occupied by a person associated with the agricultural activities.

Development control on agricultural land is the subject of a major concession of great benefit to the farming community. This is contained in Class VI of Schedule 1 to the GDO as one of the instances of "permitted development":

*"Class VI.—Agricultural buildings, works and uses*

1. The carrying out on agricultural land having an area of more than one acre and comprised in an agricultural unit of building or engineering operations requisite for the use of that land for the purposes of agriculture (other than the placing on land of structures not designed for those purposes or the provision and alteration of dwellings), so long as:—

  (a) the ground area covered by a building erected pursuant to this permission does not, either by itself or after the addition thereto of the ground area covered by any existing building or buildings (other than a dwelling-house) within the same unit erected or in course of erection within the preceding two years and wholly or partly within 90 metres of the nearest part of the said building, exceed 465 square metres;

  (b) the height of any buildings or works does not exceed three metres in the case of a building or works within three kilometres of the perimeter of an aerodrome, nor 12 metres in any other case;

  (c) no part of any buildings (other than movable structures) or works within 25 metres of the metalled portion of a trunk or classified road."

The provision, which is complex and only partially relevant for present purposes is mentioned here in order to avoid the possible misconception that the Class allows the stationing of a caravan on agricultural land in order that it can be used for the purposes of agriculture rather than for human habitation. This interpretation of the provision is incorrect because of the words which appear in parenthesis: "other than the placing on land of structures not designed for those purposes . . . ." Thus in *Belmont Farm Ltd.* v. *Minister of Housing and Local Government* (1962) (a case involving the use of an aircraft hangar for the training of horses), it was held that the question whether a structure is designed for a particular purpose is to be determined by reference to its physical appearance and layout, and not by reference to any adaption that may have been made. The following planning appeal decision involving a converted caravan further illustrates this point:

**Stationing of caravan said to be required for purposes ancillary to agricultural use of land.** A caravan was situated in a rural area subject to well-established policies restricting development unless required to satisfy a proven agricultural need. Planning permission was applied for but was refused by the local planning authority. It was submitted on appeal that Class VI of Schedule 1 to the GDO applied since the caravan was not used for human habitation otherwise than for working and preparation of light refreshments but was used to store animal foodstuffs and veterinary products. The inspector refused the appeal stating:

> "I do not consider that the development comes within any of the classes of permitted development . . . as . . . the caravan is not designed for agricultural purposes. Neither does it appear to me that the caravan is required or used for purposes of forestry. The external appearance of the caravan is unaltered from its basic shape, and being mainly white is quite prominent in these rural surroundings. Several of the internal fittings have been removed and it does not appear a very attractive habitable dwelling at present. However, it would only require the reinstatement of a few fittings to make it habitable once more. In my opinion the caravan has all the appearance of an isolated residential caravan and it thus constitutes an intrusion into the countryside.": [1981] J.P.L. 538.

The practice of installing residential caravans on agricultural land is in direct conflict with the usual policy concern of the local planning authority, as expressed in development plans, to restrict isolated caravan development. The means of reconciliation is often achieved by a grant of planning permission which is either temporary, or personal to the occupant of the caravan, or both, or by imposition of a planning condition requiring the caravan to be occupied only by a person engaged in agriculture. The former means of control is normally to be preferred for the reason illustrated by the following planning appeal decision.

**Stationing of mobile home on small agricultural unit.** Planning permission for the stationing of a caravan of the "mobile home" type was refused where the site involved half an acre of agricultural land. The appellant was over seventy years old and the inspector doubted her ability to cope with the supervision of the agricultural unit despite its very limited size. The inspector nevertheless allowed the appeal and granted a conditional planning permission, making the following observations:

> "The [local planning authority] has consistently tried to implement its policies of restricting development in this area away from any village, and I agree with them that it would be wrong for there to be any intensification of the present sporadic development in this area in the absence of proven agricultural need. Nevertheless, I consider that bearing in mind [the appellant's] age and her connections with the area, a limited period permission for, say, five years personal to [the appellant] should be a satisfactory compromise. I consider this preferable to

the imposition of an agricultural condition which would permit a continuance of a dwelling on the site after the appellant no longer required it personally.": [1974] J.P.L. 496.

In determining the existence of a need particular to agricultural land, the Secretary of State may have regard to the whole enterprise being carried out by the appellant, not merely that which is carried out on the appeal site. Thus in the appeal decision reported at [1979] J.P.L. 556, the appeal site comprised fifteen acres used for rearing cattle. This activity was carried out on several other agricultural units owned by or leased to the appellant company. The size of the appeal site raised a doubt as to whether a viable agricultural unit existed and the inspector found that it would not be large enough to keep one man fully employed. He nevertheless regarded all the lands comprised in the scattered holding as a single enterprise and assessed the agricultural need accordingly. Finding that the business was still in an early stage, he refused planning permission for the construction of a dwelling-house on the site, but permitted the stationing of a mobile home for a period of three years, anticipating that the growth of the business would make a review of a proposal for a dwelling-house appropriate at the end of that time. For further detail on assessment of needs pertaining to agricultural land see DoE Circular 24/73.

The alternative means of reconciling the conflicting claims of amenity and the needs of agriculture is by means of a condition requiring that the caravan be occupied only by a person employed in agriculture, a device also widely used in connection with the grant of planning permission for isolated housing development in the countryside. An example may be seen in *Fawcett Properties Ltd.* v. *Buckinghamshire County Council* (1960) where a grant of planning permission for a pair of cottages in a green belt area was subject to the condition that "the occupation of the houses shall be limited to persons whose employment or latest employment is or was employment in agriculture or forestry." The issue in the case was whether the condition was *ultra vires* on account of being too uncertain, but the House of Lords held it was a valid condition, Lord Denning stating that the condition would only be void for uncertainty if it could not be given any sensible or ascertainable meaning. DoE Circular 24/73 (mentioned above) recommends that the formula to be used for imposing an agricultural occupancy condition should be:

"The occupation of the dwelling shall be limited to a person solely or mainly employed, or last employed, in the locality in agriculture as defined in section 290(1) of the Town and Country Planning Act 1971, or in forestry (including any dependants of such a person residing with him), or widow or widower of such a person."

A condition in very similar terms was held to be invalid by Webster J. in *Alderson* v. *Secretary of State for the Environment* (1984), thus causing considerable excitment in the agricultural community—but was subsequently held to be valid by the Court of Appeal.

### Caravan sites

In this section, "caravan site" is not used as a legal term of art but in the more general sense in common usage, *i.e.* as a place on which several caravans, particularly of the "mobile home" type, are placed either permanently or for holiday seasonal use. This type of establishment, often supplemented by provision for touring caravans, is normally associated with the provision of facilities in the nature of sanitary and mains services for the occupants of the caravans who are allocated a "pitch" on the site. Many of the caravans are likely to be owner-occupied, the pitch being the subject of a lease or licence granted by the site operator, while others are rented or occupied under a licence together with the individual pitch on which each caravan is placed. As was pointed out in Chapter 1, these sites are of particular interest in relation to their management under the Caravan Sites and Control of Development Act 1960 and by reason of the security of tenure of the occupants under the Mobile Homes Acts 1975–1983, and Caravan Sites Act 1968, aspects which are discussed further in Chapters 4 and 5.

Planning control of caravan sites is maintained in the usual manner pursuant to the Town and Country Planning Act 1971. Planning permission will almost invariably be required to establish such a site: it *may* be required on the basis that the provision of the site infrastructure (the site facilities) amounts to "building, engineering . . . or other operations" carried out on the land, but it *will* also be required where the stationing of the numerous caravans or mobile homes amounts to a "material change in the use of the land," involving the ending of a use previously carried out there, often agricultural. The distinction between these two aspects of the need for planning permission is important, because the provision of site facilities will be within the scope of "permitted development" (under article 3 of and Schedule 1 to the GDO) if the development is carried out pursuant to any condition attached to the site licence which will be required from the district council under the Caravan Sites and Control of Development Act 1960. This is provided by Class XXIII of Schedule 1 to the GDO (see Appendix II).

If any development is proposed which exceeds that required by the conditions of an existing site licence it will normally constitute "development" and should therefore be the subject of an express grant of planning permission obtained from the local planning authority in the ordinary way.

A similar type of development is the making available of sites during the period from March to October to holidaymakers travelling in touring caravans or motorised caravans. Such sites are also often used for pitching tents. So far as planning control is concerned there is no change in the application of basic planning law principles, nor in regulation of internal management, but the security of tenure provisions which affect permanent caravan sites do not apply.

Many caravan sites have grown from mere tent sites to become used as caravan sites or for mixed use by stationing of tents and caravans. Whether there is a material change of use by such a change must always be a matter of fact and degree (see *Devon County Council* v. *Horton* (1962)), but it is interesting to note that for planning purposes, the Secretary of State has recognised a difference between touring caravans and motorised caravans. In the planning appeal decision reported at [1984] J.P.L. 132, the site was in an area of outstanding natural beauty and was used for the stationing of up to 100 tents during the summer season. Planning permission was sought for the stationing of up to 30 motorised caravans as occasion demanded. The local planning authority considered that this would involve an unacceptable visual intrusion in the landscape, though it was recognised that motorised caravans could come onto the land under the existing arrangement provided a tent was pitched by the occupants. The planning authority also took the view that there was very little difference between the visual impact of motorised caravans and touring caravans, but insisted that motorised caravans were considerably more intrusive than tents. In granting the planning permission sought, the inspector commented: "It does seem to me to be absurd that car-borne campers can use this site but persons in motorised caravans cannot do so unless they pitch a tent and sleep in it." It is also relevant to note that although the application did not relate to touring caravans, the inspector observed that "the Secretary of State has accepted . . . that there is a material difference between motorised caravans and touring caravans. . . . "Having regard to this observation, it is clearly most important to bear in mind that a proposal to use a site for stationing touring caravans in addition to motorised caravans can, in an appropriate case, be considered to amount to a material change of use requiring planning permission. Reference may be made, however, to an earlier planning appeal decision in which the Secretary of State rejected a distinction between touring and motorised caravans (see [1975] J.P.L. 362).

The policy factors relevant to the establishment of permanent caravan sites have been considered by the Department of the Environment, and views have been circulated to local planning authorities through the issue of Development Control Policy Note No. 8. This document was issued in 1969 by the (then) Ministry of Housing and Local Government, and it forms the basis of many provisions in development plans prepared by local planning authorities dealing with caravan sites. The parts of the Policy Note which are relevant to what has been stated so far are paragraphs 1–10—see Appendix III.

# 3. Enforcement of Planning Control

Where the circumstances are such that a grant of planning permission is required to station a caravan or a group of caravans on land, and the stationing is carried out without a grant being obtained, it is open to the local planning authority to seek to rectify the breach of planning control. The local planning authority has a discretionary power, conferred by the Town and Country Planning Act 1971, to issue and serve an enforcement notice. If the requirements of such a notice are not complied with, criminal proceedings may be instituted. This Chapter is therefore concerned with the principal details of enforcement proceedings, rights of appeal and other means of challenging an enforcement notice, the penalties which can be incurred through failure to comply with a notice, and with associated matters.

The provisions of the Town and Country Planning Act 1971 which deal with the enforcement aspects of development control are particularly complex. This is partly due to the amount of litigation which they have generated and partly due to the numerous amendments that have been enacted since the 1971 Act came into force. Amendments were made by the Town and Country Planning (Amendment) Act 1977, the Local Government and Planning (Amendment) Act 1981, and the Town and Country Planning Act 1984. Many of the amending provisions take effect by substitution of new provisions in the 1971 Act so that the current law is now mainly to be found in sections 87, 88, 88A, 88B, 89, 90, 91, 92, 92A, 93, and 94.

### Power to take enforcement action

Under section 87(1) of the 1971 Act local planning authorities are empowered to issue and serve an enforcement notice at their discretion; they are thus under no duty to try to remedy breaches of planning control. The subsection provides:

> "Where it appears to the local planning authority that there has been a breach of planning control after the end of 1963, then, . . . the authority, if they consider it expedient to do so, having regard to the provisions of the development plan and to any other material considerations, may issue a notice requiring the breach to be remedied and serve copies of the notice . . . "

For the purposes of this section "local planning authority" normally means the district council for the area in which the breach of planning control has occurred, or, in London, the London borough council. County councils also have enforcement powers, however, if the breach occurs in a National Park (unless a Planning Board has been established to administer the planning of the area), or in relation to a limited number of types of development (not relevant for present purposes) known as "county matters."

In the words of section 87(1) there must be a "breach of planning control after the end of 1963" for enforcement action to be competent. The meaning of "breach of planning control" is specified in section 87(3) as being either (a) a development carried out without the benefit of a grant of planning permission, where required, or (b) a failure to comply with any condition or limitation subject to which planning permission has been granted.

The inclusion of the words "after the end of 1963" seems odd at first sight, for why should it matter when the breach of planning control occurred? Until the Town and Country Planning Act 1968 there was a general limitation on the power to take enforcement action in that an enforcement notice was only effective if served within four years of the breach of planning control. This rule was changed in 1968, but protection is given to those breaches of planning control which had gained immunity from enforcement action at the time of the change in the law by requiring the breach to have occurred after the end of 1963. An enforcement notice can now be issued at any time though the "four year rule" continues to apply in the following cases, specified in section 87(4):

(a) the carrying out without planning permission of building, engineering, mining or other operations in, on, over or under land; or
(b) the failure to comply with any condition or limitation attached to a grant of planning permission for development falling within (a) above; or
(c) the making without planning permission of a change of use of any building to use as a single dwelling-house; or
(d) the failure to comply with a condition which prohibits or has the effect of preventing a change of use of a building to use as a single dwelling-house.

In the context of caravans this "four year rule" is very important. If the stationing of a caravan on land is a "use" of the land, rather than a "building" on the land, the four year rule will not apply and enforcement action can be taken at any time. If it is considered to be a building on the land the passing of at least four years will guarantee protection from enforcement action. This distinction has already been considered in the context of section 22(2)(d) of the 1971 Act (see p. 15), and it will be recalled that stationing of a caravan is normally considered to be a use of the land, though a caravan of the "mobile home" type can often be regarded as a building on the land.

### Issue, service and content of an enforcement notice

A two-stage procedure is contemplated by section 87(1) in using the words "issue . . . and serve" an enforcement notice. This involves, as the first stage, the local planning authority preparing a document for retention in its offices. This document is the enforcement notice itself. The second stage is the service of copies of the document. Section 87(5) requires copies of the enforcement notice to be served not later than 28 days after its issue on (a) the owner and occupier of the land to which it relates and (b) on any other person who has an interest in the land if that person's interest is considered by the local planning authority to be materially affected by the notice. Service of all copies of the notice must be completed at least 28 days before the notice comes into effect, the object of this latter period being to permit a recipient of a copy of the notice to appeal against it if he so wishes.

These provisions require service of a copy of the notice on the freeholder, and on any person who has a lease of the land. But is a caravan dweller an "occupier" of the land or a person "having an interest" in it, thereby entitling him to a copy of the notice? In *Stevens* v. *Bromley London Borough Council* (1972), the Court of Appeal held that owner-occupiers of caravans on an unauthorised site were, in this instance, to be regarded as "occupiers" of the land for the purposes of the enforcement provisions, but that it was a matter of fact and degree whether as licensees of their site pitches they could be classed as such. The relevant factors were considered to be (i) whether the purported occupier was a long-stay resident or merely transient and (ii) whether a substantial degree of control is enjoyed by the licensee. The court also made it clear that occupation under a tenancy agreement would constitute the caravan dwellers "occupiers" but that the two factors mentioned would be especially relevant where a licence is granted of both the caravan and site pitch. On this basis, therefore, a person who stations a caravan on a holiday site would probably be excluded. The position of trespassers who stationed caravans in a lay-by for eighteen months was considered in *Scarborough Borough Council* v. *Adams and Adams* (1983). In resisting a prosecution for failure to comply with the requirements of the notice the defendants argued that as trespassers they could not be considered occupiers of the land and that proceedings under the Town and Country Planning Act 1971 were therefore wholly inappropriate. The Divisional Court held that the local authority could serve a copy of the notice on any person they thought fit but, in any event, in this instance the trespassers were properly to be considered "occupiers" having regard to the length of time the unauthorised encampment had lasted.

As most caravan occupiers are licensees of a site pitch, the observations made in *Stevens* v. *Bromley London Borough Council* are especially pertinent. To these observations must also be added the effect of section 4(2) of the Town and Country Planning Act 1984. This provision gives a right of appeal against an enforcement notice to a person who, on the date of issue of the notice, "occupies the land or building to which the notice relates by virtue of a licence in writing." Since this right of appeal is expressly conferred on the licence holder it is reasonable to expect that he is also entitled to receipt of a copy of the notice, provided he actually occupies the land concerned.

The content of an enforcement notice is regulated by section 87(6) to (10) and (13). These provisions require that the notice must specify (i) the date on which it is to come into effect; (ii) the matters alleged to constitute the breach of planning control; (iii) the steps that are required to be taken by the local planning authority in order to remedy the breach; (iv) the time permitted for taking the required steps (different periods may be required for different steps to be taken). Further requirements are imposed by section 87(12) and by the Town and Country Planning (Enforcement Notices and Appeals) Regulations 1981 (S.I. 1981 No. 1742). These regulations require the notice to specify: (v) the reasons why the local planning authority consider it expedient to issue the enforcement notice, and (vi) the precise boundaries of the land to which the enforcement notice relates (by reference to a plan or otherwise).

With regard to (iii), the steps which can be required must be for the purpose of restoring the land to its condition before the development began or for securing compliance with any conditions or limitations subject to which planning permission was granted. These may include the demolition or alteration of any building or works, the discontinuance of any use of the land, and the carrying out on the land of any building or other operations. It will be apparent, therefore, that an enforcement notice must specify two periods: first, the date on which it is to come into effect (not being less than 28 days before it comes into effect) and, secondly, the date for compliance with its requirements.

In considering whether an enforcement notice meets the above requirements the court will permit the local planning authority some degree of latitude in drafting the notice. In *Eldon Garages Ltd.* v. *Kingston-upon-Hull County Borough Council* (1974) it was held that it was not essential for the notice to use the statutory words "breach of planning control," or to recite that the enforcing council "consider it expedient" to serve the notice or that it applies to a breach which has taken place "after the end of 1963." It is vital, however, that the notice should comply with all the statutory provisions. The essential requirement is as stated by UpJohn L.J. in *Miller-Mead* v. *Minister of Housing and Local Government* (1963) that the notice must tell its recipient "fairly what he has done wrong and what he must do to remedy it." In so doing the question arises whether the notice makes clear that the alleged breach of planning control constitutes an unlawful "operation" on the law or an unlawful "material change of use," thus following the dichotomy in the definition of development in section 22 of the 1971 Act. Despite previous cases to the contrary, notably *East Riding County Council* v. *Park Estate (Bridlington) Ltd.* (1957), the current view of this matter is that the notice need not necessarily be invalid if it makes an incorrect distinction between the two types of development. Thus in *Wealdon District Council* v. *Secretary of State for the Environment* (1983), an enforcement notice alleged that a material change of use had occurred by the stationing of a single caravan. The caravan's wheels, axle and springs had been removed, from which the Secretary of State concluded that the development was of an operational nature and that the enforcement notice should be quashed since it alleged an unauthorised material change of use. The district council succeeded in persuading the court that the enforcement notice could be amended by the Secretary of State in exercise of his power of variation under section 88A(2) (see below) and that this would not cause injustice to the owner of the land on which the caravan was stationed. The matter was accordingly remitted to the Secretary of State for reconsideration. The court accepted, however, that such a change could not always be made if, for example, the owner sought to rely on the four-year limitation period. The enforcement notice must nevertheless always specify the nature of the use to which the caravan is put (*e.g.* residential) whenever an enforcement notice specifies the breach of planning control as a material change of use: *Borough of Restormel* v. *Secretary of State for the Environment* (1983).

### Right of appeal against an enforcement notice

A right of appeal against an enforcement notice is conferred by section 88(1) on any person who has an "interest" in the land to which the notice relates, irrespective of whether that person was served with a copy of the notice. This right is not granted to everyone who might be affected by the notice, so that a squatter would be unable to use this procedure. Thus the trespassers in *Scarborough Borough Council* v. *Adams and Adams*, above, had no right to appeal (even though they were recognised to be occupiers of the land). But a tenant of a caravan is probably included, as also is a licensee who is in occupation pursuant to a written agreement: Town and County Planning Act 1984, s.4(2).

The appeal is initiated by giving written notice to the Secretary of State within the first period specified in the enforcement notice (being at least 28 days). The local planning authority will normally issue a form to be used for making the appeal at the same time as the copies of the enforcement notice are served, and are recommended by the Secretary of State to adopt this practice by DoE Circular 9/81. It is not essential to use this particular form, as any form of written notice will suffice, but it is essential that the appeal is made within the time allowed, as the Secretary of State cannot entertain appeals made out of time: *Howard* v. *Secretary of State for the Environment* (1975). The grounds on which the appeal is based may be stated in the notice of appeal or, alternatively, must be submitted to the Secretary of State within 28 days of being requested by him.

The grounds on which an appeal can be made are specified in section 88(2)(a)–(h). These are as follows:

"(a) that planning permission ought to be granted for the development to which the notice relates or that a condition or limitation alleged in the enforcement notice not to have been complied with ought to be discharged;

(b) that the matters alleged in the notice do not constitute a breach of planning control;

(c) that the breach of planning control alleged in the notice has not taken place;

(d) in the case of a notice which, by virtue of section 87(4) of the 1971 Act, may be issued only within the period of four years from the date of the breach of planning control to which the notice relates, that that period has elapsed at the date when the notice was issued;

(e) in the case of a notice not falling within ground (d), that the breach of planning control alleged by the notice occurred before the beginning of 1964;

(f) that copies of the enforcement notice were not served as required by section 87(5);

(g) that the steps required by the notice to be taken exceed what is necessary to remedy any breach of planning control;

(h) that the period specified in the notice as the period within which any step is to be taken falls short of which should reasonably be allowed."

The making of an appeal involves not only submitting the notice of appeal within the relevant time and giving the grounds of appeal, but also the payment of a fee. The amount of the fee involved is dependent upon the Town and Country Planning (Fees for Applications and Deemed Applications) Regulations 1983 (S.I. 1983 No. 1674) as amended by the Town and Country Planning (Fees for Applications and Deemed Applications)

(Amendment) Regulations 1985 (S.I. 1985 No. 1182). As the name of these Regulations implies, when a appeal is made against an enforcement notice, the appellant is deemed to have made an application for planning permission; this is expressly provided so in the 1971 Act, s.88B(3).

The effect of making an appeal is of the utmost importance. Section 88(10) expressly provides that where an appeal is made "the enforcement notice shall be of no effect pending the final determination or withdrawal of the appeal." An important tactical advantage is therefore open to the appellant, though as explained below this can be countered by the local authority by service of a stop notice.

### Resolving the appeal; powers of the Secretary of State

If an appeal is made and not subsequently withdrawn by the appellant, the Secretary of State will first consider whether the appeal is supported by a statement of grounds of appeal; if not he will request this to be supplied within 28 days. If the appellant fails to do this (because, for example, he merely wishes to delay proceedings by making a groundless appeal) the Secretary of State is empowered to dismiss the appeal forthwith by section 88(6). In the normal case, where the grounds are stated, the Secretary of State is required to give both the appellant and the local planning authority the opportunity of appearing before and being heard by a person appointed for this purpose by the Secretary of State. Such a person, an inspector in the Department of the Environment, will then proceed to conduct a public local inquiry. If, as in the majority of cases, the parties agree to dispose of the appeal without insisting on a personal appearance, each will submit written representations to the DoE in accordance with a procedure contained in Circular 38/81. The appeal will then be decided on the basis of these representations.

In cases where a public local inquiry is to be held the procedure for this is regulated by the Town and Country Planning (Enforcement) (Inquiries Procedure) Rules 1981 (S.I. 1981 No. 1743). While the details of these Rules are beyond the scope of this book, it should be noted that there are special provisions contained in the 1971 Act which apply only to enforcement notice appeals. Of particular relevance is the power contained in section 88A(2) which permits the Secretary of State (acting through the inspector) to correct any informality, defect or error in the enforcement notice or to give directions for varying its terms if he is satisfied that the correction or variation can be made without injustice to the appellant or to the local planning authority. By exercising this power the Secretary of State can, for example, correct an allegation of unauthorised "stationing" of caravans to one of "storage" of caravans, as occurred in *Burner* v. *Secretary of State for the Environment* (1983). The power cannot be used, however, to correct the notice if it involves a matter which "goes to the substance of the matter": *Miller-Mead* v. *Minister of Housing and Local Government* (1963). The power was exercised in *Wealdon District Council* v. *Secretary of State for the Environment* (1983), a case discussed above, in which it was observed, however, that a variation of the notice which specified the wrong type of unauthorised development could not often be effected under s.88A(2) without causing injustice to the appellant. The power will usually be used to alter the steps required to be taken in order to comply with the notice or to vary the stipulated time in which such steps must be taken. Thus the Secretary of State can uphold an enforcement notice in circumstances in which, had the power not existed, he might have been inclined to quash the notice.

The Secretary of State also has a power, conferred by s.88A(3), to disregard the fact that a copy of an enforcement notice has not been served on a person entitled to receive one if no substantial prejudice has been caused to any party. If a copy of the notice is served only on a caravan site operator but not on the occupiers of the caravans, the Secretary of State is unlikely to exercise his powers under this provision. Thus in the enforcement appeal decision noted at [1983] J.P.L. 271 the notice alleged breach of a condition attached to a grant of planning permission requiring the caravans on the site to be painted only with colours in the range specified by the local planning authority. Copies of the notice were not served on the owner-occupiers of the caravans concerned, whose consent would be needed before repainting works could be carried out. The Secretary of State agreed with the inspector's recommendation that the notice should be quashed and that it was inappropriate to use section 88A(3) to disregard the defect of service.

After a conclusion has been reached on the appeal the Secretary of State will direct that (a) the notice be quashed, or (b) the terms of the notice be varied, or (c) the notice be upheld. By exercise of supplementary powers under section 88B(1) he may also make a grant of planning permission for the development to which the notice relates, or for part of the development, or merely for part of the land involved. In addition he may discharge any condition or limitation subject to which planning permission was granted, and can determine any purpose for which the land may be lawfully used having regard to any past use of it and to any planning permission relating to it. The section compliments these powers by deeming an application for planning permission to have been made to the Secretary of State: section 88B(3).

From the decision of the Secretary of State there is a further right of appeal to the High Court under section 246 of the 1971 Act. The circumstances in which such an appeal may be made are briefly considered below. Of greater importance at this stage is to consider whether an enforcement notice can be challenged not only by way of appeal to the Secretary of State, but also in defence of a prosecution for failure to comply with the requirements of the notice. The penalties for failure to comply with an enforcment notice must therefore now be discussed.

## Penalties for non-compliance

The penalties which can be imposed in a case of failure to comply with an enforcement notice are regulated by section 89(1), (4) and (5). These provisions distinguish, first, between a breach of a notice requiring a use of land to be discontinued and one which does not relate to discontinuance of a use, and, secondly, between a conviction for a first offence and a subsequent conviction for continued failure to comply with a notice.

Under section 89(1) if a copy of an enforcement notice has been served on the *owner* of the land and the steps required to be taken (other than discontinuance of a use of the land) are not complied with the owner is guilty of an offence and liable on summary conviction to a fine of up to £2,000 and on

37

conviction on indictment to an unlimited fine. Section 89(4) further provides that failure to do everything in his power to secure compliance with
the notice as soon as practicable after conviction under section 89(1) renders
the owner guilty of a further offence in respect of which a maximum fine of
£100 can be imposed for every day the requirements are unfulfilled. If a conviction is obtained on indictment there is no limit to the fine which can be
imposed.

Non-compliance with an enforcement notice which requires a discontinuance of a use of land (or compliance with a condition attached to a planning permission) is dealt with by section 89(5). This section imposes
identical penalties for failure to comply, and also for permitting the use to
continue after a first conviction. These offences are committed, however,
by *any person* who uses the land or causes or permits it to be used in contravention of the notice, irrespective of whether a copy of the enforcement
notice has been served on that person.

It will be noted that section 89(5) uses the expression "causes or permits"
in attaching liability to "any person" who is in default of the requirements
of the notice. This phraseology raises a question concerning the liability of a
landowner who is burdened with a trespasser. If the trespasser stations a
caravan on the land for the purpose of habitation does the landowner commit a criminal offence if he does not take eviction proceedings against the
trespasser? In *Ragsdale* v. *Creswick* (1984) a trespasser remained in possession of the land with his caravan for approximately two years. The
defendant landowner made many efforts to persuade the trespasser to leave,
falling short of legal proceedings. The local planning authority prosecuted
the trespasser on at least one occasion as being "any person" who "causes or
permits" the breach of planning control to continue. Although a conviction
was obtained, the local planning authority decided to take no further action
and they proceeded instead against the landowner, as the trespasser had still
failed to vacate the land. The Divisional Court held that whether a person
"causes or permits" a use of land to continue is essentially a question of fact
for the magistrates' court to decide after taking into account all the circumstances of the case, but the fact that legal proceedings had not been instituted for possession did not automatically lead to the conclusion that an
offence had been committed.

Where criminal proceedings are instituted is it open to the defendant to
seek to challenge the enforcement notice in his defence? Can he allege that
the notice is invalid on any of the grounds specified in section 88(2)? In considering the answer to these questions account must be taken of section
243(1) which provides:

> "Subject to the provisions of this section—
>     (a) the validity of an enforcement notice shall not, except by way of
>         an appeal under [section 88] of this Act, be questioned in any pro-
>         ceedings whatsoever on any of the grounds on which such an
>         appeal may be brought; . . . ."

This provision is designed to ensure that a challenge to the validity of an
enforcement notice is directed to the Secretary of State rather than the
court. A person who fails to appeal in time against an enforcement notice—
or has no "interest" enabling him to appeal—is therefore unable to allege
that it is invalid on any ground specified in section 88: *R.* v. *Smith* (*Thomas*

*George)* (1984). A specific exception applies, however, to a prosecution under section 89(5). Thus section 243(2) provides that the preclusive effect of section 243(1)(*a*) does not apply to a person who has held an interest since before the enforcement notice was issued but was not served with a copy of the enforcement notice. To be able to challenge the notice in defence to a prosecution he must satisfy the court that he did not know and could not reasonably be expected to have known that the enforcement notice had been issued and that his interests have been substantially prejudiced by that omission. This would seem particularly apposite to a caravan dweller under a licence. It is also open to the defendant to challenge the notice on any ground other than those appearing in section 88(2): *Davy* v. *Spelthorne Borough Council* (1983).

An entirely different approach can be taken by a defendant by his arguing that the notice is a nullity, *i.e.* that the notice has some defect on its face or that the local planning authority has no jurisdiction to issue it. This is particularly relevant to a person who has no right of appeal to the Secretary of State due to lack of an "interest" in the land, such as the squatters in *Scarborough Borough Council* v. *Adams and Adams* (1983) (see p. 33). A notice which is a nullity has no legal effect at all and the defendant is entitled to rely on this point in his defence. He is also entitled to seek judicial review of the notice in order to have the notice quashed by the High Court in accordance with the procedure contained in the Rules of the Supreme Court, Ord. 53, and the Supreme Court Act 1981, s.31.

### Power of entry

If the steps required by an enforcement notice to be taken are not carried out within the period allowed for compliance, not only is an offence committed under section 89, but also the local planning authority have a power, conferred by section 91, to enter onto the land. This power only applies, however, if the authority have served an enforcement notice in relation to unauthorised building, etc., rather than one requiring a use of land to be discontinued.

The purpose of the power of entry is to enable the local planning authority to take the steps necessary for compliance with the notice and to restore the land to the condition it was in before the development took place. The costs of carry out these steps can then be recovered from the owner of the land in so far as they are reasonably incurred.

In *Midlothian District Council* v. *Stevenson* (1985) it was held that a local authority could enter upon land to remove caravans constituting an authorised caravan site, despite the fact that this would lead to a "discontinuance of the use of the land." The Court of Session held that the local planning authority could exercise this power since the steps required by the enforcement notice specifically required the removal of caravans on the land (as distinct from merely requiring the use to cease).

### Stop notice procedure

The making of an appeal against the service of an enforcement notice has the effect of suspending its effect until the appeal is determined: section 88(10). Sometimes the appeal is lodged merely as a delaying tactic. This tactic can, however, be countered by the local planning authority exercising their power under section 90 of the 1971 Act (as substituted by the Town and Country Planning (Amendment) Act 1977) to serve a stop notice. If, after a copy of an enforcement notice has been served, the local planning authority consider it expedient to serve a stop notice they may thereby seek to end the activity alleged in the enforcement notice to be a breach of planning control at an earlier stage than the period for compliance permitted by the enforcement notice.

The local planning authority must serve the stop notice during the first period specified in the enforcement notice and attach to it a copy of the enforcement notice. It is not necessary for the local planning authority to wait until an appeal is made against an enforcement notice; it is sufficient that the authority consider it expedient to serve the stop notice, e.g. in the interests of early termination of a breach of planning control detrimental to health or safety.

The word "activity" in section 90(1) means the stop procedure is equally applicable both to breaches of development control of a building or operational nature, and to those breaches involving a material change of use. The procedure, has, however, a limited application in the context of caravans because section 90(2) provides that a stop notice is inapplicable to (a) the use of any building as a dwelling-house, (b) the use of land as the site for a caravan by any person as his only or main residence, or (c) the taking of any steps which are required by the enforcement notice to remedy the breach of planning control. Exception (b), however, does not prevent service of a stop notice in relation to a caravan site used for holiday purposes only. A further limitation is that the procedure cannot be used to prevent a material change of use (other than the deposit of refuse or waste materials) which began more than twelve months previously. This rule is relevant to the stationing of a caravan for holiday purposes if that use commenced more than twelve months previously, and is also relevant when enforcement proceedings are taken after a temporary planning permission for a period exceeding twelve months has expired: *Scott Markets Ltd.* v. *Waltham Forest London Borough Council* (1979).

A stop notice must provide for a period of notice before it takes effect. This is a minimum period of three days and a maximum of twenty-eight days from the date of its service. It may be served on any person appearing to the local authority to have an interest in the land or to be engaged in any activity prohibited by the notice. A site notice can also be displayed on the land itself stating that a stop notice has been served and that any person who contravenes its requirements is subject to criminal proceedings.

The penalties for failure to observe a stop notice are as provided by section 90(7). An offence is thereby committed by any person who contravenes, or causes or permits the contravention of, a stop notice if such a notice has been served on him or a site notice has been displayed. The maximum penalty on summary conviction is a fine of £2,000, but an unlimited fine can be imposed on conviction on indictment. Failure to comply with the notice after first conviction is a further offence for which there is a maximum penalty of up to £100 for each day the offence continues, with an unlimited daily fine on conviction on indictment.

There is no right of appeal against a stop notice; but as there is no equivalent provision to section 243 of the 1971 Act (which applies only to enforcement notices) it is open to a person charged with an offence under section 90(7) to challenge the validity of the stop notice: *R.* v. *Jenner* (1983).

In practice, a local planning authority will not serve a stop notice unless confident that the enforcement notice on which it is dependent will be upheld by the Secretary of State. This is because if the enforcement notice is quashed by the Secretary of State the local planning authority are liable to compensate the appellant for "any loss or damage directly attributable to the prohibition contained in the notice": section 177 of the 1971 Act.

### Established use certificate

When the four-year limitation period for service of an enforcement notice was withdrawn in 1968 in relation to most developments comprising a material change of use, a significant complimentary legislative change was necessitated. A use of land which had previously gained immunity from planning control became potentially vulnerable to enforcement action, for as time went on it would become more difficult to show that it commenced before 1968 and was thereby immune from enforcement action. To avoid injustice section 94 provides for the issue of an "established use certificate" in the following circumstances:

(i) the use was begun before the beginning of 1964 without planning permission in that behalf and has continued since the end of 1963; or

(ii) the use was begun before the beginning of 1964 under a planning permission in that behalf granted subject to conditions or limitations, which either have never been complied with or have not been complied with since the end of 1963; or

(iii) the use was begun after the end of 1963 as the result of a change of use not requiring planning permission and there has been, since the end of 1963, no change of use requiring planning permission.

Any person who has an interest in the land concerned can apply for an established use certificate: section 94(2). If the local planning authority are satisfied that the claim for the certificate is made out they must issue the certificate; once issued, the certificate is conclusive evidence in defending any future enforcement proceedings: section 94(7).

It is most important to appreciate that an established use certificate does not legalise an unlawful use of the land. Its function is merely to provide a defence to enforcement proceedings. As will be seen in the next Chapter, a site licence issued under the Caravan Sites and Control of Development Act 1960 can only be issued in respect of land in relation to which an express grant of planning permission has been given, with the result that an established use certificate is inadequate for that purpose. Since most caravan sites are required to be licenced under the 1960 Act, the site operator is thereby obliged to apply for a grant of planning permission.

### Appeal to the High Court

Although the appellant against an enforcement notice has a right of appeal to the Secretary of State for the Environment under section 88 of the 1971 Act, when the Secretary of State has given his decision a further appeal is available to the High Court under section 246. This right of appeal is available to the original appellant, the local planning authority, and to any other person who has an interest in the land. The right of appeal is, however, limited to a decision on a point of law only; the merits of the Secretary of State's decision are not capable of being the subject of an appeal. The Secretary of State can be required to state a case for the opinion of the High Court as an alternative means of deciding the point of law in issue.

The procedure involved is regulated by the Rules of the Supreme Court, Ord. 94, r.12. Notice of the appeal must be entered within twenty-eight days after posting of the Secretary of State's decision letter. On reaching its decision the court cannot quash an enforcement notice in a case where the Secretary of State has made a mistake on a point of law; the notice is remitted back to the Secretary of State for further consideration in the light of the court's decision.

### Enforcement and Crown land

A particular problem of enforcement of planning control arises in connection with unauthorised development on Crown land, *i.e.* land belonging to a central government department. The difficulty is due to the limited application of the Town and Country Planning Act 1971 to Crown land. The Act does not apply to development carried out by the Crown, but according to section 266(1)(b) the Act does apply "to the extent of any interest . . . for the time being held otherwise than by or on behalf of the Crown." This means that a person (other than the Crown) who holds an interest in the land (*e.g.* a leaseholder) is subject to the full force of the legislation, but the Crown remains exempt. The reason for this was explained by Lord Denning M.R. in *Ministry of Agriculture, Fisheries and Food* v. *Jenkins* (1963), when, in commenting upon earlier legislation, he said:

> "Looking at the whole of the Town and Country Planning Act 1947 I am satisfied that the Crown does not need to get planning permission in respect of its own interest in Crown lands. The reason it is exempt is . . . by reason of the general principle that the Crown is not bound by an Act unless it is expressly or impliedly included."

The general principle has subsequently been amended by section 1 of the Town and Country Planning Act 1984 which enables the representatives of the Crown to apply for and receive a grant of planning permission.

So far as enforcement of planning control was concerned, enforcement action was not possible against a person who carried out development on Crown land unless that person held an interest in the land and the Crown consented to the issue of an enforcement notice. But enforcement action could not be taken against a trespasser or licensee on the land. Thus if caravans were stationed on the verge of land adjacent to a trunk road (the responsibility of the Minister for Transport), the local planning authority could take no action under the town and country planning legislation and had to rely on less advantageous powers under the highways legislation, as discussed in Chapter 8. Anomalously, this problem did not arise in the context of other highway land: in *Scarborough Borough Council* v. *Adams and Adams* (1983) enforcement action was held to be competent against the occupiers of caravans which were situated in a lay-by for eighteen months. In relation to Crown land the difficulty of taking enforcement action has been circumvented by section 3 of the Town and Country Planning Act 1984. If no private interest exists in the land, *e.g.* in the case of a trespasser, the local planning authority are empowered to remedy a breach of planning control by serving a "special enforcement notice" provided the Crown consents to the issue of the notice. Such a notice is similar in nature to an ordinary enforcement notice except that: (i) a copy of the notice must be served on (a) the person(s) who carried out the unauthorised development alleged in the notice, and (b) any person who is occupying the land on the date when the notice is issued, and (c) the Crown; and that (ii) there are only two grounds of appeal against a special enforcement notice. These are that "the matters alleged in the notice have not taken place or do not constitute development."

The position of licensee in possession of Crown land is, by virtue of section 4(1) of the 1984 Act, assimilated to that of any other person who holds an interest in the land, provided the licence is granted in writing. An ordinary enforcement notice can therefore be served in such a case and the licensee may appeal against the notice on any of the grounds specified in section 88(2) of the 1971 Act. This right of appeal is expressly conferred by section 4(2) of the 1984 Act.

### Enforcement by injunction

The system of enforcement of development control rests on criminal sanctions for failure to comply with an enforcement notice. Since the legislation provides only for the imposition of fines, a persistent offender can, on some occasions, take the cynical view that payment of monetary penalties is tantamount to a licence to continue in breach of an enforcement notice. In such circumstances the local planning authority may seek an injunction in the High Court restraining the offender from ignoring the requirements of an enforcement notice. Failure to comply with the requirements of an injunction is a contempt of court which can result in imprisonment for an indefinite period, effectively until the contempt is purged. The local planning authority must proceed with meticulous attention to detail in seeking this remedy since personal liberty is involved. As a result, the notice of motion to commit to prison, and the committal order, must specify exactly the contempt involved: *Chiltern District Council* v. *Keane* (1985).

This remedy is particularly relevant in the context of unauthorised caravan sites, as illustrated by *Attorney-General* v. *Bastow* (1957). The defendant was successfully prosecuted on three occasions for failure to comply with the requirements of an enforcement notice which required an unauthorised use of land as a caravan site for human habitation to cease. The defendant did not pay all the fines imposed and was imprisoned for a period as a result of this default. The Attorney-General then brought an action for an injunction on the relation of the local planning authority. The High Court held that when a public right is infringed the court has jurisdiction to grant an injunction, the public right in this instance being (per Devlin J.) that " . . . Parliament considers that the public is entitled not to have the land used in ways which may be considered to be unhealthy or offensive." The learned judge recognised that the remedies provided by the planning legislation could ultimately lead to the same result as the grant of an injunction, and he referred to the power of the local planning authority to enter onto the land and carry out the steps required by the enforcement notice. He decided, however, that notwithstanding the powers contained in the legis-

43

lation, whether an injunction should be sought or not was matter only for the Attorney-General, and then proceeded to grant the remedy sought.

The utility of this procedure was extended considerably by the decision in *Attorney-General* v. *Smith* (1958). In this instance the defendant moved the caravans from a site in respect of which he had been convicted for failure to comply with an enforcement notice onto another site. He subsequently moved the caravans to a third site. Rather than institute enforcement proceedings for a third time the local planning authority successfully petitioned the Attorney-General to proceed for an injunction on the relation of the council. This injunction was granted despite the fact no enforcement notice had been issued in respect of the third plot of land. It was sufficient that the defendant had manifested an intention to flout the town and country planning legislation. The injunction itself was expressed to restrain the defendant from using any land in the area of the local planning authority for unauthorised stationing of caravans. A county-wide injunction was granted in the later case of *Attorney-General* v. *Morris* (1973) though O'Connor J. declined to grant an injunction having effect nationwide.

Since the enactment of section 222 of the Local Government Act 1972, the local planning authority may seek an injunction by proceedings under its own name without involving the Attorney-General, a view confirmed by the House of Lords in *Stoke-on-Trent City Council* v. *B. & Q. (Retail) Ltd.* (1984). The section provides that where a local authority considers it expedient for the promotion or protection of the interests of the inhabitants of their area they may prosecute or defend or appear in any legal proceedings and may institute them in their own name. The scope of the injunction remedy has also expanded in recent years, notably as a result of the judgment of Lord Denning M.R. in *Stafford Borough Council* v. *Elkenford Ltd.* (1977) who accepted that injunction proceedings could be started before the remedy offered by the statute had even been initiated, provided that the breach of the statute was plain. An injunction was also held to be applicable in a case of failure to comply with a stop notice in *Westminster City Council* v. *Jones* (1981). Here proceedings for failure to comply with the stop notice had been initiated but not yet heard; an injunction was granted when the unauthorised development continued without regard to the enforcement notice and subsequent stop notice. A further illustration is provided by *Runnymede Borough Council* v. *Ball* (1985) in which the injunction remedy was considered appropriate by the Court of Appeal as a means of preventing the formation of a gypsy site, since prosecution proceedings would be too slow.

## Register of enforcement notices and stop notices

A person who is contemplating bringing a caravan onto an existing caravan site, or who is considering purchasing a caravan already present on the site, is well advised to make a search in the above register to ensure that there are no outstanding notices in relation to the land. Failure to make a thorough check could result in having to leave the site if any notices as may exist are enforced. While a copy of an enforcement notice has to be served on the owner and occupier of the land in question, and on any person having an interest in it (section 87(5) of the 1971 Act), no site notice has to be posted on the land. The latter step is only applicable to the service of a stop notice in circumstances when the land (or part of it) is not being used for a caravan site by persons occupying the caravans as their only or main residence (section 90(2)(b)). In many instances, therefore, the potential site resident would not discover the existence of an enforcement notice unless a prior search was made in the register of local land charges maintained under the Local Land Charges Act 1972. While a search of the last named register is made in all conveyancing transactions—and would be prudent in the present context—the search reveals only the existence but not the details of any enforcement notice that may have been issued.

The register of enforcement and stop notices is maintained pursuant to section 92A of the 1971 Act, a provision inserted by section 1 and the Schedule to the Local Government and Planning (Amendment) Act 1981. This section requires the register to be maintained by the relevant district council (or London borough). The details of the content of the register are regulated by the Town and Country Planning General Development (Amendment) (No. 2) Order 1981 (S.I. 1981 No. 1569) which inserted article 21A into the Town and Country Planning General Development Order 1977 (S.I. 1977 No. 289). The regulations require that the register shall contain the following information in relation to any enforcement notice:

(a) the address of the land to which the notice relates or a plan by reference to which its situation can be ascertained;

(b) the name of the issuing authority;

(c) the date of issue of the notice;

(d) the date of service of copies of the notice;

(e) a statement or summary of the breach of planning control alleged and the requirements of the notice, including the period within which any required steps are to be taken;

(f) the date specified in the notice as the date on which it is to take effect;

(g) information on any postponement of the date on which the notice is to take effect and the date of the final determination or withdrawal of any appeal;

(h) the date of service of any stop notice together with a summary of the activity prohibited;

(i) the date on which the local planning authority are satisfied that steps required by the notice are complied with.

The information contained in the register is entered as soon as practicable, but in any case not less than fourteen days after the event giving rise to the entry. Once entered in the register the information relevant to an enforcement notice will not be removed unless the notice is quashed on appeal or is withdrawn by the local planning authority. Since compliance with the notice does not discharge it (section 93), the entry in the register subsists, note being made of the date on which the local planning authority are satisfied that the steps required to be taken have been complied with. The enforcement notice will serve thereafter to restrain a future recurrence of the breach of planning control.

Access to the register is by personal attendance at the offices of the district council (or London borough) at any reasonable time. No charge is made for inspection.

# 4. Caravan Site Licensing: The Caravan Sites and Control of Development Act 1960

Part I of the Caravan Sites and Control of Development Act 1960 contains the statutory code which governs the arrangements for licensing of caravan sites by district councils and London boroughs. The purpose is to control many of the internal management arrangements of sites and to make provision, via site licence conditions, for matters concerning the public health aspects of caravan site use and also for matters relevant to amenity. The code thereby operates as an additional means of control over caravan sites, since the operator of such a site must comply not only with the requirements of any conditions of the grant of planning permission authorising use of the site, but must also observe the conditions subject to which the site licence is granted under the 1960 Act. As has been seen in Chapter 3, the planning aspects of the use of land as a caravan site are subject to the enforcement provisions of the Town and Country Planning Act 1971 (as amended). By contrast, the Caravan Sites and Control of Development Act 1960 incorporates a different and far less complex form of control arising from failure to obtain a site licence or failure to comply with any of the conditions attached to it, as in this instance criminal penalties are incurred without the preliminary step of service of an enforcement notice. As will be explained, it is in the conditions which may be attached to a site licence that the main interest in the 1960 Act lies. The purpose of this Chapter is therefore to discuss the pertinent sections of the Act and the salient features of the considerable body of case law which it has generated in the 26 years since it came into force on August 29, 1960.

## Scope of Part I of the 1960 Act: the need for a site licence

The basic premise of the 1960 Act is that land must not be used as a caravan site unless a site licence has been issued by the local authority for the area in which the land is situated. Thus section 1(1) provides that

" . . . no occupier of land shall . . . cause or permit any part of the land to be used as a caravan site unless he is the holder of a site licence . . . for the time being in force as respects the land so used."

Two of the expressions used in section 1(1) are defined in section 1(3) and (4) respectively.

"Occupier" means "the person who by virtue of an estate or interest in the land is entitled to possession of the land or would be so entitled but for the rights of any other person under licence granted in respect of the land."

The meaning of this provision is not immediately obvious and is perhaps best explained with the use of some examples. In the simplest case freehold land owned by X is used by him by way of grant of licences to individual caravan dwellers on specific pitches allocated to them. Here X is the occupier. Often X will grant a lease of the land to Y who then proceeds to allocate the pitches. In this case Y is the occupier, not X. Occasionally X will grant a lease to Y who sublets or grants a mere licence to occupy to Z who then proceeds to allocate the pitches. Here Z is the occupier to the exclusion of X and Y if he holds a sublease or tenancy, but not if he is only a licensee: *Hereford City Council* v. *Edmunds* (1985). It is apparent from the wording of the provision that none of these three parties can escape their responsibilities under the 1960 Act by granting a licence to the individual caravan dweller. Nor can the application of the Act to X or Y (as appropriate) be avoided by granting a *tenancy* of a site pitch to the individual caravan dweller. This is because an important proviso to section 1(3) states:

> "Provided that where land amounting to not more than four hundred square yards in area is let under a tenancy entered into with a view to the use of the land as a caravan site, the expression 'occupier' means in relation to that land the person who would be entitled to possession of the land but for the rights of any person under that tenancy."

Apart from ensuring that site operators are brought within the 1960 Act irrespective of whether they give tenancies or licences to the caravan dwellers, the proviso also means that if the whole site is less than four hundred square yards in area and is let by X to Y with a view to the use by Y as a caravan site by issue of licences to others, then X will be the occupier.

"Caravan site" is defined by section 1(4) to mean "land on which a caravan is stationed for the purposes of human habitation and land which is used in conjunction with land on which a caravan is so stationed." This definition is not a particularly helpful one for its application to commonly encountered site characteristics in practice shows that there is often some doubt as to what constitutes the extent of the site, particularly in relation to those sites which existed prior to the commencement of the 1960 Act and which came into existence without a previous grant of planning permission (where a grant of planning permission exists the boundaries of the site will normally be carefully defined by the local planning authority). Shortly after the 1960 Act came into force the courts were called upon on several occasions to determine the true effect of section 1(4). In *Williams-Denton* v. *Watford RDC* (1963) a plot of four and a half acres containing no internal boundaries consisted mainly of a neglected orchard but having some open land and a house incorporated in the plot. This became used for a caravan site by four caravans in one part of the orchard. At a later time another part of the orchard was used for the stationing of 14 caravans. The use of the latter part was in breach of planning control and became subject to enforcement action by the district council. The site operator contended that the whole of the land should be regarded as one site, not two, and that there was no breach of planning control and accordingly a site licence should be issued for the whole plot under the 1960 Act. The Court of Appeal decided that there was ample evidence to suggest that there were in reality two sites within the plot, neither being used in conjunction with the other.

A case involving a single caravan, *R.* v. *Axbridge RDC, ex p. Wormald*

(1964), raised the issue of how much land, apart from that on which the caravan stood constituted the site. The caravan was placed in a two and a half acre area, consisting mostly of sand dunes, adjacent to a bungalow, and was used to accommodate holidaymakers. Access was given to them to use the whole of the area for recreation. The owner of the land applied for a site licence which the council duly issued but it was limited to the land on which the caravan stood and to the land around it to a radius of 20 feet. The applicant contended that he was entitled to a site licence for the whole two and a half acre site and it was clear that he intended to bring more caravans onto the land. In the Court of Appeal, Lord Denning M.R. held that the recreational use of the area did not bring it within the scope of section 1(4) of the 1960 Act. He said:

> "In order that land should be 'used in conjunction with land on which a caravan is so stationed' it must, I think, be used immediately and directly in conjunction with it; for instance, land for a latrine, or on which a motor car stands, or land laid out as a playground. Such land would be part of the site, but not waste land which children or adults may run over from time to time."

The Court of Appeal therefore refused to direct the council to alter the site licence.

Once the boundaries of the site are established, do the words in section 1(4) " . . . land on which a caravan is situated . . . " infer that the process of defining the site should incorporate consideration of the number of caravans upon it? In *Hartnell* v. *Minister of Housing and Local Government* (1965) it was contended that land on which six caravans were stationed constituted a caravan site limited to that number. The question arose because the local planning authority had granted planning permission limiting the number of caravans on the site to six, the effect of which was to deprive the site operator of existing use rights he enjoyed which would permit him to bring more caravans onto the land, provided a material change of use did not thereby occur by intensification of the use (see p. 22). In determining the question it was necessary for the court to refer to section 1(4). It was held that to regard the meaning of "caravan site" as being qualified by the number of caravans situated upon the land would involve, without specific statutory authority, loss of rights by the site operator. Accordingly the governing word was "land" which refers to the piece of land on which caravans are stationed without reference to the number thereon. Less attention was paid to section 1(4) in the subsequent appeal to the House of Lords but it is worthy of note that Lord Wilberforce pointed out that the definition of "caravan site" is not determined by reference to the number of caravans on the land.

To constitute a caravan site it appears that it does not matter that the land is only in seasonal use. In *Biss* v. *Smallburgh RDC* (1964) it was claimed that 35 acres of land constituted a caravan site in circumstances where the owner permitted casual visitors to station their caravans anywhere on the land for a small charge per night. During most summer seasons the number of caravans on the land did not exceed twelve. The Court of Appeal decided that the use of the land did not end at the end of each season, nor would the fact that if on a given day no caravans were on the land prevent it from being regarded as in use as a caravan site. Nevertheless it is essential to be able to define the area of land which is alleged to constitute the site; in this case the evidence was too vague and uncertain to be able to say whether the 35 acres, or any lesser part, constituted the "site." Thus Harman L.J. said:

> "What is looked for here is a 'site' and that word seems to me to connote a place habitually devoted to some purpose. Moreover, the words in the definition about caravans being 'stationed' on the land seem to me to have like connotation. Caravans, I think, are not 'stationed' on an area where one or two of them have casually stopped for a night or so even though there may have been other caravans which have stopped in the vicinity in several years"

Of the other expressions used in section 1(1) the statutory definition of "caravan" has already been considered in Chapter 1, but there is no statutory definition of the expression "cause or permit." These words are critical to the question whether an offence is committed by failure to obtain a site licence and will now be examined, along with the criminal penalties involved.

### Failure to obtain a site licence

Under section 1(2) of the 1960 Act, an offence is committed by failure to obtain a site licence, where required, followed by a further offence if no site licence is obtained following a first conviction. The subsection is in the following terms:

> "If the occupier of any land contravenes subsection (1) of this section he shall be guilty of an offence and liable on summary conviction, in the case of the first offence to a fine not exceeding £100 and in the case of second or subsequent offence to a fine not exceeding £1,000."

Since these offences are only committed if the occupier should "cause or permit" the land to be used as a caravan site what is the position if trespassers enter onto the land, *e.g.* entry by a party of gipsies? In *Test Valley Investments Ltd.* v. *Tanner* (1964) a site owned by a development company became occupied by approximately 30 gipsies, who comprised a floating population. No attempt was made by the company to obtain a site licence and the company was successfully prosecuted for this default. The company then commenced proceedings in the county court to obtain injunctions against the trespassers but because of the floating population at the site these proved ineffective. Proceedings were brought for a second offence and the magistrates again convicted the appellant company on the basis that the company had "permitted" the use of the site, since no attempt was made to physically evict the trespassers. On appeal to the Divisional Court the company claimed it was not reasonable to resort to the remedy of self-help. The court held that (*per* Lord Parker C.J.)

> " . . . if the only steps that can be taken are steps which in all the circumstances are unreasonable you cannot be said to permit because you do not take those unreasonable steps."

In this instance it was found to be "wholly unreasonable" to resort to the remedy of self-help, as a breach of the peace was predictable.

In the *Test Valley Investments* case it was clear that the occupier company had done everything in their power after the first prosecution to remove the gipsies short of physical ejection. It does not necessarily follow, however, that the occupier must commence legal action to regain possession to avoid being guilty of, "permitting" the land to be used as a caravan site, since this depends on the circumstances. Thus in *Bromsgrove*

*District Council* v. *Carthy* (1975) the owner of the land tried patiently but unsuccessfully to persuade the gipsies to leave the site but did not seek an injunction against them. The magistrates refused to convict for "permitting" the use of the land without a site licence, and the prosecuting council appealed to the Divisional Court on the ground that it was reasonable for the defendant to take legal action against the gipsies and that she should have done so. The court held that the question whether or not legal action should have been taken was only a factor to be taken into consideration in deciding whether an offence had been committed, but it was a question which the magistrates had to consider in looking at all the circumstances of the case. In so doing they would need to assess the prospects of success in the action and the costs involved in litigation, but it was *prima facie* for the magistrates, as the tribunal of fact, to decide what steps are reasonable and what are not reasonable in a particular situation. Since the justices had directed their minds to the correct issues their decision would not be overturned.

Another aspect of prosecution for an offence under section 1 is the need for accuracy in the drafting of the information laid before the magistrates. This is illustrated by *Waddell* v. *Winter* (1967) in which the defendant placed a single caravan upon his own land and proceeded to live in it without bothering to obtain a site licence. He was charged with "permitting" the use of the land as a caravan site but he argued that since he used the site himself he was not "permitting" its use. This argument succeeded before the magistrates, and in the Divisional Court, where Lord Parker C.J. pointed out that "The offence of permitting is committed when someone is allowed to do something as a matter of permission and not as a matter of authority or mandate from the occupier." If, however, the defendant had been charged with "causing" the use of the land as a caravan site he would properly have been convicted.

Where an occupier of land is repeatedly prosecuted for offences under section 1 of the 1960 Act it is probably open to the district council concerned to seek an injunction to prevent further breaches of the law. An occupier in breach of the injunction would then be subject to imprisonment for contempt of court. There do not appear to be any reported cases where this has actually occurred, though this is probably due to the likelihood that the offender is also in breach of planning control; if the occupier has repeatedly failed to comply with enforcement notices then the enforcing council could probably seek an injunction in respect of that failure in accordance with the decisions in *Att-Gen* v. *Bastow* (1957) and *Att-Gen* v. *Smith* (1958) (see pp. 43, 44).

### Exemptions from the site licence requirement

While section 1 of the 1960 Act sets out the basic requirement for a site licence, section 2 and Schedule 1 proceed to grant a series of exemptions. The list of exemptions has already been referred to in Chapter 2 (see p. 24) where it was considered in connection with exemptions from the need to obtain an express grant of planning permission. In that context it was observed that Class XXII of Schedule 1 to the Town and Country Planning General Development Order 1977 automatically grants planning permission for the use of land as a caravan site in accordance with any of the circumstances specified in paragraphs 2-9 of Schedule 1 to the 1960 Act, or in the circumstances (other than those relating to winter quarters) specified in paragraph 10, thereof.

As the Schedule specifies a total of 12 "circumstances" those that were not mentioned in Chapter 2 now require to be considered, those contained in paragraphs 1, 11 and 11A of the Schedule:

> "1. A site licence shall not be required for the use of land as a caravan site if the use is incidental to the enjoyment as such of a dwelling-house within the curtilage of which the caravan is situated.
> 11. A site licence shall not be required for the use as a caravan site of land occupied by the local authority in whose area the land is situated.
> 11A. (*added by section 176 of the Local Government, Planning and Land Act 1980*) A site licence shall not be required for the use of land occupied by a county council . . . as a caravan site providing accommodation for gipsies."

The circumstances specified in paras. 11 and 11A are excluded undoubtedly because it is pointless for responsible public authorities who have functions under the caravans legislation (especially the power to provide caravan sites for permanent, temporary, or holiday use under section 24 of the 1960 Act) to grant licences to themselves (district councils) or, in the case of county councils, to have to seek a licence from the relevant district council. Paragraph 1, however, is worthy of note because it can be argued that, having regard to the wording of the paragraph, a site licence is, in appropriate conditions, required in connection with the use of a caravan situated in the curtilage of a dwelling-house. As has been demonstrated in Chapter 2 (see p. 18), planning permission is sometimes necessary when the use of a caravan is such that it is not incidental to the use of the dwelling-house. Where this occurs it follows that a site licence is also necessary because paragraph 1 is limited to the case where the use of the caravan is "incidental" and therefore does not confer exemption from every instance where a caravan is situated in the curtilage.

The position of travelling showmen in winter quarters (during the whole or part of the period October 1–March 31) is that no site licence is required, but an express grant of planning permission is needed since this type of use of land by travelling showmen is not granted planning permission under Class XXII of the GDO. A site licence is needed, however, if the site is not used exclusively by travelling showmen: *Holmes* v. *Cooper* (1985).

## Application for a site licence

If the use of the land is not exempt from the site licensing requirement then it is the occupier's responsibility to obtain a licence from the district council. Application may be made on a form issued by the council (there is no prescribed form); the only legal requirements are those stated in section 3(2) of the 1960 Act which requires the application to be in writing, to specify the land in respect of which the application is made, and to give the local authority such other information as they may reasonably require. No fee is payable. Before an amendment to section 3(2) was made by the Local Government, Planning and Land Act 1980, Sched. 3, para. 10, the last requirement read "such particulars . . . as the Minister may from time to time prescribe." The Minister exercised this power in making the Caravan Sites (Licence Applications) Order 1960 (S.I. 1960 No. 1474) which prescribed the form of particulars to be supplied. The Order is set out at Appendix II but it is the author's opinion that it no longer has the force of law due to the removal of the statutory power which enabled it to be made. In practice, however, the form is almost invariably still used.

An application is treated as lodged with the district council when a written request has been received for a site licence even though the full particulars have not been supplied at that stage: section 3(2). This provision permits an informal application to be recognised as an application for a licence, *e.g.* as occurred in *Chelmsford RDC* v. *Powell* (1965) in which the applicant attached a letter to an application for a grant of planning permission which stated:

> "Dear Sir,
> Please find enclosed forms and location plans. You will find also plan of all the industrial sites that surround me. I am making an application for fifty or more— as under the new Act. I also propose the following: eight toilets, six warm showers and laundry facilities, which will have ready (layout) if wanted by you. Also: concrete slabs for each caravan good paths—also anything that will better the site."

The Divisional Court held that this letter amounted to an application for a site licence on consideration of two criteria: (i) is the application capable of being an application for a site licence? (ii) would a reasonably-minded planning officer treat it as such?

As the district council are entitled to call for "such other information as they may reasonably require," it is only upon submission of that information that a statutory period of two months begins to run under section 3(4) within which time the district council must issue a licence, unless a longer period is agreed in writing.

So far it would seem that obtaining a site licence is a comparatively simple exercise. It is, however, a process which is subject to a fundamental prerequisite, for in the terms of section 3(3).

> "A local authority may . . . issue a site licence . . . if, and only if, the applicant is entitled to the benefit of a permission for the use of the land as a caravan site granted under Part III of the Act of 1971 otherwise than by a development order."

This means that the applicant cannot obtain a site licence unless an express grant of planning permission exists for the use of the land as a caravan site. While the issue of a site licence is mandatory if the planning permission requirement is satisfied, the grant of planning permission on which the site licence application depends is a discretionary decision to be made by the local planning authority, or the Secretary of State if an appeal is made to him. Often it is the pre-requisite of planning permission that will frustrate the grant of the licence. In the case of a proposed new caravan site there will often be a simultaneous application for planning permission and for the site licence; if the planning application is successful the site licence must be issued within six weeks of the grant of the planning permission or any longer period that may be agreed in writing (section 3(5)). This is in contrast to the normal rule contained in section 3(4) which requires the site licence to be issued two months after all the relevant particulars have been furnished to the district council in a case where planning permission has already been obtained by the applicant.

The importance of the express grant of planning permission cannot be over-emphasised. It is to be noted that by the specific drafting of section 3(2) a grant of planning permission by way of permitted development under a development order, *i.e.* the GDO, will not suffice, (though since the GDO exemptions follow the list of site licence exemptions this will not give rise to any difficulties), but slightly less obvious is the case of the caravan site for **which** an established use certificate has been obtained (see Chapter 3, p. 41). In the latter case, although protection from enforcement action is conferred, this is not sufficient to satisfy the requirement of section 3(3) since an established use certificate is not a grant of planning permission. It should be appreciated also that the provision can have the paradoxical effect of requiring the applicant to obtain a grant of planning permission even if the stationing and use of the caravan(s) does not amount to a development requiring planning permission; this is because the provision does not give exemption to those instances where there has been no "development" of the land in question. For further consideration of this anomaly see the discussion at [1984] J.P.L. 215 and [1984] J.P.L. 840.

When the 1960 Act first came into force there were many existing sites which did not have the benefit of planning permission. Transitional provisions were incorporated into the Act (sections 13–20) to deal with such sites under which a deemed grant of planning permission could be obtained. These provisions gave rise to considerable litigation in the first few years of the operation of the Act but in view of the time which has elapsed it is not considered relevant to examine these sections as their application is now very rarely brought into question.

Provided that the applicant has submitted all the required particulars and has a grant of planning permission, no offence will be committed if the local authority fails to keep to the statutory timetable for the issue of the licence: section 6. It has also been held by the Divisional Court in *Rees* v. *James* (1963) that section 6 indicates that a valid site licence can be issued after the statutory two months period has passed, and in that case the court proceeded to hold that a person in breach of the conditions of his site licence had committed an offence under section 9 of the Act notwithstanding its issue outside the two months period.

The obligation of the district council to issue a site licence is qualified in one respect by the provisions of section 3(6) which prevents the council from issuing a licence to an applicant who to their knowledge has held a site licence which has been revoked during the past three years. While the subsection is designed to place a control over irresponsible site operators, on a strict application it also penalises an applicant who obtained a site licence but then transferred it to another who subsequently suffered revocation within the three year period.

When an application is properly furnished, supported by an express grant of planning permission, the district council will carry out their obligation to issue a licence under section 3(4) but may enter onto the land in order to inspect it before doing so, pursuant to section 26(1). Any licence issued must be recorded in a register of site licences maintained under section 25 of the 1960 Act. This is open to inspection by the public at all reasonable times, for which no charge is payable.

### Terms and conditions of site licences

Since a site licence cannot be refused by the district council if the requirements of section 3 are complied with, interest in the outcome of an application for a site licence is focused upon the terms and conditions subject to which it is issued. As a basic proposition the site licence will be of a permanent, not temporary, nature but section 4(1) provides that if the planning permission on which it is dependant is itself temporary (a fairly frequent occurrence in the case of use of land as a caravan site), then the site licence must be expressly limited to expire at the end of the same period for which the planning permission was granted. The applicant may, however, decide to exercise his right of appeal to the Secretary of State if the planning permission has been granted for a temporary period only, and if such an appeal proves successful (either by way of extension of the period or by way of a permanent grant of planning permission), then section 4(2) requires the district council to alter the site licence to make it consistent with the planning permission. In determining whether a planning permission is temporary, regard may be had to section 29(3) which deals with grants of planning permission for intermittent periods, *e.g.* seasonal use. In such a case the planning permission is treated as permanent provided further intermittent periods are permitted by the grant.

Although section 4 is an important provision, its significance is secondary to section 5 which contains the most important feature of the 1960 Act. Under this section a site licence may be issued "subject to such conditions as the authority . . . think . . . necessary or desirable to impose . . . in the interests of persons dwelling . . . in caravans, or any other class of persons, or the public at large. . . . " (section 5(1)). The section confers very wide powers upon the district council and it further states that, without prejudice to the generality of the provision quoted, the conditions to which the licence is subject may deal with: (a) restriction of the occasions on which caravans are allowed on the land or the number of them; (b) control of the types of caravans on the land, *e.g.* by reference to size and state of repair, but not by way of the materials of which they are constructed; (c) regulation of the position of the caravans on the land and control of the presence of other structures, vehicles and tents; (d) requiring steps to be taken for preserving or enhancing amenity, *e.g.* planting of trees or bushes; (f) provision and maintenance of adequate sanitary facilities, and provision of such other facilities, services or equipment as may be specified and the maintenance of them.

Before considering the scope of the power conferred by section 5(1), other subsections which also deal with the conditions of the site licence should be mentioned. Thus under section 5(3) it is mandatory for the district council to impose a condition on the site licence requiring that a copy of the licence in force must be displayed on the land in a conspicuous place and must remain in a conspicuous place at all times when caravans are stationed on the land for human habitation. Such a condition need not be imposed, however, if the site licence restricts the number of caravans permitted on the site to three or less. Under section 5(4) a condition may require works to be carried out on the land and may prohibit or restrict the use of the land until the local authority have certified in writing that the condition has been complied with. In a case where the land is already occupied by caravan dwellers, the licence may also impose a time limit for completion of the works required. If such a condition requiring works should be imposed, the question whether planning permission is required for those works may be raised. In such a case there is no need for the applicant to also apply for a grant of planning permission since the carrying out of works required pursuant to a site licence condition is "permitted development" under Class XXIII of Schedule 1 to the GDO.

In addition to the specific powers conferred by section 5(3) and (4), an important persuasive provision is section 5(6) which empowers the Secretary of State to issue "model standards" with respect to "the layout of, and the provision of facilities, services and equipment for, caravan sites or particular types of caravan site; and in deciding what (if any) conditions to attach to a site licence a local authority shall have regard to any standards so specified." As will shortly be seen the Secretary of State has exercised this power; the current Model Standards, as they are generally known, cover a wide range of matters of relevance to caravan site control. One of these matters concerns fire precautions and is specifically mentioned at this stage because amendments were made to section 5 of the 1960 Act by section 8 of the Local Government (Miscellaneous Provisions) Act 1982 the effect of which is to incorporate new subsections (3A), (3B), (7) and (8) into section 5. These provisons require the district council to consult the fire authority (normally the county council) to determine whether the Model Standards are appropriate to the land and, if not, what fire precautions should be imposed instead. While the views of the county council do not displace the requirements of the Model Standards, the former will normally be given precedence if more onerous standards are considered necessary.

The Model Standards referred to in the previous paragraph cover, apart from fire precautions, such matters as density and space between caravans, roads and footpaths on the site, hard standings, water supply, drainage, sanitation and washing facilities, refuse disposal, etc. The current Model Standards (replacing earlier versions) were issued in 1977 and are contained in DoE Circular 119/77. These apply to permanent residential caravan sites and (with some modification) to caravan sites used for holiday purposes. In the absence of specific mention in Circular 119/77, some doubt existed as to the application of these standards to caravan sites which are used wholly or mainly for touring caravans. In 1983 further Model Standards were issued for application to such sites in the Annex to DoE Circular 23/83. Both of the sets of Model Standards are reproduced at Appendix III to which the reader should now refer. In so doing it must be appreciated that the sets of Model Standards do not have the force of law, being only an important guide for district councils, and that they are free to use their discretionary powers conferred by section 5(1). Accordingly, much of the interest in section 5 is due to the exercise of the discretionary power to attach such conditions to a site licence "as *the authority* think . . . necessary or desirable" (author's italics).

It would seem at first sight that the district council have an unrestricted power to attach any conditions they wish. This possible interpretation was, however, firmly rejected by the House of Lords in the leading case on the subject, *Mixnam's Properties Ltd.* v. *Chertsey UDC* (1964). In granting a site licence to the company, the council imposed a large list of conditions, 37 in all. Amongst those complained of in this case were:

"28. The site rents, which are to be inclusive of all services except electricity, shall be agreed with the council;

29. Security of tenure, subject to similar conditions appurtaining to a statutory

tenancy of a dwelling-house under the Rent Acts, shall be granted to all caravan occupiers."

The company sought a declaration that these conditions were *ultra vires* the powers conferred on the local authority. Lord Reid said that "general words and phrases however wide and comprehensive they may be in their literal sense must usually be construed as being limited to the actual object of the Act." Their Lordships accordingly held that the object of the Caravan Sites and Control of Development Act 1960 was to control the manner in which a caravan site is used and not to interfere with the owner's freedom of contract with persons whom he permits to stay at the site. The council had no doubt attempted to fill gaps which existed in the caravans legislation at that time relating to rent control and security of tenure but, as Lord Reid pointed out, this exceeded the intention of Parliament. Those gaps have subsequently been partially filled, the present legislation being contained in the Mobile Homes Acts 1975–83 and the Caravan Sites Act 1968, the provisions of which are discussed in Chapters 5 and 6, respectively.

In considering the scope of the power conferred by section 5(1) it is helpful to have regard not only to the House of Lords judgments but also to the decision of the Court of Appeal, which received express approval. In that court Willmer L.J. held that site licence conditions must not effect a fundamental alteration in the general law relating to the rights of the persons on whom they are imposed unless the Act clearly permitted such changes, that the use of the power must be limited by reference to the subject matter of the statute, that a condition must not be ambiguous or uncertain, and that it must not be unreasonable. In relation to the last matter he considered that site licence conditions were analogous to local authority by-laws which are subject to the rule laid down by Lord Russell C.J. in *Kruse* v. *Johnson* (1898) which renders by-laws void for unreasonableness if they are "partial and unequal in their operation as between different classes, are manifestly unjust, disclose bad faith, involve oppressive and gratuitous interference in the rights of those subject to them as could find no justification in the minds of reasonable men." A by-law (and hence a site licence condition) which offends any one of the four elements in Lord Russell's test will therefore be invalid.

A site operator may conceivably wish to lay down rules for the mutual benefit of all those who live on the site in caravans. Can the district council prevent this occurring or regulate their content by a site licence condition? Could a condition be imposed relating to the colour of the caravans or the number of them on the site? In the *Mixnam's Properties* case itself one of the conditions sought to prevent the imposition of internal site rules, except insofar as they regulated the caravan dwellers in regard to matters similar to those normally found in a tenancy agreement, and another tried to ensure that the occupier of the site could not prevent the caravan dwellers forming a tenants' association. Both of these conditions were rejected by the House of Lords. No case has yet come before the courts concerning the use of a site licence to control the colours of caravans, though the author is inclined to the view that insisting upon one colour would be *ultra vires* the district council. A condition which required that the site should be "kept free of unauthorised tents and structures" was upheld by the Divisional Court in *Carnell* v. *Jones* (1966), a case which also raised the question of whether a condition can derogate from existing use rights enjoyed by the site occupier. This question has been raised in connection with conditions which seek to impose restrictions upon numbers of caravans on the site. This problem raises special difficulties and is discussed in the next section.

Some further matters may also be noted at this stage. First, while site licence conditions will normally relate only to the site in question, it is unlikely that an attempt to impose a condition relevant to adjacent land in different ownership would be successful. Thus in *Att-Gen* v. *Maidstone RDC, ex rel. Lamb* (1973) the council attempted to impose a condition on a site licence regulating site A which required the occupier of site A to give passage over his land to the occupier of site B, also in use as a caravan site. Plowman J. held that the condition was *ultra vires* because "the power of the site licensing authority to impose conditions was limited to conditions regulating the use of the site concerned *as a caravan site* and did not extend beyond that" (original italics). Secondly it is important to bear in mind the provisions of section 5(5) which declares that:

> "For the avoidance of doubt it is hereby declared that a condition attached to a site licence shall be valid notwithstanding that it can be complied with only by the carrying out of works which the holder of the site licence is not entitled to carry out as of right."

Thus if a site licence holder is a lessee of the property and requires his landlord's consent to carry out alterations or improvements by virtue of an express provision in the lease, the existence of such a provision does not affect the validity of the site licence condition. Lastly, it is apparent from the judgment of Lord Denning M.R. in *Esdell Caravan Parks Ltd.* v. *Hemel Hempstead RDC* (1965) that the site licensing authority is not precluded from taking into account matters which are also relevant to planning considerations when seeking to impose licence conditions, as the following passage makes clear:

> "Many considerations relate both to planning and to site. Take the disposal of sewage. Suppose that the existing system in the district can take the sewage from 24 caravans but would be swamped by 78 caravans, and on that account the site authority impose a condition limiting the number to 24. That is based on 'site considerations' so as to ensure that the sewage can be disposed of. But it is also based on 'planning considerations' so as to ensure that the sewerage system is not overloaded. Take the educational facilities. Suppose that the schools are already overcrowded with children from 24 caravans but would be swamped by those from 78 caravans. That is a planning consideration, so as to ensure that the children of the district get proper education. But it is also based on site considerations. In all these matters there is a large overlap, where a condition can properly be based both on planning considerations and also on site considerations. Insofar as it can be based on site considerations, it is clearly good, even though it might also be based on planning considerations."

## Conditions regulating the numbers of caravans

The total number of caravans that can be stationed upon a site is a matter of direct concern to a site operator since income from the grant of licences or tenancies to caravan dwellers is directly proportional to the number of caravans present. In the case of sites which have been first used subsequent to the coming into force of the 1960 Act the permitted maximum will often be clear since the planning permission for the site can (and frequently will) specify by a condition that the caravans on the site are not to exceed a stated number. If the planning permission is silent as to this question, section 5(1)(a) specifically empowers the district council to place a restriction on the number of caravans on the site by means of a site licence condition.

The courts have, however, experienced some difficulty in deciding how the specific power contained in section 5(1)(a) is to be applied in cases where a caravan site has been in existence since before the coming into force of the Town and Country Planning Act 1947 (July 1, 1948), or where since that date the site occupier has acted in breach of planning control and has claimed "existing use rights" by reason of the failure of the local planning authority to correct the breach of planning control for at least four years since the breach first occurred. The problem is well illustrated by the question which arose for decision in *Esdell Caravan Parks Ltd.* v. *Hemel Hempstead RDC* (1965). In this case a site was used for caravans for many years before the Town and Country Planning Act 1947 came into force, the number not exceeding 24. The occupier of the site obtained a deemed grant of planning permission under section 17 (transitional provisions) of the 1960 Act which did not restrict the total number of caravans. A site licence was then issued which contained a condition limiting the number of caravans to 24 in circumstances where the site could easily accommodate a much larger number. Did the site licence take precedence over the planning rights of the applicant? The Court of Appeal held that the site licence condition was to prevail and that it was valid, reliance being placed on the specific power contained in section 5(1)(a). Lord Denning M.R. explained the distinction to be made in this case from the point at issue in the earlier House of Lords case of *Minister of Housing and Local Government* v. *Hartnell* (1965). In the *Hartnell* case there was a limitation on the number of caravans which was imposed by means of a condition on the *planning permission* which was obtained soon after the 1960 Act came into force but applicable to land in respect of which there were existing use rights. In that case, the imposition of the condition was *ultra vires* the local planning authority because there was no express power contained in either the Town and Country Planning Acts or the 1960 Act to impose such a condition on the planning permission: to do so would be to take away rights without compensation. The principle in issue in *Hartnell's* case also applies where a caravan site was established after July 1, 1948, and which gained immunity from planning control by being in existence for at least four years, the whole of the four-year period having elapsed before the 1960 Act came into force. Here the existing use right cannot be limited by a grant of planning permission restricting the number of caravans on the site, but the numbers could be successfully controlled by a condition on the site licence in accordance with the *Esdell* decision.

Where a limitation on the number of caravans is placed as a condition on a grant of planning permission in circumstances where the condition is valid (*i.e.* a grant in respect of a site established since the 1960 Act came into force), then the site licence conditions must not be such as to increase the number specified: *R.* v. *Kent Justices, ex p. Crittenden* (1963).

## Alteration of site licence conditions

When a site licence has been issued by the district council the conditions to which it is subject can be altered by them after obtaining representations from the site occupier pursuant to section 8(1) of the 1960 Act. This can take place at any time after the licence has been issued and may involve deletion of former conditions, amendments to them, or addition of new conditions, or a combination of these. Any such changes only become effective when written notification of them has been received by the holder of the site licence.

In exercising their powers under section 8(1), the district council are required by section 8(4) and (5) to have regard, first, to the Secretary of State's Model Standards issued under section 5(6) and also to the views expressed by the fire authority after consultation with them if there is a proposed change to a condition dealing with fire precautions and appliances. There is a right of appeal to a magistrates' court under section 8(2) against alteration of site licence conditions (as is the case with initial imposition of conditions), a matter considered in detail in the next section. When alterations are required by the council it is necessary to endorse these upon the original licence. To facilitate this, section 11(1) of the Act empowers the district council to require the licence to be delivered up to enable them to make the necessary changes under penalty of a maximum fine of £10 if the holder fails to do so "without reasonable excuse": section 11(2). While section 11(1) clearly contemplates that the licence is to be delivered up for amendment, it was held in *Turner* v. *Garstang RDC* (1965) that it was open to the council and licence holder to agree that a fresh licence be issued provided it contained conditions acceptable to both parties. In the absence of an agreement, however, the licence must be delivered up and returned in its amended form.

The initiative in seeking changes in the conditions of the site licence may also come from the site licence holder by making an application to the local authority for alteration of the conditions under section 8(2). If this is unsuccessful the applicant has a right of appeal to a magistrates' court in the same way as if the initiative has come from the district council.

### Challenging site licence conditions—appeal

An important provision of the 1960 Act confers, with one exception, a right of appeal to the magistrates' court against any conditions imposed upon a site licence. Thus section 7(1) provides that a "person aggrieved" may appeal if a licence has been issued to him, the appeal being exercisable within a period of 28 days from the date of issue of the licence. (The one exception to this rule relates to the condition that a copy of the site licence be displayed on any site upon which more than three caravans are stationed, which is mandatory). Where such an appeal is made, the applicant must satisfy the court that the condition complained of is "unduly burdensome." If the court is satisfied that this is the case it may vary or cancel the condition. The exercise of the right of appeal does not suspend the operation of the licence which will continue in full force, except in a case where an appeal is made against a condition which requires the appellant to carry out works on the land. Here the rest of the licence comes into force when received by the site occupier, but a condition requiring work to be carried out does not take effect until the end of the 28–day period allowed for appeal nor during the period which any decision on appeal is pending: section 7(2).

The critical part of section 7(1) is the interpretation of the words "unduly burdensome" an expression not defined in the 1960 Act, section 7 of which merely directs the magistrates to have regard to the Secretary of State's Model Standards in reaching their decision. The manner in which the magistrates must discharge their functions under the Act was, however, explained by Lord Parker C.J. in *Owen Cooper Estates* v. *Lexden and Winstree RDC* (1965). In this case the site occupier obtained unconditional planning permission to use a substantial area of land for a caravan site. An application of the Secretary of State's Model Standards to the area indicated that the site could accommodate 600 caravans without contravening the recommended density condition. The district council imposed a much more stringent condition on the site licence limiting the total number of caravans on the site to 200. The applicant accepted that a lower figure than 600 was desirable to maintain the character of the site but argued that 200 was too restrictive and unduly burdensome. The magistrates held that the burden of proof was on the applicant and that they would only be justified in varying the condition if it was shown that it was one which no reasonable authority could impose. Lord Parker C.J. agreed that the burden of proof was on the applicant but stated that the magistrates must approach the matter " . . . by considering if some condition of this sort is necessary for the protection of the public, something which will benefit the public and equally that it will, of necessity, by a limitation, place a burden on the appellants. It is then for the justices to decide whether the burden outweighs, or duly outweighs, the benefit." It is clear therefore that it is essentially a matter for the magistrates to decide whether the burden placed on the applicant outweighs the benefit from it to the public. In the *Owen Cooper* case itself the matter was therefore remitted back to the justices for reconsideration.

Since the "unduly burdensome" question is essentially a question of fact for the magistrates to decide, there are only a few reported instances involving the exercise of their powers. Reference may, however, be made to a number of Scottish cases in which the applicant's appeal lies to the Sheriff's Court, decisions of which are reported in the Scots Law Times. These cases are mentioned purely to illustrate judicial decision-making and are not binding on English courts. For example, in *Clyde Caravans (Langbank) Ltd.* v. *Renfrew County Council* (1962) conditions prohibiting the use of awnings and requiring the provision of hard standings under the caravans were held to be unduly burdensome. Although the provision of hard standings appeared in the Secretary of State's "Model Standards" it was held that these conditions should be regarded only as a guide when formulating conditions. In *McLellan* v. *Kirkcudbright County Council* (1962) the court held that it was able to take into account the receipts from the caravans and the plans of the occupier for improving the site when considering whether a condition is unduly burdensome. Thus where the occupier had spent £1,000 on developing the site and planned to spend £470 on providing more toilet facilities on a site having a maximum capacity of forty holidaymakers' caravans, then as receipts were only of the order of £500 per year, a condition which required installation of a hot water system in addition to further toilet facilities at a cost of over £800 was held to be unduly burdensome. Reference may also be made to the decisions in *Haslam* v. *Kirkcudbright County Council* (1962) and in *United British Caravan Co. (Caledonian) Ltd.* v. *Dunbarton County Council* (1962).

In addition to the right of appeal conferred by section 7(1), there is also a right of appeal exercisable within 28 days if the site licensing authority decide to alter any of the conditions of the site licence in accordance with the power contained in section 8, or decline to alter the conditions following an application from the licence holder. By a possible ommission from the provisions of section 8(2), which confers the right of appeal following alteration or refusal to alter, there is no further provision requiring the magistrates to apply the same test of "unduly burdensome" to the altered conditions, albeit they must have regard to the Model Standards. In *Llanfyllin RDC* v. *Holland* (1964), however, the Divisional Court indicated that the same test can be applied by the magistrates. This case is also authority for a further important point since it provides further information as to the meaning of the words "unduly burdensome." In this case the district council sought to impose new conditions concerning foul drainage which were in line with the Secretary of State's Model Standards applicable to permanent caravan sites when the site in question was only a holiday caravan site, for which less stringent conditions are recommended by the Secretary of State. The magistrates upheld the appeal of the licence holder but the local authority alleged that the magistrates could not substitute their own discretionary decision unless the local authority had not acted properly or had been guilty of outrageous behaviour or of conduct of a reprehensible character. This approach to the words "unduly burdensome" was rejected by Lord Parker C.J. He stated:

> "I can see no ground whatsoever for extending the narrow and plain meaning of the words 'unduly burdensome' in connection with the condition. No doubt any condition is burdensome, and "unduly burdensome" merely means burdensome in a respect which is unnecessary or unreasonable in all the circumstances of the case. The justices here came to that conclusion, and for my part I cannot see how it can be said that they have erred in law."

One further aspect of the appeal provisions, of crucial importance to site operators, is the question whether conditions can be challenged once the 28-day period after the first issue of the licence has expired. This point was considered in *Peters* v. *Yiewsley and West Drayton UDC* (1963) in which the holder of a site licence sought an alteration to his licence conditions after more than a year had elapsed since the licence was granted. The district council declined to alter the conditions whereupon he appealed to the magistrates. The justices declined to hear the application on the basis that to do so would confer a right of appeal against the original site licence conditions which was only available within 28 days under section 7(1). Allowing the appeal, the Divisional Court observed that it is not unreasonable that some further challenge should be available since a licence once granted was intended to be permanent. The effect therefore is that it is possible to appeal against an original site licence condition by making a subsequent application for an alteration and then to appeal against the decision of the district council if that subsequent application should prove unsuccessful.

The rights of appeal conferred by sections 7 and 8 are the only rights conferred by the 1960 Act: there is no further right of appeal to the Crown Court. There is, however, a residual right to apply to the magistrates' court to ask them to "state a case" for the opinion of the High Court in accordance with the provisions of section 111 of the Magistrates' Courts Act 1980 if the decision is considered to be wrong in law or in excess of jurisdiction. If a site licence holder wishes to avail himself of this remedy he must make his application to the magistrates within 21 days after the decision of the magistrates was given. While the magistrates are under no obligation to state a case if they are of the opinion that the applicant's application is frivolous, they may not refuse to do so otherwise, nor if directed to do so by the Attorney-General, nor if the applicant successfully petitions the High Court for an order requiring the magistrates to state the case as requested.

Where an appeal is made by way of case stated—and almost all the reported cases mentioned in this Chapter were subject to this procedure—the Divisional Court will give a ruling on the point of law in issue. The matter will then often be remitted back to the magistrates to reconsider the matter in accordance with the court's ruling, but the court may also reverse, affirm or amend the magistrates' decision or make any order it sees fit. Appeal is available from the Divisional Court to the Court of Appeal.

### Challenging site licence conditions—judicial review

While appeal to the magistrates' court offers a rapid and comparatively inexpensive means of challenging site licence conditions, it may be borne in mind that an alternative method of challenge lies in seeking judicial review. This is a remedy which is available as a general means of challenging an exercise of executive discretion in almost all administrative contexts and was used in the leading case of *Mixnam's Properties Ltd.* v. *Chertsey UDC* (1964). The remedy is currently regulated by section 31 of the Supreme Court Act 1981 and Order 53 of the Rules of the Supreme Court. Under these provisions it is open to a person having a "sufficient interest" in the matter complained of to seek the leave of the High Court to make an application for judicial review. Such an application should be made within six months of the administrative decision in issue (in this context the attachment of disputed conditions to a site licence); if leave is granted, the applicant for judicial review will be able to question the *legality*, but not the merits, of the site licence conditions. The application will be heard by the Divisional Court. If the court forms the view that the site licensing authority have exceeded their powers, *i.e.* acted *ultra vires*, the site licence conditions will be quashed, whereupon the licensing authority may substitute alternative conditions, provided they are thereby acting within the scope of their powers, or leave the matters with which they were concerned unregulated by conditions.

### Breach of site licence conditions

The penalties for breach of any condition attached to a site licence are prescribed by section 9(1) of the 1960 Act. These are the same as the penalties for failure to obtain a site licence where it is required, *i.e.* a maximum fine of £100 for a first conviction and a maximum fine of £1,000 for conviction for a second or subsequent offence. The normal rule applicable to the prosecution of summary offences is that a magistrates' court may not try a defendant unless the prosecuting authority has commenced proceedings within six months of the commission of the offence concerned: Magistrates' Courts Act 1980, s.127. In the case of a breach of section 9(1), however, the failure by the occupier of the land to comply with a site licence condition is regarded as a continuing offence to which this six months limitation rule does not apply. Thus in *Penton Park Homes Ltd.* v. *Chertsey UDC* (1973) a prosecution was brought by the district council where the occupier of a caravan site failed to comply with a condition requiring him to carry out specified works on the site within 12 months of the issue of the licence. This default on the part of the occupier continued for a period of over four years before the prosecution was brought. The occupying company appealed against a conviction in the magistrates' court on the basis that the prosecution was barred six months after the year permitted by the site licence condition for carrying out of the required works had elapsed. The Divisional Court held that the offence was a continuing one and that the prosecution could therefore be brought at any time.

Apart from the possible defence of limitation of time it is probably also open to the defendant to claim (if this should be the case) that the conditions in respect of which he is allegedly in breach are *ultra vires* and therefore of no effect. There is no reason in principle why this defence should not succeed, even if the defendant has not appealed under section 7 against the site licence conditions or sought to have the conditions quashed pursuant to an application for judicial review. In the analogous situation of a prosecution for failure to comply with a stop notice, it has been held in *R.* v. *Jenner* (1983) that the defendant can claim in his defence the notice is invalid. It is also the case that by-laws (to which site licence conditions were regarded by Willmer L.J. in *Mixnam's Properties Ltd.* v. *Chertsey UDC* (1964) as comparable) can be challenged with regard to their validity as a defence in criminal proceedings for breach: *Nash* v. *Finlay* (1901).

Persistent breach of site licence conditions may be controlled by means of a magistrates' court order revoking the licence pursuant to an application to this effect made by the district council under section 9(2). The subsection applies where a person has been convicted for failure to comply with a site licence condition on at least two previous occasions; on a third or subsequent conviction the magistrates can, if requested by the district council, order that the site licence be revoked. This will take effect on such date as is specified by the order but it will not be earlier than the final date on which the defendant's rights of appeal are exercisable (by way of case stated or otherwise). If an appeal is made, the revocation order is rendered ineffective until the appeal is determined or withdrawn. Where no appeal is in fact made, the defendant (or the district council) may apply to the court for an extension of the period before the expiration of which the order will become effective. If satisfied that adequate notice has been given to the other party, the magistrates may exercise their discretion to extend the period. Where an application for revocation is successful the occupier cannot hold a site licence under the 1960 Act for at least three years thereafter: section 3(6).

In the case of a breach of any conditions requiring works to be carried out on the site within a specified time, the district council may enter upon the site and carry out the works themselves under section 9(3). The costs incurred in exercise of this power are then recoverable from the site occupier as if the sum due was a contract debt and may therefore be the subject of proceedings to recover the sum due in the county court. This sanction for breach of site licence conditions is available to the district council irrespective of whether criminal proceedings are commenced for breach of the conditions. It will normally be the case, however, that the district council will attempt to enforce the conditions through the criminal law first.

The power of entry conferred by section 9(3) is supplementary to a more general power of entry conferred on district councils under section 26 of the 1960 Act. Quite frequently the council's officers will need to enter onto the site in order to check whether site licence conditions are being complied with, etc. Provided that 24 hours' notice has been given to the site occupier, council officers may enter onto the land at all reasonable hours if it is in use as a caravan site or if an application for a site licence has been made. This power may be used to enable the district council to determine (a) what conditions to impose on a site licence or whether to vary them; (b) whether there has been a breach of any site licence conditions; (c) whether or not circumstances exist which would authorise the taking of any action or executing works under the Act, and (d) to carry out the action or execute the works. If entry onto the land is refused, or the giving of notice would defeat the object of entry, then the district council may enter pursuant to a written warrant of a magistrate, if need be with the use of force. Any person who wilfully obstructs an entry made pursuant to section 26 is guilty of an offence and is liable on summary conviction to a maximum fine of £25.

### Powers and duties of occupier not in possession

At the commencement of this Chapter it was observed that the definition of the word "occupier" given in section 1(3) includes a person who is not in possession of the land because he has granted a licence to occupy it to another (not to be confused with a site licence under the 1960 Act) or has granted a tenancy of land which does not exceed 400 square yards in area. Since in both these circumstances the person who would, apart from these interests, be the occupier is treated as the occupier of the land, he is subject to the full force of the Act in respect of penalties for failure to obtain a site licence or to comply with any conditions subject to which it was granted. While such a person can apply for and receive a site licence in the ordinary way he is subject to the risk of prosecution where his licensee or tenant fails to comply with the site licence conditions. In order to relieve the hardship which this could cause, section 12(1) provides that where the land is subject to a licence or tenancy, there is deemed to be incorporated a condition permitting the occupier to retake possession of the land and terminate the licence or tenancy if an offence is committed under the Act. Section 12(2) further empowers the person whom the statute treats as the occupier to enter onto the land for the purpose of doing anything reasonably required for the purpose of complying with a site licence condition.

### Transfer of a site licence and transmission by operation of law

When a site licence is first issued the 1960 Act contemplates that it will continue indefinitely unless the planning permission upon which it is dependent is issued for a fixed period of time: section 4. If the holder of the licence ceases to be the occupier of the site, e.g. because of sale of his interest in the land, the new occupier must arrange to secure the transfer to him of the site licence or obtain a new licence by making a fresh application. A transfer can be achieved with the consent of the district council pursuant to section 10(1) of the Act, and this will normally be granted by the council except perhaps where the circumstances of the site demand a complete review of the site licence conditions and the change in occupier provides a suitable opportunity to do this. If the district council should decide to refuse consent to the proposed transfer there is no right of appeal against their decision. This does not work any hardship against a proposed transferee because once a transfer application has been made he is also able to apply for a new site licence under section 3 and he will be entitled to receive one by virtue of section 3(4); the district council will then have the choice of issuing consent to the transfer or granting of a new licence. If their consent is given to the transfer they need not proceed on any application for a site licence which may be made: section 10(3).

Where in the normal case a transfer is approved, the site licence must be endorsed with the name of the person to whom it is transferred and a date agreed by the parties to the transfer as the date on which the new site occupier becomes responsible for the site. These details are also registered by the district council in the register of site licences maintained by them pursuant to section 25 of the Act.

A site licence is also transferred on the death or bankruptcy of the holder. Thus, section 10(4) provides that where by operation of law a person becomes entitled to an estate or interest in land in respect of which a site licence is in force and thereby becomes the occupier of the land, he is treated as being the holder of the site licence on the day on which he became the occupier of the land. If the district council wish to record the change on the site licence itself, they are not specifically empowered to require its submission to them. They must, however, make the requisite changes if called upon to do so by the new occupier and must then record the new details in the site licences register: section 25(2).

# 5. Security of Tenure: I. The Mobile Homes Acts 1975–83

For many years the lot of the caravan dweller was disadvantageous from the point of view of his security of tenure, as no specific provisions for protection had been enacted to confer security on such a person. This meant that the landowner on whose property a caravan was situated could require the occupier of the caravan to leave the site and further require him to remove his caravan if it was owner-occupied. To guard against such an eventuality the caravan dweller needed to ensure that his licence or tenancy agreement, under which he was permitted by the landowner to use the site, was to last either for a fixed and substantial period of time or to contain a provision whereby a generous period of notice was required to be given by the landowner to bring the right of occupation to an end. In practice, such agreements were not common and the occupier would normally have the benefit of only a short-term licence, or of a periodic tenancy of a weekly or monthly nature. Since most of these arrangements were not recognised as being subject to the security of tenure provisions of the Rent Acts, the caravan dweller was without protection.

Legislative steps to remedy this situation were first taken in 1968 by the enactment of the Caravan Sites Act 1968. In broad terms, this Act offered security of tenure to all caravan occupiers, whether owner-occupiers or otherwise, but the protection granted was limited to a four-week period of notice to quit and a power of the court to suspend the operation of such a notice for up to 12 months. Provisions designed to prevent unlawful eviction and harassment were also enacted. All the relevant provisions of this Act are still in force, but so far as security of tenure is concerned, the Mobile Homes Acts 1975–83 have made further provision for the benefit of owner-occupiers of caravans. Bearing in mind that caravans, particularly of the "mobile home" variety, are often placed on permanent caravan sites in such a way that their subsequent movement is not contemplated, generous security of tenure is clearly appropriate.

The changes made by the Mobile Homes Act 1975 were designed to give security of tenure to owner occupiers for up to five years. The 1975 Act was subsequently substantially repealed and replaced by the Mobile Homes Act 1983 which confers indefinite security of tenure on caravan occupiers who qualify for protection under the terms of the Act. Some provisions of the 1975 Act are, however, still in force.

The legislation of 1983 was passed partly from necessity and partly due to the findings of research published by the Department of the Environment. The necessity element arose simply from the fact that the 1975 Act was a short-lived statute, having an in-built limitation of five years, extendable by a further three years by order of the Secretary of State. An extension order was made in 1980, but if no further legislation had been passed in 1983, owner-occupier mobile home dwellers would have been deprived of the benefits which the 1975 Act conferred on them, in particular a right to receive a written agreement from the site operator. The effect of the Mobile Homes Act 1975 was thus to permit the occupiers of caravans to obtain written agreements, but which would exist for not more than five years. This view of the limitation of the 1975 Act was confirmed by the Court of Appeal in *Taylor* v. *Calvert* (1978), in which mobile home dwellers sought agreements lasting longer than five years and referred the matter to the county court. Although they were successful at first instance in obtaining an order for longer agreement to be entered into, in some cases for up to 10 years, the site operator successfully appealed to the Court of Appeal which decided that the county court judge had no jurisdiction to grant such an order. Summarising his judgment, Lord Denning M.R. said "The long and short of it is that this Act gives security of tenure for five years with an option to extend by another three years. . . . "

Research findings into the use of mobile homes were published in the form of the "Mobile Homes Review" (1977) and the report "Mobile Homes in England and Wales" (1975), the latter being a study conducted by the Department of the Environment's Building Research Establishment. These documents and their recommendations, which are summarised in DoE Circular 12/78 (Welsh Office 9/78), revealed that at the time of the reports approximately 150,000 people occupied mobile homes as permanent dwellings many of whom had not obtained any benefits under the 1975 Act. It is to the question of security of tenure, and protection in relation to other relevant matters, of these owner-occupiers that the Mobile Homes Act 1983 is directed. The details of the legislation are explained in this Chapter, but the reader may also find it useful to refer to a joint publication of the Department of the Environment, Scottish Development Department and Welsh Office entitled "Mobile Homes—A guide for residents and site owners." This document (Housing Booklet Number 16) conveys in question and answer form a great deal of pertinent information about the Mobile Homes Act 1983. It is available free from local council offices or direct from the central government departments mentioned above.

## Scope of the Mobile Homes Acts 1975–83

In considering the application of this legislation, a primary consideration is the land to which it applies. Section 1 of the 1983 Act applies the code to a "protected site," a term which is defined by section 5 of the 1983 Act as having the same meaning as in Part I of the Caravan Sites Act 1968. That Act defines a "protected site" in section 1(2), as:

> "any land in respect of which a site licence is required under Part I of the Caravan Sites and Control of Development Act 1960 . . . not being land in respect of which the relevant planning permission or site licence—
> 
> (a) is expressed to be granted for holiday use only; or
> (b) is otherwise so expressed or subject to conditions that there are times of the year when no mobile home may be stationed on the land for human habitation."

It is clear from this definition of a protected site that the mobile homes legislation is directed only at caravan sites on which some or all of the caravans are situated and occupied throughout the year, and is also linked to the site-licensing provisions of the 1960 Act. Thus, any site which falls within the scope of the site-licensing requirements is potentially included in the Mobile Homes Acts legislation; in *Holmes* v. *Cooper* (1985), the Court of Appeal held that the 1983 Act applied to a caravan occupier who used land on which the majority of occupiers were travelling showmen, since the site had "protected" status unless all the occupants were travelling showmen. By virtue of section 5(1), the Mobile Homes Act 1983 also applies to local authority caravan sites (except those provided for gipsy accommodation), despite the exclusion of the site licensing provisions of the 1960 Act to local authority caravan sites.

The other key terms of the legislation are "mobile home," "owner," and "occupier." These terms all appear in section 1(1)(2) of the 1983 Act which applies to "any agreement under which a person ('the occupier') is entitled to station a 'mobile home' on land forming part of a protected site and to occupy the mobile home as his only or main residence." If an agreement exists, the "owner" of the site is obliged to furnish the occupier with a written statement evidencing the agreement which complies with the requirements prescribed by the Act. Of the terms quoted in this paragraph, "mobile home" has the same meaning as the word "caravan," *i.e.* as defined by section 29(1) of the Caravan Sites and Control of Development Act 1960 (as amended), while "owner" is defined by section 5(1) of the 1983 Act as "the person who, by virtue of an estate or interest held by him, is entitled to possession of the site or would be so entitled but for the rights of any persons to station mobile homes on land forming part of the site." The word "occupier" is not defined by the 1983 Act, but it is clear from section 1 of the Act that it is to be interpreted to confer security of tenure on both a licensee of a site pitch (as will commonly be the case), as well as a person who has a tenancy agreement in relation to the pitch.

It is essential to emphasise again that the Mobile Homes Act 1983 only protects owner-occupiers. Thus, a licensee or tenant of both the caravan and the property on which it stands enjoys no benefits under the 1983 Act, but if the occupier owns the caravan it does not matter whether he is a licensee or tenant of the site pitch.

Where the essential conditions for protection under the Act are satisfied, *i.e.* owner-occupation on a protected site where the caravan is the only or main residence of the occupier, the rights conferred by the Act are not lost due to the fact that the site operator has neglected to obtain a site licence under the 1960 Act: *Brice* v. *National By-Products Ltd.* (1983). This is because a site operator cannot rely on his own breach of the duty to obtain a licence under the 1960 Act as a means of depriving the caravan occupier of the protection of the 1983 Act.

The position is different, however, if the site operator has failed to obtain *planning permission* for the site; the Court of Appeal held in *Balthasar* v. *Mullane* (1985) that the caravan occupier enjoys no rights under the 1983 Act in such circumstances. This important decision effectively places an obligation on a person wishing to station his mobile home on a site to ensure that planning permission has been granted; an investigation of this matter should therefore be conducted before the mobile home is brought onto the land, or a purchase is made of one already on the site.

In *Balthasar* v. *Mullane* itself, a caravan was placed on land for a temporary but undetermined period pursuant to an oral agreement. When the landowner sought to remove the caravan from the land, the owner-occupier relied on the 1983 Act as conferring indefinite security of tenure. The plaintiff landowner had not obtained a grant of planning permission for the stationing of the caravan on the land and sought to use this default in compliance with planning control as a means of overcoming the protection conferred on the defendant by the 1983 Act. The Court of Appeal held that the plaintiff's argument succeeded and that the land on which the caravan was placed was not a "protected site." The main reason for reaching this conclusion was based on the planning control consequences of reaching a contrary view. Thus, if a caravan is placed on land which does not have the benefit of planning permission, in circumstances where planning permission is required, the local planning authority would have great difficulty in correcting the breach of planning control by enforcement action. This is because the landowner would be unable to comply with an enforcement notice if the caravan occupier could claim the benefit of the 1983 Act. The landowner could therefore be repeatedly fined for failure to carry out steps which he was legally prevented from taking.

### Scheme of protection under the 1983 Act

The concept behind the Mobile Homes Act 1983 is broadly similar in nature to that which was previously effected under the 1975 Act. The central feature is the imposition of an obligation upon the site owner to serve on the caravan occupier a written statement, containing the express terms of their agreement and including terms which are implied into the agreement by the provisions of the 1983 Act. The operative part of the 1983 Act is section 1(2) which requires the site owner to give to the caravan occupier a written statement within three months of the making of the agreement under which the occupier was authorised to station his caravan on the site. The agreement giving rise to this obligation on the site owner may be purely oral and need not be evidenced in writing and will normally arise when the caravan occupier first brings his caravan onto the site, or if the occupier purchases a caravan already on the site from a former occupier. The latter source of agreement will be less common since, as will be seen, an existing agreement with the site owner is capable of being assigned. If the site owner does not comply with his obligation, the occupier can apply to the county court for an order requiring the site owner to issue the written statement: section 1(5).

The terms which are implied into the agreement are detailed in Schedule 1 to the 1983 Act. This Schedule is divided into two Parts; the first Part gives details of terms that are always implied by the Act, while Part II describes further terms which can be implied if an application is made to the court (or to an arbitrator) within six months of the issue of the written statement. The main interest in this legislation therefore lies in the content of the implied terms; these deal not only with security of tenure but also with numerous other aspects of the relationship between the site operator and the caravan occupier, *e.g.* sale or gift of the mobile home.

Although the current scheme is similar to that introduced by the Mobile Homes Act 1975, the former Act had a fundamental weakness. Under the previous legislation it was necessary for the caravan occupier to serve a written notice on the site owner before he took up residence on the site; if he failed to serve such a notice (which was required to state that the occupier intended to occupy the mobile home as his only or main residence), he did not gain the protection of the 1975 Act. This requirement often prevented the purchaser of an on-site mobile home from getting the benefit of the Act. Thus in *Lamb* v. *Adams* (1981) the Court of Appeal held that the giving of a notice to the site owner after actual occupation of the mobile home had begun was too late and the owner of the site was not under any obligation to offer an agreement pursuant to section 1 of the Act. Shaw L.J. stated that "[T]he respondents . . . sought to argue that the objective of the Act, namely to afford protection to the owners of mobile homes, would be frustrated if too stringent a construction were put on the provisions of section 1(1). If the construction is plain, as in my view it is, it cannot be described as too stringent."

This defect in the previous law does not apply to the current scheme under which no notice need be served by the proposed occupier of the mobile home; the obligation to communicate in writing is placed, under the 1983 Act, purely upon the site owner.

### Content of the written statement

The content of the written statement is regulated by sections 1(2), 2(1) and (2), and Schedule 1 to the 1983 Act. The basic requirement is imposed by section 1(2) which requires the owner of the site to give to the occupier a written statement within three months of the making the agreement which:

> "(a) specifies the names and addresses of the parties and the date of commencement of the agreement;
> (b) includes particulars of the land on which the occupier is entitled to station the mobile home sufficient to identify it;
> (c) sets out the express terms of the agreement;
> (d) sets out the terms implied by section 2(1) below; and
> (e) complies with such other requirements as may be prescribed by regulations made by the Secretary of State."

It is to be noted, concerning (b) above, that the Act does not specifically require that the relevant site "pitch" be identified though this would be advisable.

Section 2(1) and Part I of Schedule 1 imply terms which regulate seven different aspects of the agreement. These are summarised as follows:

(i) *Duration of the agreement.* An agreement is to last indefinitely unless brought to an end by the occupier himself or by the owner following an application made to the county court or an arbitrator: Sched. 1, para. 1. The grounds on which the agreement can be brought to an end are limited (see below).

The basic principle of indefinite security of tenure is qualified by para. 2, to the extent that if the owner is a leaseholder, or has only a limited grant of planning permission for the site, the right of the mobile home dweller is limited to the length of the period of the lease or the grant of planning permission, as the case may be. The occupier should therefore make specific enquiry about this point before treating his mobile home as a permanent residence; although the site owner is obliged to disclose the length of his lease or the limitation of his grant of planning permission in the first part of the written statement, this information may not come to the attention of the occupier until after residence has been established. To find an alternative site once it has been discovered that the site owner's interest is short may prove very inconvenient.

The restriction of security of tenure which this implied term can import could also give rise to a means of circumvention of the intention of the Act, which is to confer indefinite security of tenure. It would appear that if the freeholder of the protected site grants a short lease to a nominee of his, the "owner" for the purposes of the 1983 Act would be the short leaseholder and the security of tenure of the occupiers of mobile homes on the site would end when the lease expires. Such protection as the occupiers would then enjoy would be derived only from the Caravan Sites Act 1968, the nature of which is considered further in the next Chapter. If, however, a new lease is granted before the first lease expires the occupiers would have security of tenure automatically extended to the date of expiration of the new lease: Schedule 1, para. 2(3).

(ii) *Termination by the occupier.* The occupier must give at least four weeks notice in writing to the owner to terminate his agreement: Schedule 1, para. 3.

(iii) *Termination by the owner.* This may be achieved in three circumstances:

(a) If the occupier is in breach of a term of the agreement, the owner must serve a notice on him requiring him to remedy the breach. If he fails to do so within a reasonable time the owner may apply to the county court or an arbitrator, which, if satisfied that there has been failure to comply with a notice and that it is reasonable for the agreement to be terminated, may authorise the owner to terminate if forthwith: Schedule 1, para. 4.

(b) If the court or arbitrator is satisfied that the occupier is not occupying the mobile home as his only or main residence, the court or arbitrator may authorise the owner to terminate the agreement forthwith: Schedule 1, para. 5.

(c) If the court or arbitrator is satisfied that having regard to the age and condition of the mobile home that it is having a detrimental effect on the amenity of the site, or is likely to have such an effect before the end of the next "relevant period," then the court or arbitrator may authorise the owner to terminate the agreement as at the end of a "relevant period." The term "relevant period" means the period of five years from the commencement of the agreement and each period of five years thereafter: Schedule 1, para. 6.

(iv) *Recovery of overpayments by occupier.* If the agreement is terminated, whether by the occupier or by the owner, any payments made to the owner in respect of a period of time following after the date of termination are recoverable by the occupier: Schedule 1, para. 7.

(v) *Sale of mobile home.* The occupier is entitled to sell his mobile home (and to assign the agreement) to a person approved by the owner, whose approval is not to be unreasonably withheld. The owner is entitled to a commission on the sale which must not exceed the rate prescribed by the Secretary of State by statutory instrument. A figure of 15 per cent. was previously fixed by the Mobile Home (Discounts and Commissions) Order 1976 (S.I. 1976 No. 365), but this Order has been replaced by the Mobile Homes (Commissions) Order 1983 (S.I. 1983 No. 748) which currently prescribes a figure of 10 per cent. It is to be noted that there is no obligation on the outgoing occupier to offer the mobile home for sale to the site owner at a discount: Schedule 1, para. 8.

(vi) *Gift of mobile home.* The occupier is entitled by Schedule 1, para. 9 to give the mobile home (and to assign the agreement) to a member of his family approved by the owner, whose approval is not to be unreasonably withheld. A member of the family for these purposes covers a spouse, parent, grandparent, child, grandchild, brother, sister, uncle, aunt, nephew or niece. Section 5(3) of the 1983 Act requires any relationship by marriage to be treated as a relationship by blood, and a relationship of the half blood to be treated as a relationship of the whole blood; a stepchild is to be treated as a child and also an illegitimate person treated as legitimate. Persons living together as husband and wife (though not married) are also included.

(vii) *Re-siting of mobile home.* Where the owner is (by an express term of the agreement) entitled to require that the occupier's right to station his mobile home be applicable to another part of the site, and he exercises that right, then the other part of the site must be broadly comparable to the original "pitch" and the costs and expenses of the moving of the mobile home must be borne by the site owner: Schedule 1, para. 10.

In addition to the above matters, further terms can be implied into the agreement (unless they have already been included as express terms negotiated by agreement between the parties). Inclusion of these terms (or any of them) can be achieved by either party making an application to the county court or arbitrator under section 2(2). The terms involved are described in Part II of Schedule 1. These are as follows:

1. The right to quiet enjoyment by the occupier of the mobile home.
2. Sums payable by the occupier in pursuance of the agreement and the times at which they are to be paid.
3. Review at yearly intervals of the sums so payable.
4. Provision or improvement of services available on the protected site and the use by the occupier of such services.
5. Preservation of the amenity of the protected site.
6. Maintenance and repair of the protected site by the owner, and the maintenance and repair of the mobile home by the occupier.
7. Access by the owner to the land on which the occupier is entitled to station the mobile home.

As these seven terms are so important to the parties' relationship, it would normally be expected that some or all of them would be found in the express terms of the agreement. The Part II list therefore provides an opportunity for either party to have them included after the written statement has been given to the occupier where the statement does not mention one or more of these matters. The right of application to the court or arbitrator in relation to these matters only subsists, however, for six months from the giving of the written statement; after this period has expired any variation in the terms of the agreement must be by consent of both parties. Since the right of application to the court or arbitrator is lost after six months have expired from the giving of the written statement, it is therefore imperative that the statement issued by the site owner be construed very carefully. If the express terms of the agreement do not mention the matters mentioned in Part II of Schedule 1 it will be necessary to make an application to the court or arbitrator to have the absent terms included. Variation (or deletion) of express terms which the occupier finds unacceptable may be sought by virtue of section 2(3), also by application to the court or arbitrator within six months.

A case which arose under the Mobile Homes Act 1975, *Grant* v. *Allen* (1979), shows that an amendment in relation to the rent or licence fee payable for the site pitch, can have retrospective effect. In this case, the agreement did not state how much rent was to be charged for the site pitch. When this was fixed by the court it was held that these payments were to date from the date on which the agreement was made with the site operator, not, as was contended, from the date of the court's decision.

If application is made within six months of the giving of the written statement, an opportunity can be taken to challenge express terms of the agreement which are supplementary to those implied by the Act. Thus in *Grant* v. *Allen* the site operator sought to include conditions which (amongst others) (a) permitted him to resite a mobile homes if it was "for the better management of the [site]," and (b) required payment of a commission of 12 per cent. on the making of a gift of the mobile home or its transmission on death of the occupier. In both instances the Court of Appeal decided that the rights conferred by the Mobile Homes Act 1975 on site owners were maximum rights which could not be supplemented by express terms of the agreement which were more onerous to the occupier. It is to be expected that in any future litigation under the Mobile Homes Act 1983 a similar attitude would be taken to the express terms and the Act is likely to be construed in favour of the occupier. It must be stressed again, however, that the occupier will have to comply with the terms expressly agreed unless he applies to the court or arbitrator for variation or deletion within the six-month period.

### Form of the written statement

The form of the written statement to be served by the site owner is prescribed by regulations made by the Secretary of State. These are the Mobile Homes (Written Statement) Regulations 1983 (S.I. 1983 No. 749) which came into force on the same day as the Mobile Homes Act 1983 (May 20, 1983). They are made pursuant to section 1(2)(e) of the 1983 Act and specify that a written statement has to comply with the form prescribed in the Schedule to the Regulations or must be in a form which is "substantially to the like effect." The Schedule to these Regulations requires the written statement to be divided into four parts. The full form of the Regulations is reproduced in Appendix II, but the requirements can be briefly summarised at this point. Part 1 is to contain the names and addresses of the parties, the date on which the agreement commenced, and the particulars of the land in question. If applicable, the date on which the site owner's estate or interest in the land will come to an end should also be noted, as should any similar restriction imposed by the planning permission for the site. Part 2 is to contain a summary of the rights and procedures introduced by the 1983 Act and advises the mobile home owner to consult a solicitor or citizens advice bureau if he or she is unaware of the pertinent rights or procedures. The implied terms are contained in part 3 of the form in substantially the same manner as the list to be found in Schedule 1 of the 1983 Act, with an added reference to the 10 per cent. maximum rate of commission on sale. Part 4 is to set out the express terms of the agreement which have been settled between the parties in addition to the implied terms.

## Procedure after termination of the agreement

If the site owner is successful in making an application to the county court or arbitrator to terminate the agreement by proving one of the grounds mentioned in Schedule 1, paras. 4–6, this does not entitle the site owner to immediate possession of the land on which the mobile home is situated. To achieve this the site owner must also obtain from the county court a further order (which may be sought in the same proceedings) authorising him to resume possession, otherwise an offence will be committed under section 3 of the Caravan Sites Act 1968. Such an order is capable of being suspended by the county court for up to 12 months pursuant to section 4 of the 1968 Act, except where the site owner is a local authority. It is to be noted that whereas an arbitrator can authorise termination of the agreement, the arbitrator is not empowered to make an order for possession of the site.

## Arbitration under the 1983 Act

An application to the county court under section 1(5) (failure to provide a written statement), section 2(2) (implication of terms contained in Part II of Schedule 1), or section 2(3) (variation or deletion of express terms of the agreement), may, in the alternative, be made to an arbitrator. Thus section 5(1) of the 1983 Act defines "court" to mean the county court for the district in which the site is situated or "where the parties have agreed in writing to submit any question arising under this Act or, as the case may be, any agreement to which it applies to arbitration, the arbitrator." This provision thus permits the parties to operate the scheme of the Act without the involvement of the county court; although it may produce some savings in costs arising from making of an application to an arbitrator rather than the county court, the Act does not provide any machinery for appointment of an arbitrator. This may mean, in practice, therefore, that the identity of the arbitrator is as suggested by the site owner rather than the caravan occupier. Although it does not necessarily follow that the latter is always the weaker party to the agreement, this provision could be construed as an opportunity for the site operator to gain an advantage which he would not otherwise enjoy if the 1983 Act had provided that all applications under the Act were required to be made to the county court. It should be borne in mind, however, that if the site owner is successful in gaining the arbitrator's authority to terminate the agreement he will still need to make an application to the county court for possession of the site.

Both the county court and the arbitrator are given a general jurisdiction by section 4 to determine matters arising under the Act or under the written agreement. Although both of these adjudicators are empowered to examine the merits of the application under the 1983 Act, a disadvantage in using arbitration emerges if it is desired to made an appeal from the decision of the arbitrator, if used. Thus, whereas an appeal from the county court would be available to the Court of Appeal on questions both of fact and law, an appeal from an arbitrator is available to the High Court only on questions of law: Arbitration Act 1979, s.1(2). If entering into an agreement under which an arbitrator is to act as the adjudicator in questions arising between the parties is, in effect, a concession which the potential owner-occupier must give if he is to gain a site pitch at all, it may be borne in mind that he could apply within the first six months of the agreement for the jurisdiction of the court to be substituted for that of the arbitrator, though this application (under section 2(3)) has to be made to the arbitrator. A final disadvantage is that legal aid is not available in arbitration of disputes, unlike the position which applies to the resolution of disputes in the county court. Legal advice may, however, be obtained in order to assist the occupier in the forthcoming arbitration proceedings, but this falls short of representation at the hearing.

### Agreements in existence prior to May 20, 1983

The Mobile Homes Act 1983 came into force on May 20, 1983. Where an owner-occupier of a caravan had stationed the caravan on a protected site prior to that date, he should have a received written agreement issued by the site owner under section 1 of the Mobile Homes Act 1975, unless he had failed to notify the site owner of his intention to occupy the caravan as his only or main residence prior to bringing the caravan onto the land. In either instance if the occupier continues to occupy a caravan on the site, he is entitled to receive a written statement from the site owner under section 1(3) of the 1983 Act within six months of the coming into force of the Act. Thus, for the future, all persons who satisfy the statutory requirements will have written statements containing the requirements of section 1(2) and the Mobile Homes (Written Statement) Regulations 1983, and therefore all agreements issued under the 1975 Act have been superseded.

In some instances the caravan will not have been used as the occupier's only or main residence, in which case, although the caravan is stationed on the site by agreement, it is probably not one which qualifies under the 1983 Act. If it should later be so used, the occupier may need to seek a further agreement with the site owner since the 1983 Act only applies if the occupier is "entitled" to occupy the caravan as his only or main residence, not whether, as a matter of fact, it is so used. If this occurs the site owner will have to issue a written statement under section 1(2) of the Act within three months of the change in circumstances.

A further point relevant to agreements which pre-date the 1983 Act is the possibility of a conflict between the express terms of the agreement and those which are implied under section 2(1) and Schedule 1, Part I. The Act deals with this possibility by providing in section 2(1) that the implied terms "shall have effect notwithstanding any express terms of the agreement."

### Change of occupier or site owner

It was pointed out above that the owner-occupier of a mobile home stationed on a protected site has the right to sell the mobile home or to make a gift of it to a member of his family, subject in each case to the approval of the site owner which is not to be unreasonably withheld. If this takes place it is not necessary for the purchaser or donee to negotiate a new agreement (which would necessitate a new written statement) with the site owner unless he wishes to do so. This is because the agreement which exists between the owner and the original occupier—as evidenced by the written statement—is capable of being assigned by both parties if either should sell their property. Thus section 3(1) provides that an agreement is binding on any successor in title of the owner, while section 3(2) provides that if an agreement is lawfully assigned by the occupier the assignee has the benefit of it and takes the burden of its obligations.

The position which obtains when the occupier of a mobile home dies is slightly more complicated. Under section 3(3)(a) of the Act, if the occupier dies (and at the time of death was occupying the mobile home as his only or main residence), the benefit of the agreement with the site owner passes to the deceased's surviving spouse if they were residing together at the time of death. If the deceased did not leave a surviving spouse, but is survived by a member of his or her family who was residing with the deceased at the time of death, then that person will enjoy the benefit of the agreement for the future. The scope of qualifying membership of the family for these purposes is identical to the class of persons to whom an occupier of a mobile home can give the home by way of gift under the terms implied into the agreement by Part I of Schedule 1, above, p. 72 but the 1983 Act does not state which member is entitled to the agreement if there is more than one claimant, no specific provision having been made to deal with this possible problem. In this instance the site owner cannot object to the new occupier.

If a deceased occupier left no surviving spouse and had no other member of his family residing with him at the time of his death, the mobile home will then pass to the deceased's beneficiary under his will or his intestacy. While such a beneficiary will thereby inherit the property in the mobile home, he will gain the benefit of the agreement with the site owner only to a limited extent, *i.e.* that he can sell the home and pass on the benefit of the agreement to the purchaser: section 3(3)(b) and section 3(4). It will, however, also be the responsibility of the person who inherits the mobile home to continue to pay the fees due for the use of the pitch on which the mobile home is situated. The site owner is also entitled to receive a commission of up to 10 per cent. of the purchase price. Should the beneficiary not wish to sell the mobile home but to use it as his residence, he will need to negotiate a fresh agreement with the site owner.

## The Mobile Homes Act 1975

As as pointed out above, the Mobile Homes Act 1975 was substantially repealed by the 1983 Act. The only sections of the earlier Act which are still in force are sections 7 and 8, together with some of the definitions contained in section 9. Section 8 applies the provisions of Part I of the Caravan Sites Act 1968 (to be discussed in the next Chapter) to Scotland, and is thus not directly relevant in the present context. Section 7, however, is relevant in that it confers a power on the Secretary of State to prescribe minimum standards with respect to layout and provision of facilities, services and equipment for protected sites on which mobile homes are occupied as the only or main residence of their users. This power is thus rather similar to the power of the Secretary of State to specify "model standards" under section 5(6) of the Caravan Sites and Control of Development Act 1960. It also bears a relationship to the terms of agreement between site owner and caravan occupier, whereby provision of services and facilities can be included in the agreement as implied terms on application to the county court or arbitrator under section 2(2) of and Part II of Schedule 1 to the 1983 Act. To date, the Secretary of State has not exercised his powers under this section.

# 6. Security of Tenure: II. The Caravan Sites Act 1968 and the Rent Act 1977

In the previous Chapter it was observed that the security of tenure provisions of the Mobile Homes Act 1983 are applicable only to a person who is an owner-occupier of a mobile home, thus excluding from the protection of the Act a person who rents a caravan from the site owner, or has only a licence to occupy the caravan. Such a person can rely instead upon the provisions of the Caravan Sites Act 1968 and may in some instances enjoy protection under the Rent Act 1977, a matter considered later in this Chapter.

Part I of the 1968 Act contains provisions specifically designed to protect the caravan dweller, whether or not an owner-occupier. The subsequent enactment of the Mobile Homes Acts 1975–83 has, however, provided more advantageous protection for owner-occupiers, thereby leaving the Caravan Sites Act 1968 to operate as a residual scheme of protection for those who do not fall into the owner-occupier category. The 1968 Act thus provides for a minimum standard of security of tenure based on a requirement that at least four weeks notice must be given to terminate a tenancy or licence agreement, and the conferment of a power on the court to postpone the effect of an order for possession for up to twelve months.

Despite the emphasis on security of tenure, the 1968 Act is nevertheless concerned with other matters regulating the site owner/caravan occupier relationship. Hence, in addition to prescribing a minimum length of notice for terminating an arrangement whereby a caravan is stationed on land, the Act also provides for protection against eviction without an order of the county court and for protection against acts of harassment by the site owner which are carried out in order to persuade the caravan dweller to leave the site. In relation to the latter two matters (unlawful eviction and harassment) the Caravan Sites Act 1968 is applicable to both owner-occupiers and non owner-occupiers alike, and creates criminal offences for failure to comply with its requirements. It will also be seen in the next Chapter that the second major purpose of the Caravan Sites Act 1968 was to provide for and control the use of land by gipsies. This aspect of the legislation is contained in Part II of the Act.

## Scope of Part I of the Caravan Sites Act 1968

The Act of 1968 applies to any licence agreement, or contract, whereby a person is entitled to station a caravan on a "protected site" and to occupy the caravan as his residence: section 1. It also applies if a caravan is already stationed on a "protected site" and that person is entitled to occupy the caravan as his residence by virtue of a licence or contract with the site owner. It may be observed that the legislation does not require the caravan to be the only residence of the occupier; a person can be resident in two places at once: *Fox* v. *Stirk* (1970). The term "protected site" is defined in section 1(2) of the Act to mean:

> "any land in respect of which a site licence is required under Part I of the Caravan Sites and Control of Development Act 1960 or would be so required if paragraph 11 of Schedule 1 to that Act (exemption of land occupied by local authorities) were omitted, not being land in respect of which the relevant planning permission or site licence—
> (a) is expressed to be granted for holiday use only; or
> (b) is otherwise so expressed or subject to such conditions that there are times of the year when no caravan may be stationed on the land for human habitation."

As was observed in the case of the Mobile Homes Act 1983, the legislation is directed only at caravan sites on which caravans are situated throughout the year and is also linked to the Caravan Sites and Control of Development Act 1960. The Act of 1968 applies irrespective of when occupation of the caravan began (whether before or after the enactment of the 1968 Act) and is also applicable to land owned by a local authority (including land provided for gipsy accommodation).

Other important definitions used in the 1968 Act are of the words "residential contract," "owner" and "occupier." The term "residential contract" is simply the collective term (used in section 1(1)) given to licence agreements, or other contracts, whereby occupation of a caravan as a residence is authorised by the owner of a protected site. Section 1(3) defines the "owner" of a protected site as "the person who is or would apart from any residential contract be entitled to possession of the land," while section 1(1) defines "occupier" as the person who is entitled to station and occupy the caravan as a residence (pursuant to a residential contract).

Although the Caravan Sites Act 1968 is linked to the Caravan Sites and Control of Development Act 1960 by virtue of the definition of "protected site," it appears from the decision of the Divisional Court in *Hooper* v. *Eaglestone* (1977) that the existence of a site licence is not essential for the Act to apply; it is the fact that one is "required" that brings the site within the scope of the 1968 Act. This is clearly illustrated by the facts of *Hooper* v. *Eaglestone* in which the site owner entered into a contract whereby he permitted X to occupy a caravan owned by him and agreed in the contract to supply electricity to the caravan. It transpired that he had no planning permission for the site, no site licence, and was the subject of enforcement proceedings taken by the local planning authority. To encourage the occupier to give up possession of the caravan he cut off the electricity supply, an act which constituted an offence of harassment under section 3 of the 1968 Act. The magistrates refused to convict the site owner on the basis that, as he had no site licence, the site was not a "protected site" within the 1968 Act. The Divisional Court reversed this decision, holding that it did not matter that the site owner was unable to obtain a site licence by virtue of lack of planning permission. Lord Widgery C.J. said:

> "It is quite false . . . to argue . . . that not being able to obtain a site licence at the moment [the respondent] does not have to satisfy any of the [Acts] . . . to which I have referred. The reason why he cannot get a site licence is his own fault because he is there without planning consent. The land is, in my judgment

within the definition of 'protected site' and I think that the conduct of the respondent in removing the electricity constituted an offence. . . . "

This forceful judgment clearly confers the protection of the 1968 Act on a caravan occupier where the landowner has behaved unscrupulously and has ignored the town and country planning and site licence controls. It must be observed, however, that this decision cannot be reconciled with the subsequent decision of the Court of Appeal in *Balthasar* v. *Mullane* (1985). This case, discussed in the previous Chapter in the context of the Mobile Homes Act 1983, is authority for the proposition that a site which lacks planning permission is not a "protected site." It is a pity that *Hooper* v. *Eaglestone* does not appear to have been cited in the Court of Appeal, and no reference is made to it in the judgments of Glidewell and Neill L.JJ. Further litigation on this crucial point would therefore seem inevitable.

### Notices to quit, eviction orders and court's power to postpone

The security of tenure which the Caravan Sites Act 1968 confers on an occupier of a caravan on a protected site under a residential contract is a bare requirement, contained in section 2 of the Act, that

"where a residential contract is determinable by notice given by either party to the other, a notice so given shall be of no effect unless it is given not less than four weeks before the date on which it is to take effect."

This basic rule has been specifically incorporated into the law regulating occupation of mobile homes to bring the law into line with a similar rule affecting tenancies of dwellings now contained in section 5 of the Protection from Eviction Act 1977. To avoid any doubt as to whether the latter provisions apply to caravans, section 5(5) of the Caravan Sites Act 1968 specifically excludes their application and makes independent provision via section 2.

The requirements of the section that "not less than four weeks notice" must be given is likely to be strictly interpreted by the court. Although there is no prescribed form of notice, nor even a requirement that it should be in writing, (though it would be advisable to give a written notice) it was held in *Schnabel* v. *Allard* (1967) that the notice must, if it relates to a tenancy agreement, comply with the common law rule that its expiration must coincide with the end of a period of the tenancy. Subject to this requirement, it is not necessary to give four *clear* weeks notice, and so a notice to quit given on a Saturday to expire on the fourth Saturday thereafter is valid. No notice is required, however, if the residential contract expires by effluxion of time. Once a notice has been given under section 2 or the residential contract has expired by effluxion of time, the site owner can regain possession of the site only by making an application to the county court. This is because section 3(1)(b) of the 1968 Act specifies that it is an offence to enforce any right to exclude the occupier from the protected site or from his caravan otherwise than by proceedings in the county court. The procedure which is to be followed to gain an eviction order depends on whether the residential contract was by way of a licence to occupy the site pitch, as will be the usual case, or whether a tenancy of the site pitch was granted.

In the case of a licence, the appropriate procedure is in accordance with the County Court Rules 1981, Ord. 24, rr. 1 and 2. This applies (according to

*Bristol Corporation* v. *Persons Unknown* (1973)) when a person has entered into possession of land without the licence or consent of the owner, or (as is relevant to the present context) that person has remained in occupation without his licence or consent. Under these rules, proceedings are commenced by originating application supported by an affidavit stating the interest that the applicant has in the land, the circumstances giving rise to the application, and (if appropriate), that the applicant is not aware of the names of all the persons occupying the land. If the application is successful the court will normally grant an order for possession forthwith, but may specify a later date. If the order for possession is not obeyed either forthwith or after the date fixed for possession (if stated) the applicant may ask for the order for possession to be enforced by means of a warrant of possession under the County Court Rules 1981, Ord. 26, r. 17. This will be executed by the court bailiff, though some delay can be anticipated before action is taken.

Where the site pitch is the subject of a tenancy agreement which has been terminated or of a lease which has expired, Order 24 is inapplicable as it expressly excludes tenancies. In such a case the appropriate procedure is by way of filing particulars of claim in accordance with the County Court Rules 1981, Ord. 6, r. 3, the county court having a general jurisdiction in relation to actions for recovery of land by virtue of section 21 of the County Courts Act 1984. The particulars of claim must state the land in respect of which possession is sought, its net annual value for rating, the rent payable, the grounds on which possession is claimed, and the arrears of rent (if any). Although the Caravan Sites Act 1968 does not specify grounds for possession on which the plaintiff must rely, nevertheless the court will enquire into these grounds. In the case of termination of an agreement evidenced by a written statement under the Mobile Homes Act 1983 the grounds on which that agreement had been terminated would suffice. That the court may authorise termination of the agreement and grant an order for possession in the same proceedings is clear from Order 49, rule 13(3) of the County Court Rules 1981.

Where proceedings in the county court are successful and the court grants a possession order (often referred to as an "eviction order") the court has a discretionary power (also exercisable by the registrar with the consent of the judge) conferred by section 4 of the Caravan Sites Act 1968 to postpone the effect of the order for up to 12 months from the date on which it is given. In exercise of this jurisdiction the court may select whatever period it considers to be reasonable. In considering whether or not to exercise this jurisdiction the court is required by section 4(4) to take into account the following particular matters as well as all the circumstances of the case:

(a) whether the occupier of the caravan has failed, whether before or after the expiration or determination of the residential contract, to observe any terms or conditions of that contract, any conditions of the site licence, or any reasonable rules made by the owner for the management and conduct of the site or the maintenance of caravans on the site;

(b) whether the occupier has unreasonably refused an offer by the owner to renew the residential contract or make another such contract for a reasonable period and on reasonable terms;

(c) whether the occupier has failed to make reasonable efforts to obtain elsewhere other suitable accommodation for his caravan (or, as the case may be, another suitable caravan and accommodation for it).

The court is not permitted, however, to postpone an eviction order if there is no site licence in force in relation to the site, nor if the site owner is a local authority; section 4(6)(a) and (b).

In exercise of the discretionary power to postpone the order, the court is empowered to impose terms and conditions on the occupier, e.g. in relation to payment of rent or arrears of rent in accordance with whatever the court considers to be reasonable. No order as to costs can be made, however, if a suspension of an eviction order is granted unless it appears to the court that there are special reasons for doing so after taking into account the conduct of the owner or occupier: section 4(2), (5).

Once granted, an order for postponement of an eviction order is capable of being altered following an application to the court by either party. Under section 4(3) an order can be terminated extended or reduced, or any terms or conditions subject to which it was granted can be varied (but apparently cannot be supplemented by new terms or conditions). This power cannot be used, however, to grant an extension exceeding 12 months at any one time. Neither can the discretion to postpone the eviction order be exercised in such a way that it thereby expires after the date (if any) upon which the site licence for the protected site is due to expire, i.e. where the site licence has been limited so as to be consistent with a temporary grant of planning permission for the use of the site. Subject to this requirement the court can, in theory at least, grant several postponements of an eviction order, all of them for up to 12 months.

The power to postpone the effect of an eviction order only applies in relation to protected sites. If an order for possession has been granted in relation to a site in respect of which a site licence is not required (and is therefore not a protected site) the court nevertheless has an inherent jurisdiction to postpone for a reasonable time the effect of a possession order: *Jones* v. *Savery* (1951) (in which the Court of Appeal held that a postponement of possession of a stable for three months was too generous and that one month was more appropriate to the circumstances pertaining to that case).

## Unlawful eviction and harassment

Apart from conferring a minimum standard of security of tenure upon a caravan dweller, the Caravan Sites Act 1968 also protects the occupier against action taken by the owner with a view to removing the occupier or his caravan from the site, or the carrying out of acts which encourage the occupier to leave. Section 3(1) of the Act creates three different offences which can be committed by "any person" (not necessarily only the owner of the site). These can be summarised as follows:

(a) while a residental contract exists, the occupier is unlawfully deprived of his occupation of any caravan which he is entitled to occupy as his residence on the protected site, or one which he is entitled to station on the site and occupy as his residence;

(b) after a residential contract has expired or been terminated the occupier is excluded from the site or from his caravan or the caravan is excluded from the site without a court order;

(c) while a residential contract exists, or after it has expired or been terminated, acts are done which are calculated to interfere with the peace and comfort of the occupier or persons residing with him, or services or facilities are persistently withdrawn or withheld which are reasonably required for the occupation of the caravan as a residence. In either case the person accused must be shown to have committed the acts or withdrawn the services or facilities with intent to cause the occupier to (i) abandon the occupation of the caravan or remove it from the site, or (ii) refrain from exercising any right or pursuing any remedy in respect of his occupation.

Offences (a) and (b) are both concerned with unlawful eviction of the residential occupier. For these purposes the "occupier" is given an extended meaning by section 3(2) to include the widow or widower of the person who had the benefit of the residential contract, if residing with him at the time of his death. Where there is no qualifying surviving spouse then any member of the deceased's family residing with him at the time of his death is entitled to the protection of the section. The scope of the word "family" is not defined by the 1968 Act and reference could therefore be made to the meaning given to it in section 5 of the Mobile Homes Act 1983 (see above, p. 72) or possibly to the interpretation given by the courts to the scope of "family" under the Rent Act 1977, which includes a common law spouse: *Dyson Holdings Ltd.* v. *Fox* (1975).

Prosecution for unlawful eviction is a matter for the local authority, and all local authorities are empowered to bring proceedings under the Act by section 14(2). A person who is found guilty of an offence is liable on summary conviction to a maximum fine of £2,000 or to be imprisoned for up to six months, or both: section 3(3), as amended by section 37 of the Criminal Justice Act 1982. In relation to a prosecution for unlawful eviction the Act provides the person charged with a defence contained in section 3(4). Thus if the person charged believed, and had reasonable cause to believe, that the occupier of the caravan had ceased to reside on the site at the time when the alleged act of unlawful eviction took place, then he is entitled to be acquitted. If a person charged with an offence under section 3 wishes to rely on this defence, the burden of proof lies on him to show that he had the necessary belief and that he had reasonable cause for that belief. In order to discharge this burden the accused need not show that it is beyond a reasonable doubt that he had the necessary belief but only that on a balance of probabilities he did so: *R.* v. *Carr-Briant* (1943). The defence itself contains two elements: the belief by the accused that the occupier had ceased to reside on the site forms the first part, and the reasonableness of that belief forms the second part. The defence therefore involves both a subjective element (what the accused thought), and an objective element (whether he was acting reasonably in forming his view).

Where unlawful eviction takes place from a site which is owned by a company, the defendant in a prosecution would ordinarily be the company. Section 14(1) of the 1968 Act expressly provides, however, that if an offence is committed by a company with the consent or connivance of a director, manager, secretary or similar officer of the company, or any person purporting to act as such, or is attributable to the neglect of any such officer, then that person is similarly guilty of the offence and can be punished in accordance with the penalties mentioned above. It would appear that this rule applies to local authorities as well as to commercial corporations.

The third offence created by section 3—that of harassment—was exemplified earlier in this Chapter when the case of *Hooper* v. *Eaglestone* was considered (see p. 79). In that case it was decided that cutting off the supply of electricity to a caravan on a protected site was an offence under section 3(1)(c) of the 1968 Act. The law relating to harassment is not limited to unlawful acts by caravan site owners committed against those occupying caravans under residential contracts, but applies generally to unlawful acts committed against licensees and tenants of dwelling-houses. In the latter context protection is derived from section 1 of the Protection from Eviction Act 1977, a statute which expressly excludes application to caravans by virtue of section 5(5) of the Caravan Sites Act 1968. Acts which have been held to constitute harassment for the purposes of the 1977 Act are, however, equally relevant in the present context. Indeed, before the enactment of the Caravan Sites Act 1968 the court would, where possible, construe a caravan as "premises" for the purposes of giving appropriate protection under section 30 of the Rent Act 1965, the provision which was repealed and replaced by section 1 of the Protection from Eviction Act 1977. This in fact occurred in *Norton* v. *Knowles* (1967) in which a caravan had been stationed in a field for approximately ten years and to which water, electricity and telephone services had been connected. When the site owner desired to be rid of the occupier he forcibly entered the caravan, shouted abuse at the occupant and his wife, and threatened to pull out the telephone connection and cut off the water supply and to tow the caravan away. The Divisional Court agreed with the magistrates that these were acts of harassment and that a caravan taken together with the land on which it stands constitutes "premises" for the purposes of protection under the Rent Acts and hence the site owner was properly convicted.

In order to prove an offence under section 3(1)(c) of the 1968 Act it is essential to show that the defendant intended to harass the residential occupier, mere inactivity on the part of the site owner being insufficient. In a case under the Rent Act 1965, *McCall* v. *Abelesz* (1976), the Court of Appeal gave a judgment which clearly implies that some positive act is needed or persistent withholding of services is required, and also dealt with the question whether the residential occupier is entitled to damages for breach of the section. In this instance a room in a house had been let on a weekly tenancy for a number of years. Other rooms in the house were let on similar terms. When the freehold of the house was sold to the defendant he showed no interest in the property otherwise than to receive rent by post. The previous landlord omitted to pay a large gas bill (£435) and the new landlord declined to honour it, whereupon the gas board cut off the gas supply. At a later stage the electricity and water supplies were also terminated. Other tenants of the house vacated the property leaving the plaintiff in sole possession. The supplies of services were eventually restored, in the case of the gas supply eight months after disconnection. No prosecution was brought by the local authority but a civil action for damages was brought for by the plaintiff for harassment. In the Court of Appeal, Lord Denning M.R. expressed a doubt whether an offence had been committed under section 30(2) of the Rent Act 1965 and Ormrod L.J. stated that since the gas bill was not the responsibility of the new landlords they could not be regarded as guilty of withholding the supply of an essential service. As such the lack of supply was not accompanied by an intention to cause the plaintiff to give up possession. The issue to be decided in the case, however, was whether a remedy in damages was available for breach of the anti-harassment law. It was held that a civil action for damages could not succeed relying solely on a breach of the provisions, but that an aggrieved person might conceivably succeed if he brought a civil action for breach of contract alleging a breach of the implied term that the property owner would maintain the gas and electricity supply, or alleging a breach of the convenant of quiet enjoyment which is implied in the landlord and tenant relationship. Lord Denning M.R. also expressly referred to the possibility of damages for "mental distress and upset caused by the defendant's conduct in breach of contract." In addition, it is clear that substantial damages are available if the harassment complained of is a tort, *e.g.* trespass: *Cassell* v. *Broome* (1972).

The question of a remedy in damages is especially relevant in the context of caravan use, as the nature of a caravan makes it vulnerable to interference. The Caravan Sites Act 1968 expressly preserves civil remedies by section 3(3) which, although specifying the penalties to which a person is liable for breach of the section, does so "without prejudice to any liability or remedy to which he may be subject in civil proceedings." Recent cases indicate that where an action is successfully brought for breach of contract due to harassment, punitive damages are likely to be awarded, as occurred in *Hodgson* v. *Jacobs* (1984). In this case, £2,500 damages were awarded after a landlord's campaign of harassment had finally caused a tenant to vacate the property. The court took into account the commercial gain accruing to the landlord from his wrongdoing in fixing damages at this level, but would otherwise have contemplated damages in terms of hundreds rather than thousands of pounds.

Many of the rules contained in the Caravan Sites Act 1968 concerning unlawful eviction are also applicable to harassment cases. Thus the local authority is the prosecuting authority (section 14(2)) and offences committed by a company are similarly committed by directors, managers, etc., if consented to or connived at by such officers (section 14(1)). The same penalties are applicable on conviction for breach of section 3(1)(c) *i.e.* up to six months imprisonment or a fine of up to £2,000, or both, but there is no statutory defence available to a person charged with an offence under section 3(1)(c) as there is in unlawful eviction cases. Thus if the caravan site owner believes that the caravan affected is no longer occupied as a residence, and that belief is reasonably held, and then proceeds to remove the services his actions could nevertheless constitute harassment. It is doubtful, however, whether a prosecution would succeed in such circumstances because it is essential to prove that the acts were done with the intention of causing the occupier to abandon the occupation of the caravan.

### Protection from eviction, etc., where no site licence is in force

If a caravan is stationed on land which is exempt from the need for a site licence (see p. 50) the site does not qualify as a "protected site" for the purposes of section 1 of the 1968 Act. In such circumstances the occupant will not have the benefit of the provisions of the Act and it would appear therefore that there is nothing to prevent the site owner from removing the caravan from the land on termination of the licence pursuant to which entry onto the land was permitted. There is always a risk, however, that such action by a landowner would provoke a breach of the peace. To avoid such an occurrence the most appropriate course of action would be to seek an order for possession in the county court pursuant to Order 24, rules 1 and 2 of the County Court Rules 1981. Such action (described above at p. 80) is also appropriate in the case of occupation of the land by trespassers. No notice need be given and the court has no power to postpone the effect of an eviction order otherwise than by exercise of its inherent jurisdiction.

Where the site is one for which a site licence is required but not obtained, the position is regulated by the decision in *Hooper* v. *Eaglestone* (1977) with the result that the residential occupier is entitled to the full protection of the 1968 Act, except insofar as the court does not have the power to postpone the effect of an eviction order under section 4 of the Act: section 4(6)(*b*). It is therefore no defence to an action for an injunction preventing the site operator from cutting off services to claim that, by failing to take such action, the site operator could be committing an offence under the 1960 Act: *Dean Lane Park (Merstham) Ltd.* v. *Hedge* (1968).

As a corollary to the above points the effect of a site owner invoking section 12(1) of the Caravan Sites and Control of Development Act 1960 must also be borne in mind. It will be recalled (see p. 47) that this section allows a person who by virtue of his granting (as freeholder or long leaseholder) only a licence to the site operator (or a tenancy where the site does not exceed four hundred square yards in area) is treated as "the occupier" (section 1(3)), to take possession of the land and determine the licence or tenancy if no site licence exists. Where this occurs the rights of any caravan dweller in relation to security of tenure are preserved by section 5(4) of the 1968 Act, but only to the extent that a minimum of four weeks notice to quit must be given. Protection from unlawful eviction or harassment applies in the normal way.

### Rent control under the Caravan Sites Act 1968

None of the provisions of the Caravan Sites Act 1968 expressly deals with control of rents payable (or licence fees) in cases where the Act applies. This contrasts with the Mobile Homes Act 1983, s.2(2) which empowers the court (or arbitrator) to imply into a contract a term dealing with the rent for a site pitch. The sole means under the caravans legislation, by which the court can influence the rent payable under a residential contract, is the placing of a term or condition on the occupier following exercise of the court's power under section 4 of the 1968 Act to postpone the effect of an eviction order.

It can be argued, however, that because of the provision of services, the letting of a caravan (or even the grant of a licence) constitutes a "restricted contract" within the meaning of section 19 of the Rent Act 1977, the effect of which is to confer rent control by means of reference to the rent tribunal. The extent to which the Rent Act 1977 can apply to lettings of caravans must therefore now be considered, partially because of this rent control aspect, but more especially because the application of the 1977 Act can (depending on the circumstances) confer significant security of tenure. Although there is, as yet, no specific legal authority in which it has been held that full protection (conferring indefinite security of tenure) is available under the 1977 Act, in appropriate circumstances, the weight of judicial opinion is now largely in favour of such a conclusion. It is to be hoped that the High Court will soon have the opportunity of giving a direct ruling on the matter, which seems probable following the recent case of *R. v. Rent Officer of Nottingham Registration Area, ex p. Allen* (1985), discussed at p. 89.

### Application of the Rent Act 1977

Although the Rent Act 1977 has been subsequently amended by the Housing Act 1980 it is still the principal statute on tenancies of dwellings. Section 1 of the Act provides that " . . . a tenancy under which a dwelling-house (which may be a house or part of a house) is let as a separate dwelling is a protected tenancy for the purposes of this Act." The conferral of benefits upon a caravan dweller by this Act depends upon three factors: (a) whether the occupier has a tenancy or a mere licence; (b) whether the caravan constitutes a "dwelling-house" for the purposes of this section; and (c) whether prescribed limits of rateable value are exceeded: the tenancy is protected if the limits specified by section 4 of the 1977 Act are not exceeded.

Most site pitches are occupied on a licence rather than a tenancy, and where in such a case the occupier does not actually own the caravan, it is usual that the occupation of the caravan is also by a licence rather than a tenancy. Where, however, there is a tenancy of the site pitch, it is to be expected that a tenancy of the caravan is similarly intended. The importance of this matter from the caravan dweller's point of view is that if he has a tenancy he can only be required to give up possession in accordance with section 98 of the 1977 Act, which necessitates the landlord site owner providing suitable alternative accommodation for the tenant or proving one of 20 grounds for possession specified in Schedule 15 to the Act. He must also show, in both instances (but subject to some exceptions), that it is reasonable that possession should be given of the land (and hence of the caravan).

Although a document may describe itself as a "licence" and use words inappropriate to a landlord and tenant relationship, the court will look at the substance of the matter in determining whether it is in fact a tenancy agreement and in particular whether "exclusive possession" has been granted to the occupant. One possible approach to the problem is as described by Buckley L.J. in *Shell-Mex and B.P. Ltd. v. Manchester Garages Ltd.* (1971) where he stated that:

> "one must look at the transaction as a whole and at any indications that one finds in the terms of the contract between the two parties to find whether in fact it is intended to create a relationship of landlord and tenant or that of licensor and licensee."

Thus a document which described itself as a licence was held to be a tenancy agreement in *Addiscombe Garden Estates v. Crabbe* (1958) because it contained terms more appropriate to a landlord and tenant relationship.

A test commonly used to distinguish between a lease and licence is whether "exclusive possession" has been given to the purported tenant. This is a right to exclude all persons, including the landlord, from the premises—a right which will continue to exist even if the landlord has reserved to himself a power of entry to inspect the state of repair. If no exclusive possession is given the arrangement cannot be a tenancy, and a finding that exclusive possession has been given is very strong, albeit not conclusive, evidence of a tenancy: *Street v. Mountford* (1985). A number of factors can be considered relevant in addition to the terminology used in the document and the question of exclusive possession. These are the intentions which the parties had when the agreement was made and whether a commercial charge is being made. In *Street* v. *Mountford* (1985) an agreement gave an occupier of a room an exclusive right of occupation and described itself as a "licence." The county court judge held that this was in reality a tenancy agreement, subject to the full protection of the Rent Act 1977, but the Court of Appeal overruled the county court judge and held that a licence had been created. The House of Lords restored the decision of the county court judge and decided that a tenancy had been created, ruling that intention was only relevant insofar as the question of exclusive possession was concerned.

If it is concluded that a tenancy was granted rather than a licence, the next question is whether a caravan constitutes a "dwelling-house" for the purposes of section 1 of the 1977 Act. Until very recently this question had not been placed directly before the court but the few cases in which closely related matters have been involved tended to suggest that the 1977 Act would apply. In one such case, *Makins* v. *Elson* (1977), the question arose whether a caravan could constitute a "dwelling-house" in circumstances where services of water, telephone and electricity had been attached to the caravan which rested on supports after having been jacked-up so that its wheels did not touch the ground. It had been brought onto land for occupation by its owner and his family to be used in connection with the building of a dwelling-house, a project which was not implemented as the land was sold before the development began. The owner of the land realised a large profit on its resale and the question arose whether this was chargeable to capital gains tax under the Finance Act 1965, in respect of which an exemption applied if the caravan was a dwelling-house. In the High Court, Foster J. considered that the caravan had constituted a dwelling-house and that no tax was payable, but qualified his decision by saying " . . . I do not think that the very particular facts of this case will apply to a great many others . . . ," though it is submitted that this was stated to avoid the decision in the case being treated a a simple means of avoiding the capital gains tax legislation rather than to express a general view on interpretation of the law relating to caravan use.

In *R.* v. *Guildford Area Rent Tribunal, ex p. Grubey* (1951) it was held that a letting of a caravan was subject to the jurisdiction of the rent tribunal under legislation which is now Part V of the Rent Act 1977, provided that the caravan was let for use by its occupant on land owned or controlled by the caravan owner. It would be a different matter if the caravan was let for touring purposes (but the fact that it was capable of being moved around the field in which it stood did not matter). In another more recent case, *Lloyd* v. *Mitchenall Bros. Investments* (1973), the Bristol Area Rent Tribunal fixed a rent for a furnished caravan in circumstances where the caravan was immobile, connected to all mains services, secured to the ground by props at each corner, had blocks placed under the axles and rested on a hard core base. The caravan was also rated as a residence by the local rating authority. The tribunal rejected a contention that it had no jurisdiction to fix the rent on the basis that the caravan was not a permanent dwelling. While a rent tribunal decision is not authoritative law, it is nevertheless an indication of judicial thinking.

The High Court has now accepted that a caravan can, in appropriate circumstances, constitute a dwelling-house for the purposes of section 1 of the Rent Act 1977. In *R. v. Rent Officer of Nottingham Registration Area, ex p. Allen* (1985), the landlord of a caravan sought to quash a rent fixed by the rent officer on the basis that the caravan in question was not a "house" and that the rent officer therefore had no jurisdiction to fix a rent. It was found that the caravan had been moved from time to time on the land on which it was stationed and although it had the benefit of mains services these were easily disconnected. Farquharson J. decided that the caravan did not constitute a house and quashed the rent officer's decision. He made it quite clear, however, that a caravan which is rendered completely immobile, either by the removal of its wheels or by being permanently blocked by some brick or concrete construction, was more likely to be regarded as a house in the same way as a bungalow or prefabricated dwelling would be. The mere fact that wheels remain in existence would not, however, be conclusive to a finding that the caravan was not to be regarded as a house, as it would also be relevant to inquire into the details of the occupancy of the caravan. If it was plainly used as a permanent home by the tenant there was a greater likelihood that the caravan would not be moved and could therefore be regarded as a house rather than a mere chattel on the land.

The only case in which the court has ruled that a caravan did not constitute a dwelling for Rent Act purposes is *Morgan v. Taylor* (1949), a county court decision and therefore not a binding precedent. The case is also rather unreliable in that the county court judge regarded the caravan in question as being incapable of being rated as a separate dwelling by the local authority and relied solely on this factor. This was a false premise, as the Court of Appeal subsequently held in *Field Place Caravan Park Ltd. v. Harding* (1966) that a caravan and site pitch could together be treated as a rateable hereditament.

Given that Farquharson J. clearly stated in *R. v. Rent Officer of Nottingham Registration Area, ex p. Allen* that a caravan can constitute a dwelling-house for the purposes of the Rent Act 1977, it is submitted that this is a likely finding in the case of caravans of the "mobile home" type, since they are placed on sites from which their removal is not contemplated. It is less likely, however, that a touring type of caravan would be treated in the same way, but an important factor in distinguishing between classes of caravans is likely to be whether the caravan which is alleged to be a "dwelling-house" has been rated as a separate dwelling. Where this has occurred the inference that the Rent Act 1977 applies is more difficult to resist.

### Security of tenure under the Rent Act 1977

Where a tenancy qualifies as a protected tenancy under section 1 of the Rent Act 1977, the landlord may seek to obtain possession only by an action brought in the county court. In the usual case the landlord will first terminate the contractual tenancy (*e.g.* a weekly or monthly tenancy) by giving the tenant notice to quit. This notice must be of not less than four weeks duration (Protection from Eviction Act 1977, s.5(1)), and must be in writing and contain the information prescribed by the Notices to Quit (Prescribed Information) Regulations 1980 (S.I. 1980 No. 1624) (as amended). Once the notice has expired the section 1 protected tenancy will come to an end and the tenant (if he remains in possession as he is entitled to do) will become a "statutory tenant" under section 2 of the 1977 Act. The landlord must thereafter bring an action for possession under Order 6, rule 3 of the County Court Rules 1981, and satisfy the requirements of section 98 of the Rent Act 1977. This section, together with Schedule 15 (as amended by the Rent (Amendment) Act 1985, s.1) specifies the grounds on which possession may be granted by the court; there is a discretion to order possession where any of the grounds (known as Cases 1–10) specified in Part I of the Schedule are proved and the court is satisfied that it is reasonable to make an order for possession. The effect of the order can, however, be postponed for any period the court sees fit: section 100. If the landlord can prove any of the grounds (known as Cases 11–20) specified in Part II of the Schedule, then the court has no discretion in the matter and must order that possession be granted to the landlord. The whole of Schedule 15 is reproduced at Appendix I, but it is not considered appropriate to discuss the interpretation of the 20 Cases in this book; such an undertaking would be more appropriate for a work concerned only with landlord and tenant law.

As an alternative to proving one of the 20 Cases, the landlord can offer alternative accommodation to the tenant. If the court is satisfied that the alternative accommodation is suitable for the tenant and is available at the time of the proceedings, or will be available when a possession order comes into effect, the court may grant possession to the landlord if it is also satisfied that it is reasonable to make an order in his favour. The power to postpone the effect of the order under section 100 also applies in this instance.

### Restricted contracts and the Rent Act 1977

Although indefinite security of tenure may be available to some tenants of caravans who can satisfy the requirements of the Rent Act 1977, it is more likely that only partial protection is conferred. This is because most lettings of caravans, particularly of those stationed on permanent caravan sites, are likely to fall within a category referred to in the Rent Act 1977 as "restricted contracts." This term is defined by section 19(2) of the 1977 Act as:

> "a contract, whether entered into before or after the commencement of this Act, whereby one person grants to another person in consideration of a rent which includes payment for the use of furniture or for services, the right to occupy a dwelling as a residence."

Since occupation of a caravan often involves the provision of services by the owner of the land on which it is stationed, it is into this category that many contracts will fall. A caravan constitutes a "dwelling" for the purposes of this section: *R.* v. *Guildford Area Rent Tribunal, ex p. Grubey* (above), and it is of particular significance to the present context that despite the use of the word "rent" in section 19(2), the provision is not confined to tenancies but also includes licences: *Luganda* v. *Service Hotels* (1969). Thus in the classic situation of a site owner granting a residential licence of the caravan and pitch upon which it stands, the licensee is within the scope of a restricted contract.

Where a restricted contract is granted, security of tenure is limited and depends on when the contract was first entered into. If the contract, (not being one for a fixed period), was made before the coming into force of section 69(2) of the Housing Act 1980 (November 28, 1980) the tenant (or licensee) has security of tenure under the provisions of section 103 of the Rent Act 1977. This applies if the contract has been referred to a rent tribunal and a notice to quit has been given before the tribunal's decision or within six months of the giving of the decision. Where this occurs the notice to quit is automatically suspended until the end of the six-month period, unless the tribunal substitutes a shorter period. If a notice to quit is served before any reference to the tribunal is made then section 104 permits the occupier of the caravan to apply to the rent tribunal before the notice to quit expires; if this is done the tribunal can direct that the notice to quit shall be ineffective for a period of up to six months from the date when the notice purported to take effect. The latter section also permits an occupier who has previously successfully applied to the tribunal under section 103 to gain a further extention of up to six months if the application under section 104 is made before the extended period expires.

If the restricted contract was entered into on or after November 28, 1980, the position is regulated by section 69(2) of the Housing Act 1980 which inserts a further provision (section 106A) into the Rent Act 1977. This change substantially reduced the security of tenure available under sections 103–104 of the 1977 Act by providing that on or after making a possession order and before its execution, the court is empowered to suspend the execution of the order or postpone the date for possession for a period of up to three months from the date of the making of the order. This power applies even if the original contract was for a fixed term. As the change effected by section 69(2) of the 1980 Act is a radical one it is unlikely to be commonly used in connection with occupation of a caravan under a restricted contract. This is because the powers of the court under section 4 of the Caravan Sites Act 1968—to postpone the effect of a possession order for up to twelve months—are much more likely to be invoked.

### Rent control under the Rent Act 1977

In the absence of specific legislation dealing with control of rents charged to occupiers of caravans by site owners, reference must be made to the provisions of the Rent Act 1977 (as amended by the Housing Act 1980). The 1977 Act deals with rent control of regulated tenancies in Parts III and IV of the Act and also makes provision for control of rents under restricted contracts in Part V of the Act. These provisions will apply if the caravan qualifies as a dwelling-house within section 1 of the Act: *R. v. Rent Officer of Nottingham Registration Area, ex p. Allen* (1985).

Where a tenancy of a caravan constitutes a protected regulated tenancy, the parties are free to agree on whatever rent they wish, provided a rent for the caravan has not already been registered. The initial inquiry must therefore always be directed to the question whether a rent has been registered. For the purposes of rent registration, England and Wales is divided into rent registration areas on the same basis as local authorities are arranged into counties. Rent registration functions are carried out by rent officers who are appointed and salaried by county councils; these councils provide accommodation and a secretariat within local authority offices (though technically rent officers are under the control of the Secretary of State). An application to a rent officer to have a fair rent registered can be made by either party to the tenancy at any time, even if the tenancy is for a fixed term. If no reference is made by either party to the rent officer and the land-lord seeks to increase the rent, he must comply with the formalities of section 51 of the 1977 Act which requires that the landlord and the tenant must enter into a written agreement termed a "rent agreement with a tenant having security of tenure." This is a document which is signed by both parties and which informs the tenant that his security of tenure is unaffected if he refuses to enter into the agreement and that both parties will continue to have the right to apply to the rent officer to fix a fair rent.

If either party decides to refer to the rent officer, the rent fixed will be entered in the rent register. Once a rent has been registered, at least two years must elapse before any application to revise the rent can be entertained by the rent officer unless there has been some change in the conditions determining the fair rent so as to make the registered rent no longer a fair rent. These changes can only relate to the matters specified in section 67(3) which are (a) the condition of the property (including improvements), (b) the contractual terms, (c) the quantity, quality or condition of furniture provided under the tenancy agreement, and (d) other matters taken into account when the rent was first registered.

Where a tenancy has become a statutory regulated tenancy, similar principles apply with the difference that the landlord can raise a rent which has been agreed by the parties to the level of the registered rent, if the latter is a higher figure. This is achieved by means of service of a "notice of increase" under section 45 of the 1977 Act. Where no rent has been registered, the rent payable is the same as that which was agreed under the contract and cannot be increased except as specified in sections 46 and 47. Prior to registration the rent can be increased under section 46 if the rates charged on the property have been increased by the local authority, or pursuant to section 47 where there is a change in provision of services by the landlord or the use of furniture. In the latter instance, either party may refer the matter to the county court for determination in default of agreement.

Rents charged pursuant to restricted contracts are controlled under Part V of the 1977 Act. Section 77 enables either party to a restricted contract, or the local authority, to refer the contract to the rent tribunal for the area. Prior to any such action being taken the rent payable is that which is agreed between the parties unless a rent tribunal has previously determined a rent for the property. Where an application is received under section 77, the tribunal are empowered by section 78 to (i) approve the rent charged under contract, (ii) reduce or increase the rent to such sum as they may in all the circumstances think reasonable, or (iii) dismiss the reference. In exercising their powers, the tribunal are not permitted to reduce the rent below that which would be recoverable if the property was subject to a regulated tenancy, if the circumstances are such that the property was formerly subject to such a tenancy and a rent had been fixed by the rent officer pursuant to Part IV of the Act. Once the tribunal have fixed the rent it is notified to the local authority (in this case the district council) and is then recorded in a register of rents of restricted contracts maintained pursuant to section 79. When a registration has been made either party or the local authority can refer the matter of the rent to the tribunal again at any time, but the tribunal need not entertain an application for adjustment of the rent unless at least two years have expired since the matter was last considered. The tribunal must, however, reconsider the rent if the application is made within the two year period on the ground that here has been a change in (a) the condition of the dwelling (b) the furniture or services provided (c) the terms of the contract or (d) any other circumstances taken into consideration when the rent was last considered.

### Rent book

A rent book must be issued by a landlord to any person who has a contractual or statutory right to occupy any premises as a residence if there is a weekly rent charged: Landlord and Tenant Act 1985, s.4(1). This provision covers all weekly tenancies and licences and does not depend on the application of any provisions of the Rent Act 1977. It follows therefore that if a caravan in any particular case does not qualify as a "dwelling," or is occupied pursuant to a licence which does not qualify as a restricted contract but is nevertheless used as a residence, a rent book must still be issued to the occupier. This document must contain the name and address of the landlord and information which advises the occupier of his rights under the Rent Acts as specified by the Rent Book (Forms of Notice) Regulations 1982 (S.I. 1982 No. 1474). Failure to provide a rent book where required is an offence for which there is a maximum penalty of a fine of £1,000 with a further penalty of a fine of up to £1,000 on conviction for a second or subsequent offence. It is unlikely that a defence based on the argument that a caravan does not constitute "premises" would succeed, for in *Norton* v. *Knowles* (1967) the Divisional Court found that for the purposes of the anti-harassment provisions (which apply to "premises") it did not matter that the caravan was not attached to the ground. As Salmon L.J. stated " . . . the fact that the caravan is not attached to the realty is quite unimportant."

# 7. Gipsy Caravan Sites

Gipsies are given specific recognition by the caravan sites legislation. It is the primary purpose of Part II of the Caravan Sites Act 1968 to ensure that gipsies are directed to caravan sites provided specifically for their use, thereby controlling itinerant use of land. Coupled with this objective is a legislative attempt to prevent gipsies parking caravans on highways, or on land on which they are trespassers, by making it an offence to do so in any "designated" area, *i.e.* one where the Secretary of State is satisfied that adequate site provision has been made for gipsies. The task of providing suitable sites for gipsies is allocated primarily to county councils, though once established their management is thereafter undertaken by the district councils in whose areas the sites are situated. In metropolitan areas and in London the district councils are responsible for both site provision and for management.

The law relevant to the attainment of these objectives is contained in the Caravan Sites and Control of Development Act 1960, and the Caravan Sites Act 1968, as amended, principally by the Local Government, Planning and Land Act 1980. As will be apparent from the cases and materials to be discussed in this Chapter, this legislation operates in the face of a growing gipsy population, with consequent pressure on local authorities to find suitable sites, and on gipsies themselves to avoid being in breach of the criminal law when present in a designated area.

### Background to the legislation

Prior to the enactment of the Caravan Sites and Control of Development Act 1960, gipsies were not free from difficulties but faced a less daunting task in finding suitable places to camp. Traditionally it was to rural common land that gipsies would look for sites, to a lesser extent to land on which the owner was prepared to permit a temporary encampment, and in the last resort to go onto land as trespassers. When the 1960 Act came into force, the site licensing requirements reduced in number those landowners who were willing to be accommodating to gipsies, for fear of being prosecuted for causing or permitting land to be used in contravention of section 1 of that Act. To avoid common land remaining unregulated by the site licensing provisions (due to difficulty in identifying the "occupier" for the purposes of the legislation), section 23 of the 1960 Act also empowered district councils to make orders prohibiting the stationing of caravans on common land. As a balancing device both county councils and district councils were further empowered by section 24 of the Act to provide sites where caravans could be brought (whether or not by gipsies) but they were put under no duty to provide such accommodation. Development Control Policy Note No. 8 explained the need for provision of sites for gipsies and emphasised the merits of authorised sites over sparodic encampments (see Appendix III).

Part II of the Caravan Sites Act 1968 converted the power of county councils, metropolitan district councils and London boroughs to provide sites under section 24 of the 1960 Act into a positive duty to do so, but only in relation to provision of accommodation for gipsies. The 1968 Act also enacted the provisions which enable the Secretary of State to designate the area of a local authority as one in which adequate provision for gipsies has been made, and accordingly to make it an offence for a gipsy to station a caravan on a highway, or on land on which he is a trespasser, for the purpose of residing in it for any period, if this is done within any such area. The objective was, to some extent, to give the responsible county councils an incentive to achieve designation as quickly as possible, as once this status was achieved they would then be able to take legal action to remove unauthorised caravans by seeking an order for their removal from the magistrates' court under section 11 of the Act. This would thereby substantially supplement existing powers under the Highways Acts (see Chapter 8).

While a number of sites were established for gipsies after the 1968 Act came into force (April 1, 1970), the rate at which sites were provided did not keep pace with demand. Hence DoE Circular 28/77, para. 2, recites that in 1977 about 6,000 gipsy families were travelling in England and Wales and

" . . . have nowhere they can legally go and are usually within the law only when moving along the highway. So the unauthorised encampments, which the Act was designed to eradicate, are as numerous and widespread as ever, not only causing serious worry and offence to the settled population but often offering barely tolerable living conditions for the gipsies themselves."

This state of affairs had prompted the appointment in 1976 by the Secretary of State of Mr. John Cripps (as he then was) to study the gipsy problem, his terms of reference being to "consider the effectiveness of the arrangements to secure adequate accommodation for gipsies in England and Wales, as required by Part II of the Caravan Sites Act 1968, and to report." He was directed to look in particular at the financial and administrative arrangements for provision of sites, the arrangements for designation of areas, and provisions for exemption of some local authorities from the duty imposed by the Act. The Cripps report, entitled "Accommodation for Gipsies" was published in 1977 and recommended many changes to the scheme of the Caravan Sites Act 1968. The recommendations are summarised in the Appendix to DoE Circular 57/78; some of these were accepted by the Government and were enacted by sections 173–178 of the Local Government, Planning and Land Act 1980. These sections substitute new provisions into Part II of the Caravan Sites Act 1968 to take effect in place of several of the sections which were originally enacted. Consequently, all references to the 1968 Act in this Chapter are to the amended provisions.

While many of Cripps' recommendations needed the legislative changes made by the 1980 Act in order to be effective, one important administrative change was made by DoE Circular 57/78 with immediate effect. Under paragraph 4 of this Circular, an Exchequer grant of 100 per cent. was made available to county councils to cover the capital costs of site provision. This was intended to be effective for a five-year period but was extended on enactment of section 70 of the Local Government, Planning and Land Act 1980, which placed on a permanent statutory footing the Secretary of State's power to pay grants to county councils in aid of fulfilment of their duties under the 1968 Act. Despite the changes made in 1980, the gipsy problem has not yet been rectified throughout England and Wales although a significant number of local government areas have become designated. Other areas have been the subject of less effective progress in fulfilling the statutory duty to provide suitable sites, as recent litigation by gipsies attempting to enforce the statutory duty testifies. From this, admittedly very brief, introduction to the subject we can now proceed to examine the current law.

### Duty to provide gipsy caravan sites

The main provision of the legislation relating to gipsy caravan sites is section 6 of the 1968 Act. This provides (section 6(1)):

> " . . . it shall be the duty of every [county council] metropolitan district or London borough to exercise their powers under section 24 of the Caravan Sites and Control of Development Act 1960 . . . so far as may be necessary to provide adequate accommodation for gipsies residing in or resorting to their area."

While section 24 of the 1960 Act empowered both county councils and district councils to provide sites, the 1968 Act, as amended by section 16 and paragraph 11 of Schedule 8 to the Local Government Act 1985, imposed a duty to do so on the county councils, metropolitan district councils and London boroughs. The duty is to provide "adequate accommodation" for gipsies, the word "gipsies" being defined in broad terms by section 16 of the 1968 Act as "persons of nomadic habit of life whatever their race or origin, but does not include members of organised groups of travelling showmen, or persons engaged in travelling circuses, travelling together as such." In adopting this definition the Act has followed closely the definition suggested by Lord Parker C.J. in *Mills* v. *Cooper* (1967) in which the Divisional Court held that whether a person was or was not a gipsy was capable of changing, as this depends on circumstances rather than origins.

The duty imposed by section 6(1) is subject to a qualification in the case of metropolitan districts and London borough councils. Under section 6(2), these councils do not have to provide more than 15 pitches for caravans in each of the metropolitan districts or London borough concerned.

In order to fulfil the duty imposed by section 6, the local authorities are given land management powers by section 24 of the 1960 Act. This section permits councils to acquire land already in use as a caravan site, or which has been used as a caravan site (section 24(2)). It is implicit in section 24(2) that there is a power to acquire any other land voluntarily for the purpose of providing a caravan site, but councils are expressly empowered to acquire land compulsory for this purpose by section 24(6), whether or not already in use as a caravan site. No duties are imposed in relation to provision of caravans; indeed section 24(7) provides that local authorities have no powers to provide caravan accommodation in discharge of their duties under the section.

In addition to the power to provide caravan sites for gipsies, all local authorities have powers under section 6(4) of the 1968 Act to provide working space and facilities for the carrying on of activities normally carried on by gipsies. They may also provide any services or facilities for the health or convenience of gipsies under section 24(2) of the 1960 Act, and in so doing are directed to "have regard to" the Secretary of State's Model Standards for Caravan Sites. The Secretary of State has, however, accepted that the conditions sought by the Model Standards do not apply to gipsy caravan sites: DoE Circular 28/77, para. 7.

### Notification and consultation where proposal to acquire land exists

When a county council propose to provide a gipsy caravan site on any land they must consult with the district council in whose area the proposed site is situated and with any other councils, authorities, or persons they consider appropriate. It is important that the district council which is affected by the proposal should be permitted to object to the scheme, since it is the district council which will have to manage the site once it has been provided. The duty to consult is imposed by section 8(1) of the 1968 Act and will normally involve further consultation with neighbouring district councils and with those persons having interests in neighbouring land, but it was held in R. v. Sheffield City Council, ex p. Mansfield (1978) that the local authority had a "latitude" as to whom they choose to consult. There is no obligation to advertise the proposal in a newspaper, nor is there any general legal requirement to take into account any objections which are received from consultees, thought there is clearly a moral obligation to do so. A special procedure applies, however, if the district council for the area, or a neighbouring district council, lodge an objection which cannot be resolved by negotiations. In this instance, section 8(2) permits the objecting district council to notify the Secretary of State of the existence of the objection. On receipt of an objection, the Secretary of State must give it consideration and then give a direction to the county council under section 8(3). This direction must be one of the following: (a) to abandon the proposal; (b) to proceed with the proposal; or (c) to make an application for planning permission (to be decided by the Secretary of State) for the proposed use of the land as a gipsy caravan site. In exercise of his discretion under section 8(2) the Secretary of State is obliged to consider all three options on their merits, as illustrated by R. v. Secretary of State for the Environment and Cheshire County Council, ex p. Halton Borough Council (1984). In this case the district council vigorously opposed the proposals of the county council on the grounds that to provide a gipsy caravan site on the selected land was: (a) contrary to the provisions of the structure plan; (b) a loss of land suitable for permanent housing purposes; and (c) unnecessary in view of existing site provision. The Secretary of State ruled that he could not, on the merits, direct the county council to abandon the proposal, nor did he see fit to require an application for planning permission to be made to him as he considered that the issues involved raised only local planning matters and were not of national significance. His decision not to require a planning application was based on advice on policy contained in paragraphs 29 and 30 of DoE Circular 28/77, which emphasise that where such an application raises local issues these should be determined locally. As a result he decided to direct the county council under section 8(3)(b) to proceed with the project. The district council succeeded in having this direction quashed since the minister had not given any reasons for failure to direct in accordance with section 8(3)(c), which in view of the national (rather than purely local) policy issues raised would appear to have been the most appropriate decision. By rigidly applying his policy contained in DoE Circular 28/77 he had fettered his discretion and had thereby acted unlawfully.

In a case where it is the district council which seeks to provide a site in exercise of the power conferred by section 24 of the 1960 Act, the only mandatory consultation requirement imposed by the caravans legislation is in accordance with subsection 2A (inserted by section 8 of the Local Government (Miscellaneous Provisions) Act 1982). This requires the district council to consult the fire authority (normally the county council) in relation to the measures to be taken for preventing and detecting the outbreak of fire, and the provision and maintenance of fire fighting equipment. Further consultation is, however, required in relation to the grant of planning permission which may be needed for the use of the land as a gipsy caravan site, a requirement equally applicable to county councils which must therefore consult the district council. As will be seen in the next section, this mutual consultation requirement leads to the question whether alternative sites can be suggested by a council which seeks to oppose a grant of planning permission.

### Planning permission for gipsy caravan sites

When a local authority wish to provide a caravan site facility for gipsies, in many instances this will involve a need for planning permission as the change in the use of the land will be a material change for the purposes of section 22 of the Town and Country Planning Act 1971. There is no need, however, for a county council to seek a grant of planning permission from the relevant district council since the county council can (in common with district councils) grant planning permission to themselves by operating a procedure contained in the Town and Country Planning General Regulations 1976 (S.I. 1976 No. 1419). Under regulation 4, the county council seeking planning permission must first pass a resolution to seek permission for the caravan site in question and then notify the district council, (and vice versa if it is a district council proposal), and persons who have interests in the land concerned if it has not already been purchased by the council. Representations can be made by persons affected, and by the council which had been notified, within a period of 21 days from the date of notification. After this period has expired the initiating council can then pass a further resolution, the effect of which is that planning permission is deemed to be granted by the Secretary of State. In cases where the councils concerned cannot agree and an objection is made, the Secretary of State may be petitioned by the opposing authority to call in the application for decision by himself after convening a public local inquiry. In these cases section 8(3)(b) of the Caravan Sites Act 1968 will normally have been applied by the Secretary of State (see above). However, in cases where the Secretary of State has directed the county council to proceed under section 8(3)(b), it is unlikely that the Secretary of State would subsequently intervene to consider the question whether planning permission should be granted.

When objection is made to a planning proposal, whether arising under section 8(3)(c), or under regulation 4 of the Town and Country Planning General Regulations, it is normally amenity issues that are contested. On some occasions, however, the opposing council may seek to object on the basis that there are more suitable locations for the development elsewhere. In *Bennett* v. *Secretary of State for Wales* (1981) the inspector who held a public local inquiry into the objections of a district council to a county council proposal, ruled that " . . . it is beyond the scope of the present inquiry to consider the merits of other sites and perhaps propose a completely fresh location." Glidewell J. held that the consideration of alternative sites was not normally to be undertaken but in the case of a proposal such as this, where the need for a development outweighs its disadvantages, then such consideration should be given. He therefore quashed the decision of the Secretary of State to grant planning permission.

Proper consideration was given to the question of an alternative site in the appeal decision reported at [1982] J.P.L. 469, in which an application for planning permission was made to the Secretary of State pursuant to section 8(3)(c). The application failed, largely due to the impact the proposed gipsy site would have on the settled community; after declining the application, the Secretary of State ordered the applicant county council to abandon the proposal by giving a direction under section 8(3)(a).

### Enforcement of the duty to provide sites

One of the most important aspects of the law relating to provision of sites for gipsies is the question whether a recalcitrant local authority, which is under a duty imposed by section 6 of the Caravan Sites Act 1968, can be forced to carry out that duty. As will shortly be seen, there have been several attempts by gipsies in need of caravan sites to enforce the duty in the courts.

Quite apart from the possibility of a civil action to enforce the duty, it is to the powers of the Secretary of State in this regard that attention must initially be given. Under section 9 of the 1968 Act, the Secretary of State may:

> " . . . if at any time it appears to him necessary to do so, give directions to any local authority to whom s.6(1) of this Act applies requiring them to provide, pursuant to that section, such sites or additional sites for the accommodation of such numbers of caravans as may be specified in the directions. . . . "

The section goes in to provide that the Secretary of State may enforce the direction by application to the court for an order of mandamus.

Since the Secretary of State is given a power to enforce the duty imposed by section 6, it is to the Secretary of State that those persons seeking accommodation should initially refer. In practice, however, the Secretary of State has shown reluctance to use his powers under section 9, even where there have been long delays in provision of sites. Private individuals have therefore attempted to enforce the duty themselves by action in the High Court. In *Kensington and Chelsea London Borough Council* v. *Wells* (1974), a group of gipsies went onto land owned by the council, which then brought an action for possession. The gipsies brought a "cross action" against the council, seeking a mandatory injunction that the council should carry out their duties, or in the alternative that the proceedings for possession should be restrained until the council had complied with their duty. The Court of Appeal noted that in the three and a half years since the 1968 Act came into force, the council had apparently done nothing to provide any sites for gipsies. Nevertheless, the court held that the gipsies could not enforce the duty of the council to provide accommodation for them and that the council was entitled to possession. This conclusion was based upon the House of Lords decision in *Pasmore* v. *Oswaldtwistle Urban District Council* (1898) in which it was held that where an Act of Parliament itself provides a remedy for failure to perform a statutory duty, it is not open to a private individual to enforce the duty by his own legal action, even though the duty was imposed for his benefit. The court also expressed the *obiter* opinion that no breach of section 6 occurred until the Secretary of State had actually issued a direction under section 9. Although this opinion has subsequently been held to be incorrect, the court has also held in *Greater London Council* v. *Jones* (1973) that failure by a local authority to carry out the duty imposed by section 6 does not give gipsies an implied licence to enter upon land owned by the defaulting local authority for the purposes of establishing an encampment.

If the Secretary of State fails to give a direction under section 9 in circumstances where there is a shortage of sites, can he be forced to do so by legal action? In *R.* v. *Secretary of State for Wales, ex p. Price* (1984), the Secretary of State was requested by a gipsy to make a direction under section 9 in circumstances where the county council concerned had provided a number of sites in the county as a whole but there were no such facilities in the area in which the gipsy lived. The Secretary of State replied explaining that such a direction would only be made in "exceptional circumstances" and was satisfied that the council were attempting to carry out their duty under section 6. In an application for judicial review of this decision, the applicant alleged that (a) the Secretary of State's decision was one to which he could not have come if he had correctly applied the law; (b) the Secretary of State was not entitled to refrain from exercising his powers unless he considered that "exceptional circumstances" existed; and (c) the fact that sites were available elsewhere in the county was irrelevant. McCullough J. held that the duty imposed by section 6 was to be read as subject to an implied qualification that the duty of the county council was to do "that which was practicable or reasonably practicable or reasonable or that it must use its best endeavours." The corresponding position of the Secretary of State was to consider whether, in the light of the difficulties in finding sites, overcoming local opposition, the time taken to acquire the land and obtain planning permission, it could really be said that the council had not performed its duty. Acknowledging that these difficulties confront county councils, the Secretary of State is entitled not to interfere unless some other exceptional factor existed which warranted a direction under section 9. The learned judge accordingly ruled that the Secretary of State had not acted illegally in failing to issue a direction under section 9 and that he was also entitled to take into account the council's record in providing sites elsewhere in the county, as the council was not obligated to provide sites in every part of their area. Although the action against the Secretary of State failed in this case it does, however, confirm that it is possible to seek judicial review of the exercise of his powers. It may be fairly concluded, however, that on McCullough J.'s approach the prospects of success are not very hopeful.

In the most recent cases on this problem, the court has reached conclusions favourable to the gipsies involved. In *R.* v. *Secretary of State for the Environment, ex p. Ward* (1984), two London borough councils provided a site for gipsies in partnership. Conditions at the site were considered to be such that it was unsuitable for human habitation and one of the councils resolved to close it when their lease of the land expired. The applicant in this case, a gipsy resident at the site, petitioned the Secretary of State to make a direction under section 9, but the Secretary of State declined to exercise his powers. An application was made for judicial review seeking to require the Secretary of State to make a direction under section 9 and for the councils to carry out their duty under section 6. Woolf J. considered that he was not bound by the decision in *Kensington and Chelsea London Borough Council* v. *Wells* when the application was one for judicial review (as distinct from an ordinary action) and held that the councils were in breach of their duty under section 6 in giving up responsibility for the site. He thus directed the councils to reconsider the position irrespective of the fact that the Secretary of State had not intervened, but held that it was premature to interfere with the Secretary of State's decision as he had yet to thoroughly investigate the situation before a decision on whether to give a direction under section 9 could be made.

An excellent summary of the law relating to the provision of caravan sites for gipsies was given by Mann J. in *R.* v. *Secretary of State for the Environment, ex p. Lee* (1985), in which judicial review was sought in respect of an allegation that a county council had failed to perform its duty under section 6 and that the Secretary of State had improperly failed to exercise his discretion under section 9 of the 1968 Act. The council had succeeded in providing a considerable number of pitches for gipsies since the Caravan Sites Act 1968 came into force, total provision being 123. Census figures showed, however, that the demand amounted to at least 273 pitches. The Secretary of State refused to give a direction under section 9 as he was satisfied that the council were doing all that was practicable to carry out their duty. Mann J. accepted that the applicant could seek judicial review and considered all the previous cases. He disagreed with McCullough J. in the *Price* case in relation to the nature of the duty imposed on the council, preferring a view expressed by Woolf J. in the *Ward* case. This was to the effect that the council's duty:

" . . . is qualified by the fact that what is or is not adequate accommodation is a question in the first instance for the authority concerned, which has to make a value judgment, taking into account all the circumstances. It is also qualified by the fact that except in exceptional circumstances, the court will not seek to enforce that duty, but leave the matter to the Secretary of State, who can be expected to only exercise his powers when it is appropriate to do so."

The correct approach to the problem was to ask the simple question whether there was adequate accommodation for gipsies in the area. If the answer was "no," as it was in this case, then whether the applicant was entitled to a remedy was a matter of discretion. On the basis of this approach, Mann J. found that throughout the time when the legislation had been in force (over 14 years), supply of sites was consistently behind demand. He therefore made a declaration that the county council had failed to carry out its duty and quashed the decision of the Secretary of State not to intervene under section 9.

## Compulsory purchase of land for gipsy caravan sites

The difficulty of finding suitable sites for gipsies inevitably involves the use of compulsory purchase powers by local authorities. All county councils, district councils, and London borough councils have powers of compulsory purchase conferred on them by section 24(5) of the Caravan Sites and

Control of Development Act 1960. If a local authority wish to exercise this power, they must first gain the consent of the Secretary of State (section 24(6)) after which the procedure to be applied is in accordance with that prescribed by Part II of the Acquisition of Land Act 1981. The council will initially make a compulsory purchase order in the form prescribed by the Compulsory Purchase of Land Regulations 1981 (S.I. 1981 No. 6). Thereafter, advertisement of the making of the order takes place in a local newspaper in two successive weeks, saying that the order may be inspected at the local authority's offices and giving not less than 21 days in order to lodge objections to the order. A notice is served on every owner, lessee and occupier of the land (except a tenant for a month or less) giving the same information. Objections to the order are made in writing, which, together with the order, are submitted to the Secretary of State. There then follows a period during which efforts may be made by all parties to resolve the objections. If they remain unresolved, the Secretary of State will convene a public local inquiry, or allow the objectors the opportunity of appearing before an inspector appointed by him. There is a discretion to disregard an objection if it is merely concerned with the compensation that will ultimately be payable. Most cases will result in a public inquiry at which the objectors will be allowed to give evidence, as may other parties if the inspector decides to permit them to be heard.

The inquiry is conducted in accordance with the Compulsory Purchase by Local Authorities (Inquiries Procedure) Rules 1976 (S.I. 1976 No. 746), which governs the procedural steps involved. The inspector will ultimately prepare a report of the proceedings which will include his findings of fact and a recommendation as to whether or not the order should be confirmed. The final decision is made by the Secretary of State, who is not bound by the report, though it is unusual for him not to follow it. The Secretary of State may modify the order if he sees fit, but in so doing can only reduce the area of land which is to be acquired and cannot increase it. If the order is confirmed, the authority can thereafter proceed to acquire the land involved on payment of compensation.

An objector to the compulsory purchase order may seek to persuade the inspector that a more suitable site is available elsewhere. In *Brown* v. *Secretary of State for the Environment* (1979), the inspector found that there were several sites under consideration by the county council, one of which was already owned by them. He reached the conclusion that the site subject to the compulsory purchase order was the most unsuitable of all the sites concerned. Despite this view, the Secretary of State decided to confirm the order and ruled that the existence of alternative sites was irrelevant to his decision, since his function was only to consider the merits or otherwise of the land subject to the order. In quashing the Secretary of State's decision, Forbes J. decided that the Secretary of State had misdirected himself in refusing to consider alternative sites and had thereby omitted a material consideration. He also decided that it was wholly unreasonable for the Secretary of State to confirm a compulsory purchase order when the acquiring authority already owned land suitable for the purpose.

## Management of sites by district councils

When a caravan site has been established, by any local authority, it is the function of the district council for the area in which the site is situated to manage the site. Thus section 7(1) of the 1968 Act expressly limits the duty of county councils to the task of finding and providing adequate accommodation for gipsies, while expressly placing a duty on district councils to carry out the management powers conferred by section 24 of the 1960 Act.

Most of the arrangements for local authority site management are not regulated by law but by recommendations of Department of the Environment, mainly contained in DoE Circular 28/77. The only significant provision in relation to management contained in the statutes concerns the levying of charges for site use and joint management of sites. Under section 7(2) of the 1968 Act charges for using a gipsy caravan site (or its services and facilities) are determined by the county council and these are collected by the district council. The charges are required to be "reasonable," (section 24(3) of the 1960 Act), but if the district council incur a loss in the course of management of the site, allowance being made for administrative expenses, the county council must reimburse the district council to the extent of the loss. Management of a site by a district council can, with the approval of the county council, also be conducted on an agency basis on behalf of another district council if the two district councils agree: section 7(3). This is likely to occur where the two district councils are neighbours.

DoE Circular 28/77 envisages that management of sites can take place on the basis that some of the sites are provided for emergency purposes only while progress is made in provision of permanent sites. Emergency sites are therefore provided for the purpose of "stopping-over" only, but in such cases the minimum requisite is provision of an immediate regular refuse collection facility, and as soon as possible thereafter to provide "other basic facilities such as a water supply and elementary sanitation": para. 33. The Circular also envisages that most sites will be for the use of gipsies who intend to occupy a pitch for their semi-permanent use, but that permanent sites should have a proportion of pitches available for gipsies needing only a short-stay facility: para. 37. Part V of the Circular, entitled "Practical Aspects of Site Provision and Management" should be consulted for extensive detail of standards of site provision and recommended site layouts.

### Unlawful gipsy encampments: designation under section 12 of the Caravan Sites Act 1968

The Department of the Environment has stated that the objective of the 1968 Act is to ensure that a countrywide network of permanent sites for gipsies is provided, both for gipsies residing in or resorting to any particular area: DoE Circular 28/77, para. 37. To ensure that, once provided, these facilities are used, and with the objective of controlling the formation of gipsy encampments otherwise than on the sites provided, the 1968 Act empowers the Secretary of State to designate areas under section 12. In general terms, a designated area is one in which it is illegal to station gipsy caravans except on local authority sites. Within such an area local authorities can take steps to remove illegally stationed caravans.

Under section 12(1), (2), (2A) the Secretary of State can, on an application being made to him, designate by means of an order the area of a county council, metropolitan district council or London borough, or (since 1980) the area of a non-metropolitan district council. In the last instance the designation of a district council can be achieved only by a joint application by the district council and the county council in whose area the district is situated. Under section 12(2A) (inserted by section 16 of and paragraph 11 of Schedule 8 to the Local Government Act 1985) two or more metropolitan district councils can also seek designation by making a joint application. The Secretary of State cannot, however, make a designation order unless it appears to him that one of the conditions stated in section 12(3) is satisfied. These are either (i) that adequate provision has been made in the area for accommodation of gipsies residing in or resorting to the area, or (ii) that in all the circumstances it is not necessary or expedient to make any provision.

The criteria applied by the Secretary of State in reaching a decision on an application for designation under section 12 are not specified in the Act, but are stated in Annex 2 to Circular 8/81. This document was issued by the Department of the Environment after the enactment of the Local Government, Planning and Land Act 1980 had made amendments to the 1968 Act, including the substitution of the present section 12. The Circular explains that the Secretary of State must be satisfied that " . . . the sites provided are sufficiently diverse and suitably designed and managed to meet the accommodation needs, within reason, of gipsies residing in or resorting to [the area]. Once designated, an authority should be able to handle any reasonable and foreseeable demands within its own area. . . . " Local authorities seeking designation should be able to demonstrate that they have (a) residential sites (long-stay sites with full facilities), (b) transit sites (short-stay sites with minimum facilities), and (c) emergency stopping-places (land with few or no facilities, to deal with unexpected incursions).

It is tempting to think that once designation has been achieved this puts to an end the duty under the 1968 Act to provide further sites. That this is incorrect has been emphasised by the Secretary of State in DoE Circular 28/77 (para. 23). This paragraph explains that designation must be seen only as a means of acquiring additional powers to ensure that gipsies use the accommodation available to them. Indeed, a designated authority may have to increase the provision they have made if there is a subsequent expansion of the gipsy population in the area, and the Secretary of State is able to use his powers under section 9 to direct a county council to do so. The Secretary of State may also revoke a designation order acting on his own accord under section 12(4). Notwithstanding these powers it is pertinent to note that in the course of his judgment in *R. v. Secretary of State for the Environment, ex p. Ward* (1984), Woolf J. observed that a local authority could expect to be able to rely on the continuation of the designated status unless there was a change of circumstances since the making of the designation order.

The position of London boroughs and metropolitan districts must be considered in the light of section 6(2) which limits the duty of these councils to provision for 15 caravans in each of those boroughs or districts. However, it does not necessarily follow that provision of spaces for 15 caravans amounts to "adequate provision" of sites for the purposes of designation under section 12. This is because section 12 designation is dependent upon an assessment of a factual state of affairs and is not directly linked to fulfillment of the section 6 statutory duty. The Secretary of State also regards the statutory figure of 15 as a minimum standard: DoE Circular 28/77, para. 21. Almost all of the London boroughs have now succeeded in acquiring designation status but few metropolitan districts have been designated. On

February 24, 1986, the list of designated areas in England and Wales was as follows:

| Area Designated | S.I. No. |
|---|---|
| (1) The London boroughs of: | |
| Barking | 1973 No. 449 |
| Bexley | 1975 No. 648 |
| Camden | 1981 No. 665 |
| Croydon | 1974 No. 919 |
| Enfield | 1975 No. 316 |
| Greenwich | 1974 No. 920 |
| Hammersmith | 1975 No. 1082 |
| Havering | 1973 No. 445 |
| Hillingdon | 1984 No. 1296 |
| Islington | 1981 No. 666 |
| Kensington and Chelsea | 1975 No. 647 |
| Lambeth | 1979 No. 419 |
| Lewisham | 1979 No. 428 |
| Merton | 1973 No. 881 |
| Newham | 1973 No. 446 |
| Redbridge | 1973 No. 447 |
| Richmond-upon-Thames | 1973 No. 1944 |
| Sutton | 1974 No. 921 |
| Waltham Forest | 1973 No. 448 |
| Wandsworth | 1981 No. 1592 |
| Westminster | 1974 No. 1788 |
| (2) The former county boroughs of: | |
| Bolton | 1974 No. 4 |
| Bury | 1973 No. 879 |
| Leeds | 1973 No. 880 |
| Lincoln | 1974 No. 5 |
| Manchester | 1972 No. 1943 |
| Oxford | 1974 No. 922 |
| Plymouth | 1972 No. 1451 |
| St. Helens | 1972 No. 1450 |
| Stoke on Trent | 1972 No. 1449 |
| Wolverhampton | 1972 No. 1945 |
| (3) Countywide designations: | |
| Dorset | 1978 No. 1221 |
| Oxfordshire (part) | 1974 No. 922 |
| West Sussex | 1982 No. 69 |
| (4) District designations: | |
| Aylesbury, Chiltern & South Bucks | 1981 No. 1337 |
| Ashford | 1985 No. 1391 |
| Boston | 1984 No. 1469 |
| Chester | 1984 No. 1958 |
| Chesterfield, Bolsover and N.E. Derbyshire | 1985 No. 1952 |
| Dartford | 1982 No. 1501 |

| Area Designated | S.I. No. |
|---|---|
| Epsom & Ewell | 1985 No. 407 |
| Gravesham | 1983 No. 1945 |
| Hartlepool & Stockton-on-Tees | 1985 No. 1885 |
| High Peak | 1984 No. 67 |
| Huntington | 1984 No. 1959 |
| Hyndburn | 1983 No. 410 |
| Ipswich, Babergh, Mid Suffolk & Suffolk coastal | 1985 No. 1652 |
| Kennet, North Wiltshire, Thamesdown & W. Wiltshire | 1982 No. 68 |
| Kingston upon Thames | 1984 No. 16 |
| Luton | 1985 No. 1218 |
| Middlesbrough | 1985 No. 324 |
| Milton Keynes | 1982 No. 1255 |
| Northampton, Wellingborough & South Northamptonshire | 1985 No. 382 |
| Nuneaton & Bedworth | 1983 No. 388 |
| Oldham | 1983 No. 387 |
| Oswestry | 1982 No. 1799 |
| Peterborough | 1985 No. 1764 |
| Rochdale | 1984 No. 200 |
| Salisbury | 1983 No. 1392 |
| Selby | 1984 No. 1797 |
| South Bedfordshire | 1982 No. 1570 |
| South Derbyshire | 1984 No. 967 |
| Tonbridge & Malling | 1985 No. 972 |
| Trafford | 1984 No. 1358 |
| Wealdon, Rother, Eastbourne Hastings | 1985 No. 324 |
| West Lindsey | 1984 No. 1780 |
| Windsor & Maidenhead | 1985 No. 1795 |

When a local government area has become a designated area, section 10 of the 1968 Act applies to thereafter. This section provides:

" . . . it shall be an offence for any person being a gipsy to station a caravan for the purpose of residing for any period
(a) on any land situated within the boundaries of a highway; or
(b) on any other unoccupied land; or
(c) on any occupied land without the consent of the occupier."

If a gipsy is found guilty of an offence under this section he is liable to a maximum fine of £50 on conviction in the magistrates' court. If he continues in breach of the section, after having been convicted, he is guilty of a further offence and liable to a fine of up to £5 per day for each day the offence continues. The section does, however, provide a defence if breach of the section occurred as a result of an emergency. Thus under section 10(2), a gipsy who is subject to proceedings must prove that the caravan was illegally stationed in consequence of illness, mechanical breakdown or other immediate emergency and that he removed it (or intended to remove it) as soon as reasonably practicable. Prosecutions under section 10(1) can be brought by all local authorities (section 14(1), though a duty imposed by section 12(6) of the Act, to take "reasonably practicable" steps to inform gipsies within an area which has been designated of the effect of designation, applies only to county councils, metropolitan districts and London borough councils.

### Removal of unlawful encampments and occupants

A remedy open to local authorities in attempting to deal with unauthorised gipsy encampments lies in seeking an order of the magistrates' court authorising the removal of the caravans and persons residing therein. This remedy is available if an offence under section 10 of the 1968 Act appears to have been committed, irrespective of whether proceedings are brought by the local authority in relation to that offence. Thus if the magistrates' court is satisfied that a caravan is stationed on land in contravention of section 10 it may make an order requiring the removal of the caravan and occupants; in so doing the court's order need not precisely identify the caravan concerned. The magistrates are empowered by section 11(2) to authorise the local authority to take such steps as are reasonably necessary to ensure compliance with the order, and may specifically authorise the authority to enter onto the land and to take specified steps for securing entry to the caravan and to render it suitable for removal from the land.

When an order under section 11 is made the order must not be executed by entering onto any occupied land (*i.e.* occupied otherwise than by gipsies), unless at least 24 hours notice is given to the owner and occupier concerned. No such notice need be given, however, if the authority have made reasonable enquiries and have not been able to discover their names and addresses. These parties are also entitled to notice of any proceedings under the section, and are entitled to be heard, the local authority being placed by section 11(9) under a similar obligation to notify them of commencement of the proceedings so far as is possible after making reasonable enquiries.

A substantial part of section 11 is concerned with the problem of serving notice of the proceedings on the caravan occupier. It was held in *R. v. Havering JJ., ex p. Smith* (1974) that this must be effected before the hearing as it may be the case that the caravan occupier has not committed an offence under section 10, *e.g.* because of illness causing an enforced stop. The amendments to section 11 introduced by section 174 of the Local Government, Planning and Land Act 1980, are directed to providing a method of service of the notice of the proceedings in a manner which will achieve the desired result, *i.e.* impart the necessary information and at the same time overcome the problems facing local authorities in seeking to serve the notice. Thus under section 11(6), the notice (in the form of a summons requiring the recipient to attend the court to answer to the complaint made by the local authority) need not name any of the occupants of the caravan. If it is impracticable to serve the notice personally, section 11(7) provides that service is effected if a copy of it is merely attached to the caravan in a prominent place. Where, as will often be the case, the identity of the occupiers is unknown, service is effected if a copy of it is attached in a prominent place to every caravan which is situated on the land at the time when notice is given. Section 11(8) further requires the local authority to take reasonably practicable steps to display a notice on the land itself in such a position that it is likely to be seen by any further gipsies that may come onto the land to camp.

If the magistrates' court issues the order sought by the local authority, further provision is made by section 11 to ensure that execution of it is not hindered. It is therefore an offence intentionally to obstruct any person who is carrying out the requirements of an order of the court, in respect of which a maximum fine of £400 can be imposed if found guilty on summary conviction: section 11(4). In recognition of the possibility of a breach of the peace occurring in securing the removal of caravans, section 11(5) provides that a police constable in uniform can arrest without a warrant any person who he reasonably suspects to be guilty of the offence of obstruction.

### Site licences for local authority gipsy sites

In general, no site licence is needed under section 1 of the Caravan Sites and Control of Development Act 1960. The Local Government, Planning and Land Act 1980 provides in section 176 that a site licence is not required by a county council for the use of land as a caravan site which provides gipsy accommodation. This provision incorporated paragraph 11A into Schedule 1 to the 1960 Act (exemptions from site licencing requirements), and supplements the provisions of paragraph 11, which states that no site licence is needed by a district council in relation to land used as any type of caravan site which is provided by the district council.

These provisions do not, however, take account of the possibility that land may be made available for use by gipsies otherwise than by local authorities. In such instances a site licence will be necessary, and must be provided by the local authority if planning permission is obtained for the use of the land. If a site licence is granted in such circumstances the issuing authority should bear in mind the Secretary of State's view that the Model Standards for Caravan Sites issued under section 5(6) of the 1960 Act do not apply to sites for gipsies: DoE Circular 28/77, para. 7.

### Caravans on commons

It was stated in the introductory paragraphs of this Chapter that, prior to the 1960 Act, gipsies traditionally used rural commons for encampment purposes. While this was undoubtedly the case, there was no free-for-all situation at that time as there existed restrictions on the use of commons. One restriction arose from section 193 of the Law of Property Act 1925. This provision, which is still in force, grants rights of access to the public for "air and exercise" on commons, principally in urban areas, but section 193(4) makes it an offence punishable by a maximum fine of £50 to " . . . draw or drive upon any land to which this section applies any carriage, cart, caravan, truck or other vehicle. . . . "

Commons in all areas could also be affected by the making of a scheme under the Commons Act 1899. Part I of this Act, which deals with controls over the use of commons, empowers all district councils to make a scheme for the regulation and management of any common within their district with a view to making of by-laws and regulations for the prevention of nuisances and the preservation of order on the common. Enquiry as to whether a scheme exists in relation to any particular common should be made of the district council concerned. Where by-laws have been made they will typically prohibit (amongst other things) the stationing of a caravan on the common. The penalty for breach of the by-laws (if any) is a maximum fine of

£100 together with a daily fine of £5 for every day the offence continues after conviction: Local Government Act 1972, s.237.

The object of section 23 of the Caravan Sites and Control of Development Act 1960 was to ensure that no land, except that specified in Schedule 1, should be outside the site licensing system. The section therefore permits a district council to make an order which prohibits the stationing of caravans on common land for human habitation. This power cannot be exercised, however, if either section 193 of the Law of Property Act 1925, or a scheme under the Commons Act 1899, already applies to the land. The council is also prohibited from making an order if they have already issued a site licence in respect of the land, *i.e.* where the "occupier" has been ascertained for the purposes of the 1960 Act. It will be appreciated from the fact that as the definition of a "common" given in section 23(8) includes town and village greens, the exercise of these powers has greatly reduced access to commons for parking of caravans. Breach of any order made under the section is an offence for which a maximum fine of £50 may be imposed. Having regard to this penalty, copies of an order must be displayed on the land itself.

Objections to the making of an order under section 23 can be made in accordance with the provisions of Schedule 2 to the 1960 Act. This contains arrangements for newspaper notification of the making of the order and for objections to be made within 28 days. The order can be confirmed by the council itself if no objections are received within the 28 day period, but if objections are received these must be forwarded with the order to the Secretary of State for the Environment who may cause a public local inquiry to be held. The Secretary of State may therefore confirm the order, whether or not subject to modifications, or he may reject it.

As these provisions do not carry heavy penalties for their breach, a local authority wishing to clear an encampment on common land may wish to commence civil proceedings to evict illegally stationed caravans. In *Costello* v. *Dacorum District Council* (1983) the local authority obtained a 10–year lease of privately-owned common land for the express purpose of enabling them to evict the gipsies who were using the land. The Secretary of State had previously issued a temporary grant of planning permission (for three years) authorising the use of the common as a caravan site. The Court of Appeal held that the local authority had acted within their powers under section 120(1)(*b*) of the Local Government Act 1972, which enabled them to acquire land for the purposes of the "benefit, improvement or development of their area. . . . " and they were therefore entitled to proceed with their objective to clear the site.

### Self-help for gipsies

While much of this Chapter has been concerned with the duties of public authorities in relation to gipsies, mention should be made of the steps which are open to gipsies to take themselves. Provided planning permission is obtained (where required) and the requirements of the Caravan Sites and Control of Development Act 1960 are complied with, gipsies are free to establish their own sites. The difficulties which local authorities experience in finding suitable sites are, however, equally applicable to gipsies themselves with the result that many applications for planning permission are doomed to failure despite the exhortations of the Department of the

Environment, particularly in DoE Circular 28/77. It was recognised in this Circular that gipsies may wish to make provision for their own accommodation, and paragraphs 40–41 give the following advice:

*"Gipsy-owned caravan sites.*
40. Some gipsies have from time to time sought planning permission and site licences for the development of their own sites for the accommodation of gipsy families. Other have expressed a desire to acquire land on which to settle individually or in a family group, but have found the procedures or the lack of finance too daunting. In the present financial situation and in view of the urgent need for more sites, local authorities may wish to consider the advantages of encouraging self help in this manner. It may involve a sympathetic and flexible approach to applications for planning permission and site licences, for example by allowing sites to be established with only minimum facilities in the first instance and to be developed by degrees thereafter. In some cases, too, there may be suitable land in local authority ownership which could be offered to gipsies for purchase or lease.
41. There have been cases where gipsies have bought a plot of land and stationed caravans on it only to find that the necessary planning permission and site licences are not forthcoming. Even if the objections are insuperable local planning authorities might not consider it expedient to take enforcement action until sites are available in the area for such families."

Following the publication of the Cripps Report "Accommodation for Gipsies" the following advice was issued to local planning authorities in DoE Circular 57/78:

"4.13. . . . The Secretaries of State agree that it would be to everyone's advantage if as many gipsies as possible were enabled to find their own accommodation, rather than having to rely on local authorities to provide it at the public expense.
The Secretaries of State . . . look to local authorities to make a positive effort to identify pieces of land in their ownership, however small, which might be suitable for a single family or a group of related families, or as a commercially operated site. Authorities may also consider the purchasing of land for lease or resale to the gipsies. Where a gipsy already owns or intends to purchase land, he should be able to get help from the local authority in understanding the planning and licensing procedures.
The Property Services Agency already offer the local authorities surplus government land which is not required for other government departments; the Secretaries of State urge authorities, in considering whether they require such land, not to overlook the need for land for gipsies. The Property Services Agency cannot sell land to a gipsy direct: surplus land not required by either government departments or local authorities is sold by public auction or tender so that any interested party has an opportunity to acquire it. Gipsies could compete for the purchase of the land but only in the same way, by bidding or tendering for it; this is likely to prove difficult for them.
. . . The Secretaries of State . . . appreciate that sites suitable in other respects may conflict with Green Belt or other planning policies. But the special need to accommodate gipsies—and the consequences of not accommodating them—should be taken into account as a material consideration in reaching planning decisions."

This advice of this Circular was specifically applied in the planning appeal decision reported at [1981] J.P.L. 616, but other reported decisions tend to indicate that amenity and other considerations may outweigh (despite the advice of DoE Circulars 28/77 and 57/78) the need for sites. This is illustrated by the following appeal decisions:

**Stationing of mobile homes for Romany family.** Application was made to station a mobile home on an area of backland behind extensive rear gardens of continuous residential development. The inspector found that the proposed development would "be most undesirable in terms of augmenting existing sporadic development in a backland rural setting and of detracting from the character and appearance of the surroundings as a result." The report continues:

"I have considered the recommendations of the Cripps Report and the content of Circular 57/78 very fully and I am aware of the present shortfall in the provision of permanent gipsy caravan sites in the district but I do not believe that private sites should be permitted irrespective of planning merit as a means of short term alleviation of this problem. I recognise that there is clearly a genuine desire and intent on the part of the appellant to settle permanently on the site but I nevertheless do not consider that the circumstances of family need in this case at present justify setting aside the planning objections purely on the basis of the Romany background concerned": [1982] J.P.L. 472.

**Private gipsy site in proposed green belt area.** In this appeal the issue was whether there was sufficient justification to override the presumption against new development in a proposed green belt area. The inspector stated that he was "mindful of the advice contained in DoE Circulars 28/77 and 57/78 urging flexibility in the approach to the very special problems of gipsy caravan site locations," and considered the site a suitable one despite the green belt proposal. He declined to allow the appeal, however, on the grounds that (a) the application was a speculative one submitted by the Romany Guild, supported by the Gipsy Council, relating to land owned by a trust the director of which was an absentee, thus giving rise to anxiety over the efficient management of the site; (b) the details of the use of a proposed work area associated with the site had not been made available and it would be irresponsible to give a "blanket" permission which could give rise to environmental problems: [1984] J.P.L. 210. For a further example see [1984] J.P.L. 830.

In several other reported instances the appeals have been concluded in favour of the applicants. The following planning appeal decision provides an example.

**Gipsy caravan site in potential green belt area.** In this appeal the inspector recognised that demand for gipsy caravan sites greatly exceeded supply, the problem being acute in the area of the appeal site. With the guidelines of DoE Circulars 28/77 and 57/78 in mind he stated "I consider that there should be an initial presumption in favour of the . . . proposal; only if other material considerations are overriding should permission be withheld." As the site was sufficiently removed from permanent residential development with no highway objections, the application was permissible notwithstanding the green belt proposal: [1983] J.P.L. 570. Other examples of successful appeal decisions are reported at [1981] J.P.L. 539, [1983] J.P.L. 563 and [1983] J.P.L. 566.

# 8. Caravans Situated on the Highway

When a caravan is parked on land forming part of a public highway instead of on land which is privately owned, what legal issues are raised? What is contemplated here includes the common situation where a touring caravan is placed on the public highway outside a dwelling-house due to lack of space in the area of land comprising the curtilage of the house. For example, where a house is terraced, the highway may be used for parking the caravan, much like a private car. Similarly, when the caravan is being used for touring purposes can it be parked for any length of time in a lay-by or on the verge of the main part of the carriageway? How do the controls, if any, affect gipsies?

Having discussed in the previous Chapter the provisions of the Caravan Sites Act 1968 which affect gipsies, it is appropriate to consider their position when in transit but temporarily parked on a highway, and the special provisions designed to prevent itinerant use of highway land by gipsies. The meaning of the word "highway" is also considered here.

### Gipsy caravans stationed on the highway

When the area of a local authority has become designated under section 12 of the Caravan Sites Act 1968, controls over the use of land by gipsies come into immediate effect. Under section 10(1)(a) it is an offence for a gipsy to station a caravan within the boundaries of a highway in a designated area for the purpose of residing for any period. Most of the details of this offence, the defence of illness, mechanical breakdown, etc., were considered above at p. 106, so that is only relevant at this point to give consideration to the scope of the words "within the boundaries of a highway." "Highway" is not defined in the Caravan Sites Act 1968, nor is it fully defined in the main statute dealing with highway law, the Highways Act 1980. Section 328 of the 1980 Act merely provides that "highway" means "the whole or part of a highway other than a ferry or waterway." The absence of a full definition means that the common law rules governing the scope of a highway must be applied. In *ex p. Lewis* (1888), the word was defined as "a way over which there is a public right of passage and re-passage without let or hinderance." The width of the highway includes not only the surface habitually used by the public in exercising the right of passage or repassage (the made-up area), but also the whole space between the fences which enclose it: *Attorney-General* v. *Benyon* (1969). A verge was held to be part of the highway in *Rodgers* v. *Ministry of Transport* (1952); so, also, was an area of land formerly used for highway purposes but which is no longer specifically used as such due to carriageway re-shaping: *Suffolk County Council* v. *Mason* (1979). In this case, the House of Lords endorsed the previously established principle of "once a highway, always a highway" until such time as it is formally stopped up or extinguished.

If a gipsy caravan is stationed on a highway outside a designated area, no offence is committed under section 10 of the 1968 Act. Nor is any offence committed if the caravan is stationed on the highway in a designated area otherwise than for the purposes of residing for any period. Whether any other offence is committed depends largely upon the application of principles of highway law which also apply equally to other road users. A number of these principles are based on provisions contained in the Highways Act 1980, the relevant provisions of which must now be examined.

### Camping on highway land

A particular statutory offence is contained in section 148 of the Highways Act 1980. The relevant part of this section provides:

"If without lawful authority or excuse—
(d) a hawker or other itinerant trader pitches a booth, stall or stand, or encamps, on a highway he is guilty of an offence and liable to a fine not exceeding £400."

This provision is derived from section 127 of the Highways Act 1959 the drafting of which specifically included after the word "trader" the words "or a gipsy." In its current form, the section has omitted the specific reference to gipsies (on the basis that the inclusion was discriminatory), so that making an encampment on a highway is only an offence under this section if the person charged with the offence is either a "hawker" or an "itinerant trader." Apart from the reduction of its scope by the removal of the specific reference to gipsies, the section has also been rendered less effective than it would first appear by the decision of the Divisional Court in *Smith* v. *Wood* (1971). Although this case concerned a prosecution of gipsies under section 127 of the Highways Act 1959, the decision is of general relevance to the application of the section due to the interpretation the court placed upon the word "encamps." The meaning of this word came to be considered when a party of gipsies established a camp on a lay-by and were charged under section 127 of the 1959 Act with having been encamped during the period November 6–18, 1969, the camp having been first established prior to November 6. In their defence they submitted to the magistrates that there was no case to answer because the offence contemplated by the section related to the single act of establishing a camp and not to the continuing act of remaining encamped. The magistrates convicted the gipsies, but on appeal the Divisional Court quashed the convictions on the basis that although "encamps" could be interpreted to mean either setting up a camp or living in a camp, in the context of the section it meant only the former. In giving judgment for the defendant gipsies, Lord Parker C.J. recognised that the decision was highly inconvenient from the point of view of the prosecuting local authority. It appears from this decision, therefore, that in order to gain a conviction under what is now section 148 of the Highways Act 1980, the prosecutor must specify the precise date on which the act of encampment took place, a matter which may not be easy to determine.

### Structures placed on the highway

A provision of the Highways Act 1980 which seems, at first sight, to have little relevance to the stationing of a caravan on a highway, but which has

113

been held to be relevant by the High Court, is section 143. This section enables the highway authority to serve a notice on any person who has control or possession of a "structure" which has been "erected or set up on a highway" requiring that person to remove it within the time specified in the notice. If it is not removed in accordance with the notice no criminal offence is committed, but the highway authority may take steps to remove the structure after not less than one month has expired since the notice was first served.

The application of the section depends on the meaning of the word "structure." This is defined in section 143(4) as including "any machine, pump, post, or other object of such a nature as to be capable of causing obstruction, and a structure may be treated as having been erected or set up notwithstanding that it is on wheels." Whether this includes a caravan was considered in *R. v. Welwyn Hatfield District Council, ex p. Brinkley* (1982). In this case a group of caravans was situated on the verge of a road for 13 months. The highway authority (which was the district council acting under powers delegated by the county council), served a notice under section 143 of the 1980 Act. An attempt was made to have the notice quashed on the ground that a caravan was not a structure for the purposes of the 1980 Act. In deciding the matter the court had regard to the definition of a "caravan" given in section 29(1) of the Caravan Sites and Control of Development Act 1960 (as amended) as " . . . any structure designed or adapted for human habitation which is capable of being moved from one place to another. . . . " and concluded that the fact that the caravan was capable of being moved about did not prevent it being a structure for the purposes of section 143 of the 1980 Act. The notice served by the highway authority was thus upheld, but Forbes J. was careful to confine his judgment to specific circumstances.
He stated:

> "I accept that to be a structure within the definition of that term, as it appears in the Highways Act, there must be some degree of more than casual resting there. I do no think it can be said that one is erecting a structure on wheels on a highway merely because one parks a car there. I do not think that a car would be a structure within that meaning even though it is constructed."

Being in no doubt that a caravan is capable of causing an obstruction (as required by section 143(4)), he concluded:

> "Whether the disposition of a caravan can properly be called the erecting or setting up of a structure on the highway would depend on whether it has been there merely for a short period of time, and there is an intention to move it on fairly quickly, or whether it has been deposited there for a considerable period."

It is only in the latter case that the highway authority is justified in serving a notice under this section.

## Obstruction of the highway

One of the most commonly used provisions of the Highways Act 1980 is specifically designed to deal with obstructions. Section 137, formerly section 121 of the Highways Act 1959, is in the following terms:

> "(1) If a person, without lawful authority or excuse, in any way wilfully obstructs the free passage along a highway he is guilty of an offence and liable to a fine not exceeding level 3 on the standard scale [currently £400].

(2) A constable may arrest without warrant any person whom he sees committing an offence against this section."

The provision has been the subject of a large amount of litigation involving many different types of alleged acts of obstruction and different aspects of the offence. For instance, the use of the word "wilfully" in section 137(1) tends to suggest that the defendant must intend to make the highway less convenient. It was held, however, in *Arrowsmith* v. *Jenkins* (1963), that an offence is committed under the section if the defendant merely does something (or omits to do something) and intends to carry out the act or omission which in fact causes an obstruction to occur, even if there was no specific intention to create the obstruction.

To constitute an "obstruction" there must be a substantial interference with the right of free passage over the highway and it must not be purely temporary in nature: *Seekings* v. *Clarke* (1961). It follows, therefore, that very minor interferences can be ignored as well as those which arise from objects which are placed in position for very limited purposes. Subject only to these considerations, it was held in *Wolverton Urban District Council* v. *Willis* (1962) that (i) every member of the public is entitled to unrestricted access to the whole of a footway; (ii) any encroachment which restricts the full exercise of that right is an unlawful obstruction; (iii) a member of the public who is restricted in the use of the footway is therefore obstructed because he is denied access to the whole of the footway.

Since the scope of section 137 is so wide, the courts have imposed a limitation on its operation by insisting that there must be proof that the use of the highway in question by the defendant is an unreasonable use. In *Nagy* v. *Weston* (1965) it was held that whether a use of the highway is unreasonable and therefore amounts to an obstruction is purely a question of fact depending on all the circumstances of the case. The magistrates must therefore take into account the length of time the obstruction continues, the place where it occurs, the purpose for which it has occurred, and whether it does in fact cause an actual obstruction, as opposed to a potential obstruction.

Within the present context, the temporary parking of a caravan in a lay-by is unlikely to be considered an obstruction within the section, since a lay-by is constructed for the specific purpose of providing a resting place. Its use as such is thus not an unreasonable use of the facility. It may be more difficult, however, to show "reasonable use" of the highway where the caravan is parked partly on a footpath or pavement.

### Civil action for recovery of possession of the highway

The statutory provisions contained in the Highways Act 1980, ss. 137, 143 and 148, provide the powers most likely to be used to deal with a stationary caravan or group of caravans situated on land forming part of a highway. It is clear, however, that the provisions are not free from difficulties from the point of view of the highway authority and in practice it may be necessary to consider alternative remedies. A variety of other matters are relevant to the issue of controlling unauthorised encampments, one of which involves the use of a procedure originally designed to overcome the problem of recovering possession of property occupied by squatters. This procedure is available in both the county court and the High Court, under the County Court Rules 1981, Ord. 24 and the Rules of the Supreme Court, Ord. 113, respectively.

The procedure is employed with a view to obtaining an order for recovery of possession of the land described in the order. It is initiated by a person who alleges that his land is occupied by a person or persons (not being a tenant or tenants holding over after the termination of a tenancy) who entered into or remained in occupation without his licence or consent. In High Court proceedings the applicant must file an affidavit with his originating summons for possession, the affidavit stating (a) his interest in the land, (b) the circumstances giving rise to the application, and (c) that he does not know the name of any person occupying the land who is not named in the summons. Copies of these documents must be served on any person who is in fact named in the summons, but if there are persons unknown in occupation it is sufficient to attach them to the caravan unless the court directs that some other method of service is to be used. Following service of the summons and affidavit, the court will not normally make an order for possession unless at least five clear days have elapsed since service, and may exercise the power to order that possession be given to the applicant on a specified date.

The utility of this procedure in cases of unauthorised stationing of a caravan on a highway was confirmed by the Court of Appeal in *Wiltshire County Council* v. *Frazer* (1983). In this case an unauthorised encampment of several caravans and tents occurred on land owned by the county council, which was the highway authority. An application was made by the council under RSC, Order 113, which was granted by the High Court. On appeal against the making of the possession order, the defendants argued that the procedure of Order 113 was inapplicable in the present context as no real obstruction of passage along the highway has been caused by the encampment, and that section 143 of the Highways Act 1980 (control of authorised structures placed on highway land) offered a more appropriate remedy. The Court of Appeal held that there was no requirement that the highway authority should only employ such remedies as are granted by the Highways Act 1980, and, as freeholders of the highway verge concerned, were entitled to proceed under Order 113. The fact that no blockage of the highway had occurred was also held to be irrelevant since no distinction was to be made between the occupiers of the unauthorised encampment and squatters in a dwelling-house. Both groups of persons are trespassers and therefore equally subject to the procedure of Order 113.

### Breach of local by-laws

All local authorities have powers to make by-laws for local application. There are many statutes which confer by-law-making powers and these can be exercised at the discretion of each authority. Most such powers are only of limited scope, being expressly conferred for a specific purpose, e.g. to regulate the conduct of person using common land by seeking to prevent nuisances and preserve order, pursuant to sections 1 and 10 of the Commons Act 1899. There is no specific statutory power enabling a local authority to make by-laws to regulate the stationing of caravans on highway land within its area, but resort may be had to a general power conferred by section 235 of the Local Government Act 1972. This provision enables London boroughs and district councils to make by-laws "for . . . good rule and government . . . and suppression of nuisances." As this power is so widely drafted it could be used to regulate stationing of caravans on highways, provided that any by-laws which are made are approved by the Secretary of State for the Environment and are not *ultra vires, i.e.* they must not be void due to the by-law-making authority having exceeded the scope of its powers. This means that the by-law must not be judged to be "unreasonable" within the meaning given to this word by Lord Russell C.J. in *Kruse* v. *Johnson* (1898). There it was held that by-laws would only be unreasonable if they are "partial and unequal in their operation as between different classes, are manifestly unjust, disclose bad faith, involve oppressive and gratuitous interference in the rights of those subject to them as could find no justification in the minds of reasonable men."

The police as well as the local authority concerned can prosecute for breach of a by-law, prosecution power having been conferred on the former by section 12 of the Local Government (Miscellaneous Provisions) Act 1982. If a conviction is obtained in the magistrates' court, the offender is subject to a maximum fine of £100 under section 237 of the Local Government Act 1972. If, however, he remains in breach of the by-law he is guilty of a further offence and on further conviction can be fined up to £5 per day for each day the offence continues. A persistent offender can also be restrained by means of an injunction, issued by the High Court, which is obtained if a successful action is brought by the local authority suing in the name of the Attorney-General (commonly known as a "relator" action) and with his consent. Breach of the injunction is a contempt of court for which imprisonment can be ordered.

## On-street parking of a caravan in an urban area

In seeking to control the parking of a caravan in an urban area, the first consideration will be whether the parking of any vehicle on the highway concerned is regulated by an order made by the local highway authority under section 1 of the Road Traffic Regulation Act 1984. Breach of such an order may attract a "parking fine" of up to £400 under section 5, 98 and Schedule 7 (though customarily punished by a fixed penalty fine of £10) and may lead to the removal of the caravan by the highway authority in exercise of their powers under section 99 of the 1984 Act.

Where no such order exists in relation to the highway involved, reference must be made to the powers described in the previous parts of this Chapter. Although most can be used without delay, they are particularly likely to be utilised in the context of the stationing of a touring caravan which has been detached from its towing vehicle and is left stationary for weeks or months at a time. One further matter requires mention, however, which arises under the Road Traffic Act 1972. Section 36B of this Act (which was inserted by section 7 of the Road Traffic Act 1974) will, when brought into force by a statutory instrument, create the new offences of parking a vehicle wholly or partly (a) on the verge of an urban road, or (b) on any land which is situated between two carriageways of urban road and which is not a footway, or (c) on a footway comprised in an urban road. In this section "urban road" means a road which is subject to a 30 m.p.h. or 40 m.p.h. speed limit, and "footway" is, effectively, the pedestrian part of a way comprised in a highway which consists of a carriageway for vehicles and pavement area. The latter is the footway area. No offence will be committed, however, if the caravan is parked contrary to this section under the direction of a police constable in uniform, or for emergency purposes, or for the purposes of loading and unloading. In the last instance the caravan must be attended throughout and it must also be the case that the loading or unloading of it could not have been satisfactorily carried out if it had not been parked on the footway or verge. The maximum penalty for breach of the section following conviction in the magistrates' court will be a fine of £100.

### Stopping on a clearway

In the same way that orders are made under the Road Traffic Regulation Act 1984 to regulate traffic in urban areas, the same powers can be used to make "clearway" orders. These orders, made in accordance with the Various Trunk Roads (Prohibition of Waiting) (Clearways) Order 1963 (S.I. 1963 No. 1172) forbid stopping on the main carriageway of specified roads. This does not apply to use of lay-bys provided on such roads. It is not certain, however, whether an offence is committed by parking on the verge adjacent to the main carriageway rather than in a lay-by. The maximum penalty for breach of a clearway order is a £400 fine, though this offence is customarily punished by a fixed penalty fine of £10.

### Highway encampments and the town and country planning legislation

Before leaving the highway aspects of caravan use a few words should be added, in the interests of clarity, on the role of the town and country planning legislation.

A breach of planning control can occur if the use of land comprising a highway is an act of "development" within the meaning of section 22(1) of the Town and Country Planning Act 1971, i.e. where a material change in the use of the land involved is effected. Reference has already been made to the case of Scarborough Borough Council v. Adams and Adams (1983) (see p. 33), in which the Divisional Court held that caravan dwellers who lived in their caravans in a lay-by for eighteen months were occupiers of the lay-by for the purposes of service of copies of an enforcement notice under section 87 of the 1971 Act. It is apparent from that case that trespassers can also be served with copies of an enforcement notice and can be convicted for failure to comply with the requirements specified in the notice. By virtue of the changes made by section 3 of the Town and Country Planning Act 1984, similar action can also be taken in respect of highway land comprised within the boundaries of a trunk road or special road. Since such land is vested in the Crown, the local planning authority could serve a special enforcement notice in relation to unauthorised development on the land.

The advantages of seeking to control the use of highway land via the town and country planning legislation lie in the more effective enforcement powers available to the local planning authority compared to the comparatively weak provisions of the Highways Act 1980.

# 9. Regulation of Tent Sites and Miscellaneous Statutory Provisions

As the title of this Chapter indicates, it is intended to serve a two-fold purpose. The first arises from the need to include within the scope of this book a short account of the law relevant to tent sites. This is a direct result of the observation that was made in Chapter 1, that until the enactment of the Caravan Sites and Control of Development Act 1960, the law relating to caravan sites and to tent sites was concomitant. Secondly, there are a number of statutory provisions which are relevant to caravans (and sometimes also to tents) which have not been discussed elsewhere, largely due to their *ad hoc* nature relative to the material considered so far. The opportunity is therefore now taken to collate the relevant provisions as a miscellaneous class.

### Legal control of tent sites

The definition of "caravan" in section 29(1) of the Caravan Sites and Control of Development Act 1960 specifically excludes a tent, thus leaving tent sites to remain controlled under the previous legislation, the Public Health Act 1936, section 269. This provision is still in force in relation to what the section terms "moveable dwellings," of which tents are the principal remaining group.

The section requires that a licence be obtained from the local authority when land is to be used for camping on more than 42 consecutive days or for more than 60 days in any period of 12 months. Such a licence can be obtained by *either* the occupier of the relevant land (the owner of land which is not subject to a lease is by section 269(8) deemed to be the occupier of it), *or* the persons(s) wishing to erect or station the tent(s) on the land. Application for a licence is made on a form obtainable from the local authority (the district council or London borough), though no prescribed form is in use nor is any fee payable to the local authority. In dealing with the application, the local authority have four weeks in which to reach a decision; unless the application is rejected or granted subject to conditions during this period the licence is deemed to be granted unconditionally: section 269(4). The onus is therefore on the local authority to notify the applicant of refusal of the application within the period, or that the licence is granted subject to conditions.

In the same way that the conditions attached to a caravan site licence are especially important, so also are the conditions attached to a tent site licence. The power to attach conditions is regulated by section 269(1) which empowers the local authority to attach "such conditions as they think fit"

119

in relation to the following matters, depending on whether the applicant is the occupier of the land or a person proposing to erect or station tents on the land. In the former case the conditions can regulate:

"the number and classes of moveable dwellings which may be kept thereon at the same time, and the space to be kept free between any two such dwellings, with respect to water supply and for securing sanitary conditions."

In the latter case the conditions are less wide-ranging being applicable to:

" . . . the use of (the moveable dwelling) (including the space to be kept free between it and any other such dwelling) and its removal at the end of a specified period, and for securing sanitary conditions."

If a licence is refused by the local authority, or granted subject to conditions which the applicant does not wish to accept, there is a right of appeal to the magistrates' court under section 269(4). This right is further regulated by section 300 of the 1936 Act which requires the appeal to be made within 21 days of the service on the applicant of the authority's decision. A further right of appeal is also available under section 301 to the Crown Court exerciseable by a "person aggrieved" of the magistrates' decision. Appeal by way of case stated to the Queens Bench Division of the High Court is also available from either the magistrates' court or Crown Court if it is considered that an error of law has been made. An example of the use of the right of appeal by case stated is *Pilling* v. *Abergele Urban District Council* (1950) in which a licence was refused by the local authority on the ground that "the site is unsuitable because such use would be detrimental to the amenities of the district, particularly on account of the close proximity of other dwellings." As the 1936 Act is a statute dealing with public health and sanitary conditions, the Divisional Court held that the magistrates had erred in law in refusing the licence in this ground as this was a matter to be considered under the town and country planning legislation. The applicant's appeal by way of case stated therefore succeeded.

Failure to obtain a licence is an offence under section 269(7), as also is failure to comply with any condition subject to which the licence was issued. The maximum penalty is a fine of £100 plus a further fine of £2 for each day the offence continues after the first conviction. No express power is granted to the local authority to revoke the licence, though a power to do so may perhaps be regarded as inherent in the power to issue licences under the section.

### Exemptions from site licence requirements

The broad effect of section 269 of the Public Health Act 1936 is reduced by two other provisions of the section. Under section 269(5) no licence is needed in relation to a moveable dwelling (in this case a tent) which (a) is kept by its owner on land occupied by him in connection with his dwelling-house and is used for habitation only by him or members of his household, or (b) is kept by its owner on agricultural land occupied by him and is used for habitation only at seasonal intervals and only by persons employed in farming operations on that land. Further exception is also given in the case of a moveable dwelling which is not in use for human habitation and no other moveable dwellings are being used as such on the same land. Since the enactment of the Caravan Sites and Control of Development Act 1960, these exemptions are far less significant now than when they formerly applied also to caravans. Of lasting significance, however, is section 269(6) which empowers the Secretary of State to grant a certificate of exemption to any organisation which he is satisfied takes reasonable steps to ensure that, while camping, their tents are not used so as to give rise to any nuisance and that the sites they own or provide, or which are used by the members are properly managed and kept in good sanitary condition. The organisations which have received exemption certificates to date are the following:

Army Cadet Forces Association
Boy Scouts Association
Boys' Brigade
Girl Guides Association
London Union of Youth Clubs
Camping Club
Caravan Club
Salvation Army
National Council of YMCA
Church Lads' Brigade

For the purposes of section 269, the grant of a certificate of exemption has the same effect as if a licence had actually been issued authorising the use of land belonging to, provided by, or used by its members, for the purposes of erecting tents (or any other moveable dwelling not being a caravan). Unlike the issue of a licence by a local authority, the Secretary of State is expressly empowered by section 269(6) to withdraw the licence at any time.

### Tent sites and planning permission

Development control applies to the use of land for a tent site in the same way that it applies to stationing of caravans for human habitation. The Town and Country Planning Act 1971 therefore operates to require a grant of planning permission to be obtained if the use of the land involves a "material change of use" within the meaning of section 22(1) of that Act. There are, however, some significant differences between tent site control and caravan site control. The most important of these is that a grant of planning permission is not a pre-requisite to the issue of a licence under section 269 of the Public Health Act 1936. The absence of this link means that tent sites can, on occasion, prove difficult to control when an encampment has become established by entry of tent-dwellers onto the site during the 42 day period allowed before a licence is necessitated under section 269(2). This problem is thus a repetition of that formerly faced by local authorities dealing with caravans prior to the enactment of the Caravan Sites and Control of Development Act 1960.

In an attempt to rectify this difficulty, a Caravan and Tent Sites Bill was promoted as a Private Members Bill by Peter Hubbard-Miles M.P. in July 1983. The Bill sought to unify the site licensing system of caravans and tent sites, by bringing tent sites within the scope of the Caravan Sites and Control of Development Act 1960 from which they are specifically excluded by section 30 of that Act. Had the Bill succeeded, the result would have been to end the dual system of licensing which took effect when the 1960 Act came into force on August 29, 1960. Lack of Parliamentary time prevented com-

121

pletion of a Second Reading of the Bill but it is understood that the Government is committed to introducing a further legislative proposal having a similar objective.

A further significant difference relates to enforcement of planning control. Whereas a caravan can, in appropriate circumstances, be considered to be a building on land, it is most unlikely that a tent could qualify as a building. Thus the use of land for a tent site is not subject to the four-year rule under section 87(4) of the Town and Country Planning Act 1971 which places a limitation on enforcement action. Such action can therefore be taken at any time. It is also possible to serve a stop notice in relation to be an unauthorised tent site, a step which is expressly excluded by section 90(2) of the 1971 Act in relation to a caravan which is being used as a permanent residence.

Two classes of "permitted development" under article 3 of Schedule 1 to the Town and Country Planning General Development Order 1977 (S.I., 1977 No. 289) apply to tent sites. Class IV.2 applies to a wide range of temporary uses of land, and permits land to be used for a tent site on up to 28 days in any calendar year. Of specific application is Class V of the GDO, under which planning permission is deemed to be granted for the use of land, other than buildings, not being within the curtilage of a dwelling-house, "for the purposes of recreation or instruction by members of an organisation which holds a certificate of exemption granted under section 269 of the Public Health Act 1936, and the erection or placing of tents on the land for the purposes of that use." Since this provision is directly linked to section 269 of the 1936 Act, the effect is that the exempted organisations listed above need neither a licence to use the land for camping, nor any express grant of planning permission. It is to be noted that no restrictions are imposed as to the length of time land can be used by the organisation concerned, nor the numbers of members using it.

### Tents, caravans and public health legisation

Section 268 of the Public Health Act 1936 applies several parts of that Act to tents and caravans ("tents, vans, sheds and similar structures used for human habitation") which would otherwise only apply to houses and buildings. The section provides that some sections of Part II of the Act, and Parts III, VII and XII, are all applicable to tents, vans, etc., thus empowering district councils and London boroughs to exercise statutory powers to control the public health matters to which the provisions apply. The provisions are especially useful in relation to caravan sites, which enjoy exemption from the site licensing requirement of the Caravan Sites and Control of Development Act 1960.

The matters concerned are as follows: Part II deals with filthy or verminous premises or articles and verminous persons, Part III with nuisances and offensive trades, Part VII with provisions (now mostly repealed and replaced by subsequent legislation) regulating notification of births, maternity and child welfare and child life protection, and Part XII with numerous general provisions, *e.g.* in relation to legal proceedings. Mention should also be made of the former Part V, which has been repealed and replaced by the Public Health (Control of Disease) Act 1984. Section 56 of this Act applies the provisions of Part II of the 1984 Act (which deals with notifiable diseases) to "tents, vans, sheds," etc., used for human habitation, and confers a by-law-making power on local authorities for the purposes of preventing the spread of infectious diseases by occupants of "tents, vans, sheds and similar structures used for human habitation."

Coverage of all the public health issues and procedures raised by the application of the relevant parts of the 1936 Act (as amended) would be outside the purpose of this book. It is pertinent, however, to make some statements in relation to statutory nuisances, as much of section 268 of the 1936 Act is concerned with controlling these. Sub-section (2) classifies as a statutory nuisance the following:

> " . . . a tent, van, shed or similar structure used for human habitation—
>> (a) . . . which is in such a state, or so overcrowded, as to be prejudicial to the health of the inmates; or
>> (b) . . . the use of which, by reason of the absence of proper sanitary accommodation or otherwises, gives rise, whether on the site or on other land, to a nuisance or to conditions prejudicial to health."

Where the local authority are satisified that a statutory nuisance exists they are required by section 93 of the 1936 Act to take steps to end the nuisance. The procedure involves service of an "abatement notice" on the person by whose actions or failure to act the nuisance arises, or who is permitting the nuisance to continue. If the nuisance arises from a structural defect the owner of the premises must be served with a notice. The owner must also be served if the person responsible for the nuisance cannot be found, though in this event the occupier may (as an alternative to the owner) also be served. By section 268(2), the "occupier" of a tent, van, etc., is deemed to include any person for the time being in charge of the offending structure. By a specific provision contained in section 268(3), a further discretion is given to the local authority if the nuisance arises under section 268(2)(b) above. In this instance a notice can be served on the occupier of the land on which the tent, van, etc., is erected or stationed.

The abatement notice will require its recipients to abate the nuisance and to execute such works and take such steps as may be necessary for that purpose: section 93. The notice must allow reasonable time for compliance with its requirements: *Bristol Corporation* v. *Sinnott* (1918). If the notice is not complied with the local authority must thereafter institute proceedings which can be either of a summary nature or involving the High Court. In either case, where a notice is served in accordance with the discretionary power conferred by section 268(3) on the occupier of the land, a defence is available if the occupier can prove that he did not authorise the stationing on the land of the tent, van, etc.

Summary proceedings are commenced by the local authority making a complaint to a magistrate who will thereafter issue a summons to the persons who received the abatement notice to appear before the magistrates' court. If, after hearing the complaint, the court is satisfied that the nuisance exists, the court may make one or more of a number of orders specified in section 94 of the 1936 Act. These are:

(a) A nuisance order. This requires the defendant to comply with all or any of the requirements of the abatement notice, or otherwise to abate the nuisance within a time specified in the order, and to execute any works necessary for the purpose. The order may, either additionally or in the alternative, prohibit a recurrence of the nuisance and require the defendant to execute any works necessary to prevent a recurrence within a time specified in the order: section 94(2).

(b) An order imposing a fine on the defendant, not exceeding £1,000: section 94(2).

(c) An order requiring the defendant to pay to the local authority the reasonable expenses of making the complaint and conducting the proceedings before the court: section 94(3).

(d) An order prohibiting the use for human habitation of the tent, van, etc., at such places or within such areas as may be specified in the order: section 268(5).

If a nuisance order is not complied with, a further offence is committed, punishable on conviction in the magistrates' court by a fine of up to £2,000 and by a further fine of up to £50 for each day the nuisance order is not complied with after that conviction: section 95(1). The local authority are also empowered by section 95(2) to enter onto the land concerned in order to abate the nuisance and then recover their reasonable expenses of so doing from the person in default: section 96.

The alternative to summary litigation is to take proceedings in the High Court. Section 100 of the 1936 Act empowers a local authority to commence such proceedings, even though the authority have not suffered any damage from the alleged nuisance. One pre-condition must be fulfilled, however, which is that the local authority must be of the opinion that summary proceedings would not afford an adequate remedy, though there is no obligation on the local authority to pursue the matter in the magistrates' court first before reaching the conclusion that summary proceedings are ineffective to abate the nuisance. The main advantage of using High Court procedure lies in the power of the High Court to grant an injunction; if the defendant fails to comply with the terms of any injunction that may be granted the court may order that the defendant be committed to prison for contempt.

An important procedural point arising in proceedings under section 100 was considered in *Warwick District Council* v. *Miller-Mead* (1962), a case in which an attempt was made to control an alleged statutory nuisance on a caravan site by service of an abatement notice followed by proceedings in the magistrates' court. Proceedings were later instituted in the High Court but it appeared that the council had not met to pass the resolution to proceed under section 100 until three days after the proceedings were initiated. The defendant thus claimed that the council had not formed the necessary opinion, as required by the section, that the summary proceedings would be ineffective. The Court of Appeal held that it was not necessary in all cases for the formal resolution of the council to precede the issue of the writ, provided that the formal resolution is passed prior to the commencement of proceedings before the court.

Special provision for recurring nuisances was made by the Public Health (Recurring Nuisances) Act 1969. If a local authority is notified that a nuisance has occurred on any premises (the word "premises" includes land by virtue of section 343(1) of the 1936 Act), and is likely to recur on the same premises, section 1 of the 1969 Act enables them to serve a "prohibition notice" prohibiting a recurrence of the nuisance and requiring its recipient to take such steps as may be necessary to prevent a recurrence. Such a notice can specify any works which the local authority consider are necessary for the purpose, and may expressly require those works to be carried out. The advantage of this procedure is apparent from section 1(3) which empowers a prohibition notice to be served irrespective of whether the nuisance is actually in existence at the time of service, and irrespective of whether an abatement notice has been previously served in relation to it. Enforcement of the requirements of a prohibition notice is similarly not dependent upon recurrence of the nuisance, since a complaint can be made to a magistrate under section 94 of the 1936 Act if the requirements of the prohibition notice have simply not been complied with. If the magistrates' court is satisfied that the nuisance has recurred (even if not still in existence at the date of the hearing), or that the defendant has not complied with the requirements of the prohibition notice, the court may make an order under sections 94 or 268(5), provided it is proved that the nuisance is likely to recur.

As a postscript to the subject of statutory nuisances, reference must also be made to the power conferred by section 268(4) of the 1936 Act on local authorities for the purposes of making by-laws. The subsection provides as follows:

> "A local authority may make by-laws for promoting cleanliness in and the habitable conditions of, tents, vans, sheds and similar structures used for human habitation, . . . and generally for the prevention of nuisance in connection therewith."

The procedure for making by-laws and powers of enforcement in connection with their breach have already been considered (see p. 116), but it is understood that this particular power has not been widely exercised by local authorities.

### Premises prejudicial to health or a nuisance

Notwithstanding the availability of the powers described in the previous section, local authorities (district councils and London borough councils) are empowered to take direct remedial action in relation to any premises which appear to the authority to be in a "defective state" so as to be prejudicial to health or a nuisance. This power is conferred by section 76 of the Building Act 1984, which requires that before the power can be exercised it must also appear to the authority that unreasonable delay would be occasioned by relying on the procedures of sections 93–95 of the Public Health Act 1936. If the local authority wish to exercise this power, a notice must be served on the person who would normally be the recipient of an abatement notice under section 93, the present notice stating that the local authority intend to remedy the defective state and specifying the defects they intend to remedy: section 76(1).

After service of such a notice, a statutory period of seven days starts to run, during which a counter-notice can be served by the person concerned stating that he intends to remedy the defects himself: section 76(3). If no such counter-notice is served, the local authority can enter onto the land and carry out the works necessary to remedy the defective state after nine days have expired from service of the first notice: section 76(2). If a counter-notice is served, however, no further action can be taken by the local authority unless the works are not begun to be executed within a reasonable time or are not proceeding at a reasonable pace; in these circumstances the local authority can proceed to carry out the works themselves. At whatever stage the power to execute works is exercised by the local authority, the expenses of so doing are recoverable from the person who was served with the first notice.

The final part of section 76 of the Building Act 1984 makes a reference to a similar power conferred by housing legislation. Thus, section 76(7) says that the powers conferred by section 76 "may be exercised notwithstanding that the local authority might instead have proceeded under section 9 of the Housing Act 1957" (now replaced by section 189 of the Housing Act 1985). These provisions are concerned with the power of a local authority to order the repair of a house which is "unfit for human habitation" by means of the service of a "repair notice" unless the local authority are satisfied that it is not capable of being rendered fit for human habitation at a reasonable cost. Caravans and tents are expressly included in the scope of this section by virtue of section 205 of the 1985 Act which applies to a "hut, tent, caravan, or other temporary or moveable structure which is used for human habitation and has been in the same enclosure for a period of two years next before action is taken".

The meaning of "fitness for human habitation" is governed by section 604 of the 1985 Act. Thus a tent or caravan is unfit for human habitation if it is not reasonably suitable for occupation, having regard to the following matters: (a) repairs; (b) stability; (c) freedom from damp; (d) internal arrangement; (e) natural lighting; (f) ventilation; (g) water supply; (h) drainage and sanitary conveniences; (i) facilities for storage, preparation and cooking of food and the disposal of waste water.

### Application of building regulations to caravans and mobile homes

Although statutory powers exist to apply building regulations to them the existing building regulations system of building control is inapplicable to caravans and mobile homes. The Building Regulations 1985 (S.I. 1985 No. 1065) were made pursuant to the Building Act 1984 which under section 1(1) relates to "the design and construction of buildings and the provision of services, fittings and equipment in or in connection with buildings." This Act is a consolidating statute, imposing a system of control, operated by district councils and other approved inspectors, designed to regulate the "health, safety, welfare and convenience of persons in or about buildings . . . or matters connected with buildings": section 1(1). In inner London the relevant legislation is contained in the London Building Acts (Amendment) Act 1939 and the London Building (Constructional) By-laws 1972, the system being administered by London boroughs. These provisions are likely to be repealed to create a unified nationwide system under section 46 of and Schedule 3 to the 1984 Act.

Details of the existing building control scheme are largely irrelevant for present purposes, for two reasons. First, it is only if a mobile home or caravan is modified or added to in such a way that it is no longer capable of conforming to the definition of a "caravan" in section 29(1) of the Caravan Sites and Control of Development Act 1960 that the Building Regulations 1985 could become applicable. This is made clear by Regulation 9 of and

Schedule 3 to the 1985 Regulations, as these provisions specifically exclude the application of building regulations to:

> "(a) a building intended to remain where it is erected for less than 28 days, or
> (b) a mobile home within the meaning of the Mobile Homes Act 1983."

Secondly, under the Health and Safety at Work, etc., Act 1974 section 74 (now re-enacted as section 121 of the Building Act 1984), the potential scope of building regulations was greatly extended. The Secretary of State for the Environment may now make building regulations for application to "any permanent or temporary building, and, . . . any structure or erection of whatever kind or nature." This is expressed by section 121(2) of the 1984 Act as including a "vehicle, . . . or other moveable object of any kind." The appropriate exercise of these powers would bring caravans and mobile homes directly within the building control system, but at the time of writing no steps have been taken so to do. As was mentioned in Chapter 1, construction standards for caravans and mobile homes are currently dependent only upon compliance with British Standard 3632 of 1970.

## Homelessness

Provision of accommodation for persons who are homeless is regulated by Part III of the Housing Act 1985, which replaced the Housing (Homeless Persons) Act 1977. This Act places local authorities (district councils and London borough councils) under a duty to secure that accommodation is made available for a person who is homeless, or to take reasonable steps to secure that accommodation does not cease to be available to a person threatened with homelessness. This duty, imposed by sections 65 and 66 of the 1985 Act, is a qualified one, in that accommodation need not be provided unless the applicant is in "priority need" of accommodation, and did not become homeless intentionally.

A person is considered to be homeless under section 58(1)(2) of the 1985 Act if he has no accommodation which he, together with any other person who normally resides with him as a member of his family or in circumstances in which the housing authority consider it reasonable for that person to reside with him, is entitled to occupy by virtue of an interest in it, a court order, or a licence. He is also homeless if he has no accommodation which he is occupying by virtue of any enactment or rule of law giving him the right to remain in occupation or restricting the right of any other person to recover possession. Homelessness also arises under section 58(3) if a person has accommodation but cannot secure entry to it, or that occupation of it will lead to violence or threats of violence from some other person residing in it. In R. v. *Hillingdon London Borough Council, ex p. Puhlhofer* (1986), the House of Lords held that whether or not a person has accommodation is essentially a question of fact for the local authority to decide; what the local authority has to consider is whether the applicant has accommodation within the ordinary meaning of the word. Thus where a family of two adults and two children lived in one room, the family was not homeless because the room was capable of accommodating them.

A particular relevance in the context of mobile homes is section 58(3)(c) of the 1985 Act. This provides that a person is homeless if he has accommodation but:

"it consists of a moveable structure, vehicle or vessel designed or adapted for human habitation and there is no place where he is entitled or permitted both to place it and to reside in it."

This provision makes it clear that owner-occupier caravan and mobile home residents can come within the homelessness legislation.

Priority need is established if (a) a person has dependent children residing with him; or (b) he is homeless (or threatened with homelessness) by reason of flood, fire, or any disaster; or (c) he (or any person residing with him) is vulnerable as a result of old age, mental illness or handicap or physical disability, or other special reason; or (d) he resides (and can be reasonably expected to reside) with a pregnant woman, or if a pregnant woman is the applicant: section 59.

The third requirement, that the applicant should not have become homeless intentionally, is governed by section 60 which provides that a person becomes intentionally homeless if he deliberately does or fails to do anything in consequence of which he ceases to occupy accommodation which is available for his occupation and which it would have been reasonable for him to continue to occupy.

The duty of a local authority on receipt of an application for assistance under the 1985 Act is to inquire into the matter in accordance with section 62(1). Where the applicant is found to be homeless, in priority need, and not homeless intentionally, the duty is to secure that accommodation becomes available for his occupation: section 65(2). Although the Act does not so specify, the discharge of this duty in relation to a mobile home owner who has no place to station his mobile home would probably be best discharged by providing a pitch on a local authority caravan site provided under section 24 of the Caravan Sites and Control of Development Act 1960. In a case where the applicant cannot satisfy all the requirements of the 1985 Act, the duty of the local authority is only to furnish the applicant with appropriate advice and assistance (section 65(4)), exception being made in the case of a person in priority need. In this instance the duty is to provide temporary accommodation for such period as they consider will give him a reasonable opportunity of securing accommodation for himself and to provide appropriate advice and assistance: section 65(3).

### Provision of caravan accommodation

Although county and district councils both have power to provide caravan sites under section 24 of the Caravan Sites and Control of Development Act 1960, section 24(7) specifically excludes any power to provide caravans "under this section." Whether local authorities can provide caravan accommodation under any other provision is not clear. It is possible that section 9 of the Housing Act 1985 empowers local authorities to provide accommodation of the "mobile home" type, since the words used in the section are "houses" and "buildings," the section normally being regarded as empowering local authorities to provide bricks and mortar housing. The Mobile Homes Review (1977) explains, however, (para. 2.5.2.) that "[T]he Department has taken the view for the purposes of loan sanction and subsidy that mobile homes constitute housing accommodation provided they are in some way securely fixed to the soil. How local authorities meet that requirement has been left to them."

# 10. Rating of Caravan Sites

Who is responsible for the rates assessed on a caravan site?—the site operator or each individual caravan dweller? This and many other questions are raised by rating matters, for example whether there are any rules which are relevant to leisure caravans. Most fundamentally, the question arises whether in fact a caravan is capable of being the subject of a rating assessment, bearing in mind that a caravan is, for most purposes, normally to be regarded as a chattel placed on the land but not part of the land itself.

The law relevant to rating is contained principally in the General Rate Act 1967, as amended by numerous subsequent statutes, *e.g.* the General Rate Act 1970, the Rating Act 1971, the Local Government Acts 1972–4, the Local Government, Planning and Land Act 1980, the Local Government Finance Act 1982 and the Rates Act 1984. In addition, special provision is made in relation to specific types of caravan site by the Rating (Caravan Sites) Act 1976. These statutes combine to provide a code of law regulating the levying of rates, that well known (if only on account of its notoriety) form of local taxation designed to provide a source of revenue for the purposes of meeting a part of the expenditure of the authorities which levy them or on whose behalf the rates are levied.

The authorities which levy rates are the district councils and the London borough councils. These authorities, known as "rating authorities," also collect rates for county councils and the parish and community councils, these non-rating authorities being termed "precepting authorities."

The tax itself is capable of being levied on any property which section 19 of the General Rate Act 1967 terms a "hereditament." All hereditaments are assessed by reference to their "net annual value," a figure determined on the basis of the rent which a hypothetical yearly tenant would be willing to pay. In the words of section 19(3), this is the amount "equal to the rent at which it is estimated that the hereditament might reasonably be expected to let from year to year if the tenant undertook to pay all the usual tenants' rates and taxes and to bear the cost of the repairs and insurance and other expenses, if any, necessary to maintain the hereditament in a state to command that rent." In the case of dwellings (including caravans), the figure to be determined initially is the "gross value" which under section 19(6) is calculated on the assumption that the landlord will bear the cost of repairs, insurance and other expenses. From this figure certain fixed deductions are permitted (depending on the gross value, as determined) in order to reach the figure which is thereafter the rateable value of the property. The scale of deductions is as specified by the Valuation (Statutory Deductions) Order 1973 (S.I. 1973 No. 2139).

Administration of the rating system is the function of valuation officers of the Inland Revenue. The valuation officer for the district in which any given hereditament is situated will propose an assessment for entry in the valuation list or propose an amendment to an existing entry. Owners and occupiers are required to be notified of the proposal and may make objection to it within 28 days (section 70(2)), though a subsequent proposal for alteration can be made. Many such objections are then resolved by agreement between the valuation officer and objector, but in default of agreement a proposed entry in (or alteration of) the valuation list may be the subject of an appeal by the ratepayer to the local Valuation Court. A further appeal may be made to the Lands Tribunal whose decision is final, subject, however, to a right of appeal by way of case stated, exercisable within six weeks of the decision, on a point of law only. This appeal lies direct to the Court of Appeal.

### Rateable occupation

In accordance with Part III of the General Rate Act 1967, the levying of rates is by reference to the occupation of real property, rather than by its ownership. In order to be in "occupation" of property and therefore liable for the rates levied upon it, four tests must be satisfied. These have evolved from case law, no provision having been made in the General Rate Act 1967 to define "occupation." In *R. v. St. Pancras Assessment Committee* (1877) it was established that to be in occupation there must first of all be *de facto* possession (but not necessarily continuous physical possession), and that there must be an element of permanence to that possession. This is supplemented by the requirement that the occupation must be beneficial (but not necessarily profitable) to the occupier (see *Jones* v. *Mersey Docks and Harbour Board Trustees* (1865)) and must be exclusive as well as actual. The last feature is well illustrated by *John Laing & Son Ltd.* v. *Assessment Committee for Kingswood Assessment Area* (1949). A construction contract was scheduled to involve development activities for at least a year. To facilitate the development the developer erected various site huts on the land, on which an assessment was made. The company claimed that as the contract included terms for continual inspection of the building work by the owner of the land, the occupation was not exclusive. It was held by the Court of Appeal that the developer had maintained exclusive occupation despite the element of control exercised by the landowner, since the latter's presence related only to the performance of the contract.

In the context of caravans the Court of Appeal has held that the application of these principles is such that in many instances it will be the caravan dweller who is in rateable occupation. In *Field Place Caravan Park Ltd.* v. *Harding (Valuation Officer)* (1966) a caravan site was in use for both permanent residential caravans and for leisure caravans used for holidays and week-ends. While no distinction was drawn between these two types of use, the valuation officer assessed the owners of the caravans for rating purposes, in preference to the caravan site operator. In reaching the conclusion that most of the caravans were rateable, Lord Denning M.R. disregarded the caravans which had not been parked on the site for at least a year, which he considered to be "too transient to attract rateability."

In taking this view in relation to transience, Lord Denning M.R. impliedly endorsed the view of the Lands Tribunal in *Tawell & Son* v. *Buckingham (Valuation Officer)* (1963) in which a caravan placed on a site for a year was held to be sufficient to establish rateable occupation. Subsequently, in *Moore* v. *Williamson (Valuation Officer)* (1973), the Lands Tribunal rejected four to five months on the site as being too transient.

Of the remaining group of caravans, Lord Denning M.R. considered as a typical example a four-berth caravan measuring 21 feet by 7 feet 3 inches, parked on a pitch measuring 55 feet by 31 feet. This was enclosed by a low fence and gate and was connected to the electricity supply and had a soak-away system. The wheels of the caravan were still present but it was stabilised by a series of jacks. It was found as a fact that this caravan could not be moved in less than half an hour and the site operator had retained the right to insist on its being moved to any position on the site. Both the site operator and the caravan dweller claimed that the site pitch was a rateable hereditament but that the caravan itself was not. Accordingly, they argued that there were two separate units of occupation, the pitch and the caravan and only the former was rateable. Lord Denning M.R. said:

> "I cannot accept this view. You have only to look at the whole curtilage and its fence, its mown grass, sometimes its garden, all appurtenant to the caravan, and you realise that it is all one unit occupied for dwelling purposes by the owner of the caravan and his family. It is clearly one unit of occupation capable of being one rateable hereditament."

A further argument advanced by the ratepayer was that even if the caravan and site pitch amounted to one unit of occupation, the site operator had paramount occupation in that he had retained a right of access to the site pitch, to inspect the area under the caravan and to cut the grass if such was deemed necessary, but had no right to enter the caravan. Dismissing this argument, Lord Denning M.R. considered that the dictum of Lord Russell in *Westminster City Council* v. *Southern Railway Company* (1936) was applicable:

> " . . . the effect of the alleged control upon the question of rateable occupation must depend upon the facts in every case; and in my opinion in each case the degree of the control must be examined, and the examination must be directed to the extent to which its exercise would interfere with the enjoyment by the occupant of the premises in his possession for the purposes for which he occupies them, or would be inconsistent with his enjoyment of them to the substantial exclusion of all other persons."

In giving a concurring judgment, Salmon L.J. took into account the rights of the caravan site operator and decided that "The mere fact that the site occupier has . . . rights . . . does not, in my judgment, compel the finding that his occupation is paramount to that of the caravan dweller." He added "Whether or not an occupation is paramount must be a question of fact and degree."

In applying these principles to the modern mobile home there must always be borne in mind the question of "fact and degree" of occupation described by Salmon L.J. Nevertheless it is likely that in most instances the mobile home dweller will be found to be in rateable occupation and thus the burden of the rate assessment will normally fall on him rather than the site operator. It is unlikely that the fact that the mobile home occupier occupies his pitch under a licence (rather than a tenancy) will affect the position: *Forces Help Society and Lord Roberts Workshops* v. *Canterbury City Council* (1978).

Although no distinction was drawn by the Court of Appeal in *Field Place*

*Caravan Park Ltd.* v. *Harding* between permanent residential caravans and leisure caravans (because all the caravans under consideration had been on the site for at least a year, and in most instances several years) a statutory distinction has subsequently been drawn by the Rating (Caravan Sites) Act 1976. This Act applies to "leisure caravans"; its effect is explained below.

### As a caravan is a chattel why is it rateable?

One of the main issues faced by the Court of Appeal in the *Harding* case was the problem that, in principle, rating applies to land and not to chattels placed on it. While this was once considered to be a rigid rule, its effect was considerably mitigated by the House of Lords in *London County Council* v. *Wilkins (Valuation Officer)* (1956) (a case involving contractors' site huts), in which the House reached the conclusion that a chattel could be rated with the land on which it is placed if it is to be enjoyed with the land. In a statement particularly apt to the present context Lord Radcliffe said:

> "a structure placed on another's land can with it form a rateable hereditament, even though the structure remains in law a chattel and as such the property of the person who placed it there."

In deciding to apply this view to the caravans in the present case Lord Denning M.R. said:

> "The correct proposition today is that, although a chattel is not a rateable hereditament by itself, nevertheless it may become rateable together with land, if it is placed on a piece of land and enjoyed with it in such circumstances and with such a degree of permanence that the chattel with the land can together be regarded as one unit of occupation."

Further observations were made by Salmon L.J. in relation to the fact that the caravans were on wheels rather than resting directly on the ground. He considered that this factor was relevant only in so far as it may be relevant to the question of transient occupation of the site. But once it was established that the occupation was not too transient to attract a rating assessment the presence of wheels was no longer relevant. Salmon L.J. thus refused to draw a distinction between a caravan dweller and a person living in a hut or a bungalow on the land, holding that it would be "an affront to common sense" to hold that the hut or bungalow occupiers were rateable but the caravan dwellers were not.

### Rating and leisure caravans

Special provisions contained in the Rating (Caravan Sites) Act 1976 can be invoked by the valuation officer, if he thinks fit, which will displace the principles described above. The 1976 Act applies only to caravan sites which comprise an area of not less than 400 square yards and contains pitches for "leisure caravans." The term "pitch for a leisure caravan" is defined in section 6(c) of the 1976 Act as one which is not allowed to be used for human habitation throughout the year due to a site licence condition or condition attached to a grant of planning permission.

The main effect of the 1976 Act is that under section 1 the valuation officer is empowered to make a single entry in the valuation list which will comprise the land occupied by the site operator and some or all (as the valuation officer sees fit) of the leisure caravans which would otherwise be treated as separate hereditaments. If this occurs the liability for rate payments, (so far as collecting the tax is concerned), becomes that of the site operator rather than the leisure caravan occupier.

Where section 1 has been implemented by the valuation officer and a particular leisure caravan pitch has become, or is proposed to become, entered with other land in the occupation of the site operator as a single hereditament, section 1(7) nevertheless enables the leisure caravan occupier to seek a separate entry. Such a proposal must then be treated in accordance with the provisions of the General Rate Act 1967, ss.69–74. These sections regulate applications for alteration of the valuation list and include a right of appeal to a local valuation court if the proposal is not accepted by the valuation officer.

In order that leisure caravan occupiers are aware of any changes in the valuation list which arise under section 1 of the 1976 Act, section 2 goes on to provide for the display of a site notice and to require the site operator to provide information at the request of a caravan dweller. The relevant procedures are initiated by the valuation officer, who is placed under a duty by section 2(1) to give at least one month's written notice to the site operator of his proposals to exercise his powers under section 1 of the Act. This notice must state how many leisure caravans occupied by persons other than the site operator are to be included in the entry and how much of the rateable value proposed for the hereditament as a whole is attributable to those caravans and their pitches.

Thereafter a duty is placed by section 2(2) on the site operator to display a site notice during the period April 1–October 31, while the proposed entry is still current and after it has been effected. This notice must state (a) the part of the site which is affected (or that the whole site is included as a single entry); (b) the number of leisure caravans involved and the amount of the rateable value attributable to them, together with their pitches; and (c) the current rate in the pound at which the general rate for the rating area is charged under the General Rate Act 1967. If any details specified in the notice regulated by sections 2(1) and 2(2) are altered then the valuation officer must serve a further notice on the site operator who in turn must display a further site notice: section 2(3). All site notices displayed under section 2 must be displayed on the site at a conspicuous place where they are likely to be seen by the leisure caravan dwellers who are affected: section 2(4).

If a leisure caravan dweller so requires, the site operator must furnish him with a written statement of the information required to be displayed by a site notice, or any supplementary notice: section 2(5).

Criminal sanctions can be imposed on a site operator who fails to comply with his duties under section 2 without reasonable excuse. On conviction in the magistrates' court he is subject to a maximum fine of £400 (level 3 on the standard scale regulated by section 37 of the Criminal Justice Act 1982).

## The basis of valuation

There are many principles to be applied in determining the rateable value of a hereditament. Specific examination of them lies beyond the scope of this book, the present purpose being limited to a summary of some of the principles involved and an account of some decisions of the Lands Tribunal and Court of Appeal in instances where a caravan site has been the subject of a rating dispute.

133

Valuation principles are based primarily on the judgment of Scott L.J. in *Robinson Bros. (Brewers) Ltd.* v. *Houghton and Chester-le-Street Assessment Committee* (1937). These may be summarised as follows:

1. Each hereditament must be independently assessed.
2. The hereditament to be valued must be assumed to be vacant and to be available for letting.
3. It must always be "the actual house or other property for the occupation of which the occupier is to be rated and it is to be valued as it in fact is *rebus sic stantibus*," and not by reference to its value if structurally altered or put to some different mode of use.
4. "Every intrinsic quality and every intrinsic circumstance which tends to push the value up or down" must be taken into consideration.
5. The value arrived at should represent "the figure at which the hypothetical landlord and tenant would . . . come to terms as a result of bargaining for that hereditament in the light of competition or its absence in both demand and supply, as a result of "the higgling of the market."
6. The actual rent at which a hereditament is let or the actual rents at which similar hereditaments in similar economic sites are let so that they are truly comparable are not necessarily conclusive evidence, but may be the best evidence, of value.
7. Where the best evidence is not available, the motive likely to induce potential tenants to bid for the hereditament is a relevant factor in estimating what the amount of such bids might reasonably be expected to be, *e.g.* the making of profit or the carrying into effect of a power or duty.
8. If there is no better evidence, assessments put upon comparable properties may be looked at as evidence in the nature of an admission by the party who determined them.

The effect of these principles was later summarised by Lord Denning M.R. in *R.* v. *Paddington (Valuation Officer), ex p. Peachey Property Corporation Ltd.* (1965) in the following terms:

> "The rent prescribed by the statute is a hypothetical rent, as hypothetical as the tenant. It is the rent which an imaginary tenant might be reasonably expected to pay to an imaginary landlord for a tenancy of this dwelling in this locality, on the hypothesis that both are reasonable people, the landlord not being extortionate, the tenant not being under pressure, the dwelling being vacant and to let, not subject to any control, the landlord agreeing to do the repairs and pay the insurance, the tenant agreeing to pay the rates, the period not too short or yet too long, simply from year to year."

The emphasis placed upon the rack rent of a hereditament by Scott L.J. in the *Robinson Bros.* case was later qualified by the Court of Appeal in *Garton* v. *Hunter (Valuation Officer)* (1969), a case which concerned a caravan camping site. The site had been let to the ratepayer at a rent of £5,000, a figure which the Lands Tribunal regarded as a rack rent. This figure was adjusted to £5,750 to take into account a surrender of an existing lease. The ratepayer contended that the valuation should be £5,100 and relied on a calculation based on a percentage of the capital cost of the land and of erecting the buildings on it, a formula known as "the contractor's basis." The valuation officer sought to fix the valuation on a "profits basis" and proposed a figure of £8,700. The Lands Tribunal rejected both the contractor's basis and profits basis means of valuation and held that the rack rent figure, as adjusted, was the best evidence available; evidence in relation to other means of calculating was thus excluded. In the Court of Appeal Lord Denning M.R. held that the best evidence rule as stated by Scott L.J. was wrong and that the correct view was that all relevant evidence can be admitted. Lord Denning M.R. thus reformulated the rule by stating " . . . when the particular hereditament is let at what is plainly a rack rent, or when similar hereditaments in similar economic sites are so let, so that they are truly comparable, that is admissible evidence of what the hypothetical tenant would pay; but it is not in itself decisive. All other relevant considerations are admissible." The matter was thus remitted to the Lands Tribunal for further consideration with a direction to admit evidence of other means of valuation.

The following decisions of the Lands Tribunal illustrate the relevance of factors which have been put forward by ratepayers and valuation officers as pertinent to assessment.

**Carter** v. **Squire (Valuation Officer)** (1968). A caravan site was situated in a former stone quarry, thereby being enclosed on three sides, access to the site being gained over a rough approach road. The caravans on the site were placed in close proximity. The local valuation court assessed the caravans at between £80 and £90 gross value depending on the size of the caravans, whereas the valuation officer had proposed valuations of between £70 and £83. The ratepayers claimed that on another site (over 100 miles away) the valuation for the same size of caravans was £62 instead of £80, and also compared the assessments with those placed on prefabricated bungalows which had gross values of £65.

The valuation officer had relied on site rents to calculate the gross values, but had disregarded prefabricated bungalows as comparables as he considered that these structures attracted a different section of the community notwithstanding that they had been taken into account in relation to the caravan site with which comparison was sought to be made. The Lands Tribunal held that assessments on prefabricated bungalows should be taken into account and that the underlying principles of valuation should be consistent throughout the country, allowing for different amenities. In this case the overall area was held to be more important to the valuation than the length of the caravans; as the pot-holed approach road and close proximity of the caravans were detrimental, the gross valuations were reduced to between £60 and £72.

**Baker (Valuation Officer)** v. **Horwell and Halton Borough Council** (1975). A local valuation court had reduced the valuation officer's assessments on 10 separately assessed caravans and their pitches by 25 per cent. The ratepayers had successfully argued that the site lacked amenities, that the local authority had not exerted control over the site pursuant to the conditions of the site licence, that there was effectively a nil return for the rates paid, and that the valuations should reflect the restrictive conditions imposed by the site operator and also the lack of security of tenure.

The Lands Tribunal allowed the appeal of the valuation officer, holding that the best evidence was derived from the actual rents paid for pitches as

135

these reflected local conditions, advantages and disadvantages. The Tribunal rejected the considerations accepted by the local valuation court and held (i) that the lack of action by the local authority was a matter to be pursued with the authority and could not be taken into account; (ii) the hypothetical tenancy was to be considered without regard to restrictions imposed by the site operator or to problems of security of tenure, since the hypothetical tenancy has to be regarded as an agreement reached between two persons, both of whom must be considered to be acting reasonably.

**Hart v. Smith (Valuation Officer)** (1978). A leisure caravan was permanently situated on the caravan site operator's land. A dispute arose in relation to the rating of the caravan and pitch, the dispute being limited to the rating year prior to the coming into force of the Rating (Caravan Sites) Act 1976. The ratepayer appealed against a decision of the local valuation court to assess the hereditament at gross value £67, rateable value £37, for which decision no reasons were given. The appellant argued (i) that the caravan site in issue in *Field Place Caravan Park Ltd.* v. *Harding* (*Valuation Officer*) (1966) was more advantageous to the occupiers than the present site; (ii) that the assessment was too high when compared with small houses (not being prefabricated bungalows) in the locality; and (iii) that the composite assessment for the whole site proposed pursuant to the 1976 Act showed an average rateable value of only £22.37 per caravan.

The Lands Tribunal rejected all the ratepayer's arguments ruling (i) that direct comparison with the *Field Place* site was no guide, as that site was in a different part of the country; (ii) that no valid comparison can be made in respect of a caravan and a house, the Tribunal having previously so held in *Leighton* v. *Thomas* (*Valuation Officer*) (1976); and (iii) that it was not realistic to derive the rental of a separately let caravan by taking a mathematical fraction of the caravan site as a whole. The Tribunal considered, however, that the amenity of the site was below average and reduced the assessment to gross value £60, rateable value £33.

Reference may also be made to the following Lands Tribunal decisions:

*Racine* v. *Buncombe* (*Valuation Officer*) (1967)
*Hanstock* (*Valuation Officer*) v. *Dawson* (1970)
*Reason* v. *Atkinson* (*Valuation Officer*) (1977)
*Price* v. *Smith* (*Valuation Officer*) (1977)
*Holderness District Council* v. *Hingley* (*Valuation Officer*) (1979)
*Rye Bay Caravan Park Ltd.* v. *Morgan* (*Valuation Officer*) (1979).

# Appendices

# Appendices

# Appendix I: Statutes

## Caravan Sites and Control of Development Act 1960 (8 & 9 Eliz. 2, c. 62)

An Act to make further provisions for the licensing and control of caravan sites, to authorise local authorities to provide and operate caravan sites, to amend the law relating to enforcement notices and certain other notices issued under Part III of the Town and Country Planning Act 1947, to amend sections twenty-six and one hundred and three of that Act and to explain other provisions in the said Part III; and for connected purposes.

[29th July, 1960]

PART I

CARAVAN SITES

*Licensing of caravan sites*

**Prohibition of use of land as caravan site without site licence**

1.—(1) Subject to the provisions of this Part of this Act, no occupier of land shall after the commencement of this Act cause or permit any part of the land to be used as a caravan site unless he is the holder of a site licence (that is to say, a licence under this Part of this Act authorising the use of land as a caravan site) for the time being in force as respects the land so used.

(2) If the occupier of any land contravenes subsection (1) of this section he shall be guilty of an offence and liable on summary conviction, in the case of the first offence to a fine not exceeding one hundred pounds and, in the case of a second or subsequent offence, to a fine not exceeding [level 4 on the standard scale.]

(3) In this Part of this Act the expression "occupier" means, in relation to any land, the person who, by virtue of an estate or interest therein held by him, is entitled to possession thereof or would be so entitled but for the rights of any other person under licence granted in respect of the land:

Provided that where land amounting to not more than four hundred square yards in area is let under a tenancy entered into with a view to the use of the land as a caravan site, the expression "occupier" means in relation to that land the person who would be entitled to possession of the land but for the rights of any person under that tenancy.

(4) In this Part of this Act the expression "caravan site" means land on

139

which a caravan is stationed for the purposes of human habitation and land which is used in conjunction with land on which a caravan is so stationed.

AMENDMENT
The maximum fine in subs. (2) was raised to the current amount at level 4 on the standard scale by the Criminal Justice Act 1982, s.38, and a reference to that amount substituted for the original reference to £250 by s.40 of that Act.

### Exemptions from licensing requirements

2. No site licence shall be required for the use of land as a caravan site in any of the circumstances specified in the First Schedule to this Act and that Schedule shall have effect accordingly.

### Issue of site licences by local authorities

3.—(1) An application for the issue of a site licence in respect of any land may be made by the occupier thereof to the local authority in whose area the land is situated.

(2) An application under this section shall be in writing and shall specify the land in respect of which the application is made; and the applicant shall, either at the time of making the application or subsequently, give to the local authority such [other information as they may reasonably require.]

(3) A local authority may on an application under this section issue a site licence in respect of the land if, and only if, the applicant is, at the time when the site licence is issued, entitled to the benefit of a permission for the use of the land as a caravan site granted under Part III of [the Act of 1971] otherwise than by a development order.

(4) If at the date when the applicant duly gives the [information required by virtue of] subsection (2) of this section he is entitled to the benefit of such a permission as aforesaid, the local authority shall issue a site licence in respect of the land within two months of that date or, if the applicant and the local authority agree in writing that the local authority shall be afforded a longer period within which to grant a site licence, within the period so agreed.

(5) If the applicant becomes entitled to the benefit of such a permission as aforesaid at some time after duly giving the [information required by virtue of] subsection (2) of this section the local authority shall issue a site licence in respect of the land within six weeks of the date on which he becomes so entitled or, if the applicant and the local authority agree in writing that the local authority shall be afforded a longer period within which to grant a site licence, within the period so agreed.

(6) Notwithstanding anything in the foregoing provisions of this section, a local authority shall not at any time issue a site licence to a person who to their knowledge has held a site licence which has been revoked in pursuance of the provisions of this Part of this Act less than three years before that time.

AMENDMENTS
The words within square brackets in subss. (2), (4) and (5) were substituted by the Local Government, Planning and Land Act 1980, Sched. 3, para. 10.

The reference to the Town and Country Planning Act 1971 was substituted by virtue of para. 2 of Sched. 24 to that Act.

## Duration of site licences

4.—(1) Where permission for the use of any land as a caravan site has been granted under Part III of [the Act of 1971] otherwise than by a development order, and has been so granted in terms such that it will expire at the end of a specified period, any site licence issued in respect of the land by virtue of the existence of that permission shall expire, and shall be stated to expire, at the end of that period; but, subject as aforesaid, a site licence shall not be issued for a limited period only.

(2) If after a site licence is issued the terms of the said permission are varied by the Minister on an appeal under [section 36 of the Act of 1971], the local authority who issued the licence shall make in the site licence any alteration required to secure that its terms comply with the provisions of the foregoing subsection.

## Power of local authority to attach conditions to site licences

5.—(1) A site licence issued by a local authority in respect of any land may be so issued subject to such conditions as the authority may think it necessary or desirable to impose on the occupier of the land in the interests of persons dwelling thereon in caravans, or of any other class of persons, or of the public at large; and in particular, but without prejudice to the generality of the foregoing, a site licence may be issued subject to conditions—

(a) for restricting the occasions on which caravans are stationed on the land for the purposes of human habitation, or the total number of caravans which are so stationed at any one time;

(b) for controlling (whether by reference to their size, the state of their repair or, subject to the provisions of subsection (2) of this section, any other feature) the types of caravan which are stationed on the land;

(c) for regulating the positions in which caravans are stationed on the land for the purposes of human habitation and for prohibiting, restricting, or otherwise regulating, the placing or erection on the land, at any time when caravans are so stationed, of structures and vehicles of any description whatsoever and of tents;

(d) for securing the taking of any steps for preserving or enhancing the amenity of the land, including the planting and replanting thereof with trees and bushes;

(e) for securing that, at all times when caravans are stationed on the land, proper measures are taken for preventing and detecting the outbreak of fire and adequate means of fighting fire are provided and maintained;

(f) for securing that adequate sanitary facilities, and such other facilities, services or equipment as may be specified, are provided for the use of persons dwelling on the land in caravans and that, at all times when caravans are stationed thereon for the purposes of human habitation, any facilities and equipment so provided are properly maintained.

(2) No condition shall be attached to a site licence controlling the types of

141

caravans which are stationed on the land by reference to the materials used in their construction.

(3) A site licence issued in respect of any land shall, unless it is issued subject to a condition restricting to three or less the total number of caravans which may be stationed on the land at any one time, contain an express condition that, at all times when caravans are stationed on the land for the purposes of human habitation, a copy of the licence as for the time being in force shall be displayed on the land in some conspicuous place.

[(3A) The local authority shall consult the fire authority as to the extent to which any model standards relating to fire precautions which have been specified under subsection (6) of this section are appropriate to the land.]

(3B) If—

(a) no such standards have been specified; or

(b) any standard that has been specified appears to the fire authority to be inappropriate to the land,

the local authority shall consult the fire authority as to what conditions relating to fire precautions ought to be attached to the site licence instead.]

(4) A condition attached to a site licence may, if it requires the carrying out of any works on the land in respect of which the licence is issued, prohibit or restrict the bringing of caravans on to the land for the purposes of human habitation until such time as the local authority have certified in writing that the works have been completed to their satisfaction; and where the land to which the site licence relates is at the time in use as a caravan site, the condition may, whether or not it contains any such prohibition or restriction as aforesaid, require the works to be completed to the satisfaction of the authority within a stated period.

(5) For the avoidance of doubt, it is hereby declared that a condition attached to a site licence shall be valid notwithstanding that it can be complied with only by the carrying out of works which the holder of the site licence is not entitled to carry out as of right.

(6) The Minister may from time to time specify for the purposes of this section model standards with respect to the layout of, and the provision of facilities, services and equipment for, caravan sites or particular types of caravan site; and in deciding what (if any) conditions to attach to a site licence, a local authority shall have regard to any standards so specified.

[(7) The duty imposed on a local authority by subsection (6) of this section to have regard to standards specified under that subsection is to be construed, as regards standards relating to fire precautions which are so specified, as a duty to have regard to them subject to any advice given by the fire authority under subsection (3A) or (3B) of this section.]

[(8) In this section "fire precautions" means precautions to be taken for any of the purposes specified in paragraph (e) of subsection (1) of this section for which conditions may be imposed by virtue of that subsection.]

AMENDMENTS

Subss. (3A), (3B), (7) and (8) were inserted by the Local Government (Miscellaneous Provisions) Act 1982, s.8.

## Failure by local authority to issue site licence

6. Where a local authority, being required under section three of this Act to issue a site licence in respect of any land, fail to do so within the period

within which they are required to issue a site licence by that section, no offence under section one of this Act shall be committed in respect of the land by the person by whom the application for the site licence was made at any time after the expiration of the said period and before a site licence is issued in pursuance of the said application.

## Appeal to magistrates' court against conditions attached to site licence

7.—(1) Any person aggrieved by any condition (other than the condition referred to in subsection (3) of section five of this Act) subject to which a site licence has been issued to him in respect of any land may, within twenty-eight days of the date on which the licence was so issued, appeal to a magistrates' court acting for the petty sessions area in which the land is situated; and the court, if satisfied (having regard amongst other things to any standards which may have been specified by the Minister under subsection (6) of the said section five) that the condition is unduly burdensome, may vary or cancel the condition.

(2) In so far as the effect of a condition (in whatever words expressed) subject to which a site licence is issued in respect of any land is to require the carrying out on the land of any works, the condition shall not have effect during the period within which the person to whom the site licence is issued is entitled by virtue of the foregoing subsection to appeal against the condition nor, thereafter, whilst an appeal against the condition is pending.

## Power of local authority to alter conditions attached to site licences

8.—(1) The conditions attached to a site licence may be altered at any time (whether by the variation or cancellation of existing conditions, or by the addition of new conditions, or by a combination of any such methods) by the local authority, but before exercising their powers under this subsection the local authority shall afford to the holder of the licence an opportunity of making representations.

(2) Where the holder of a site licence is aggrieved by any alteration of the conditions attached thereto or by the refusal of the local authority of an application by him for the alteration of those conditions, he may, within twenty-eight days of the date on which written notification of the alteration or refusal is received by him, appeal to a magistrates' court acting for the petty sessions area in which the land to which the site licence relates is situated; and the court may, if they allow the appeal, give to the local authority such directions as may be necessary to give effect to their decision.

(3) The alteration by a local authority of the conditions attached to any site licence shall not have effect until written notification thereof has been received by the holder of the licence, and in so far as any such alteration imposes a requirement on the holder of the licence to carry out on the land to which the licence relates any works which he would not otherwise be required to carry out, the alteration shall not have effect during the period within which the said holder is entitled by virtue of the last foregoing subsection to appeal against the alteration nor, thereafter, whilst an appeal against the alteration is pending.

(4) In exercising the powers conferred upon them by subsection (1) and subsection (2) of this section respectively, a local authority and a magis-

trates' court shall have regard amongst other things to any standards which may have been specified by the Minister under subsection (6) of section five of this Act.

[(5) The local authority shall consult the fire authority before exercising the powers conferred upon them by subsection (1) of this section in relation to a condition attached to a site licence for the purposes set out in section 5(1)(e) of this Act.

AMENDMENT

Subs. 5 was inserted by the Local Government (Miscellaneous Provisions) Act 1982, s.8.

## Provisions as to breaches of condition

9.—(1) If an occupier of land fails to comply with any condition for the time being attached to a site licence held by him in respect of the land, he shall be guilty of an offence and liable on summary conviction, in the case of the first offence to a fine not exceeding one hundred pounds, and, in the case of a second or subsequent offence, to a fine not exceeding [level 4 on the standard scale.]

(2) Where a person convicted under this section for failing to comply with a condition attached to a site licence has on two or more previous occasions been convicted thereunder for failing to comply with a condition attached to that licence, the court before whom he is convicted may, if an application in that behalf is made at the hearing by the local authority in whose area the land is situated, make an order for the revocation of the said site licence to come into force [on such date as the court may specify in the order, being a date nor earlier than the expiration of any period within which notice of appeal (whether by case stated or otherwise) may be given against the conviction]; and if before the date so specified an appeal is so brought the order shall be of no effect pending the final determination or withdrawal of the appeal.

The person convicted or the local authority who issued the site licence may apply to the magistrates' court which has made such an order revoking a site licence for an order extending the period at the end of which the revocation is to come into force, and the magistrates' court may, if satisfied that adequate notice of the application has been given to the local authority or, as the case may be, the person convicted, make an order extending that period.

(3) Where an occupier of land fails within the time specified in a condition attached to a site licence held by him to complete to the satisfaction of the local authority in whose area the land is situated any works required by the condition to be so completed, the local authority may carry out those works, and may recover as a simple contract debt in any court of competent jurisdiction from that person any expenses reasonably incurred by them in that behalf.

AMENDMENTS

The words within square brackets in subs. (2) were substituted by the Courts Act 1971, Sched. 8.

The maximum fine in subs. (1) was raised to level 4 on the standard scale by the Criminal Justice Act 1982, ss.38 and 46.

### Transfer of site licences and tranmission on death, etc.

10.—(1) When the holder of a site licence in respect of any land ceases to be the occupier of the land, he may, with the consent of the local authority in whose area the land is situated, transfer the licence to the person who then becomes the occupier of the land.

(2) Where a local authority give their consent to the transfer of a site licence, they shall endorse on the licence the name of the person to whom it is to be transferred and the date agreed between the parties to the transfer as the date on which that person is, for the purposes of this Part of this Act, to be treated as having become the holder of the licence.

(3) If an application is made under subsection (1) of this section for consent to the transfer of a site licence to a person who is to become the occupier of the land, that person may apply for a site licence under section three of this Act as if he were the occupier of the land, and if the local authority at any time before issuing a site licence in compliance with that application give their consent to the transfer they need not proceed with the application for the site licence.

(4) Where any person becomes, by operation of law, entitled to an estate or interest in land in respect of which a site licence is in force and is, by virtue of his holding that estate or interest, the occupier of the land within the meaning of this Part of this Act he shall, for the purposes of this Part of this Act, be treated as having become the holder of the licence on the day on which he became the occupier of the land, and the local authority in whose area the land is situated shall, if an application in that behalf is made to them, endorse his name and the said date on the licence.

### Duty of licence holder to surrender licence for alteration

11.—(1) A local authority who have issued a site licence may at any time require the holder to deliver it up so as to enable them to enter in it any alteration of the conditions or other terms of the licence made in pursuance of the provisions in this Part of this Act.

(2) If the holder of a site licence fails without reasonable excuse to comply with a requirement duly made under this section he shall be liable on summary conviction to a fine not exceeding ten pounds.

### Responsibility of occupier of land subject to a licence or special tenancy

12.—(1) It shall be a condition of any licence or of any such tenancy as is mentioned in subsection (3) of section one of this Act that if any person in exercise of rights under the licence or tenancy does anything which would constitute an offence under that section if that person were the occupier of the land, the person who is the occupier of the land may take possession of the land and terminate the licence or tenancy; and in determining whether the occupier of the land has permitted the land to be used as a caravan site account shall be taken of any powers exercisable by him under this subsection.

(2) The occupier of any land subject to a licence or subject to any such tenancy as is mentioned in subsection (3) of section one of this Act shall have the right, as against any person claiming under the licence or tenancy, to enter on the land and do anything on the land reasonably required for the

145

purpose of complying with any conditions attached to a site licence issued with respect to the land.

\*     \*     \*

*Caravans on commons*

## Power of rural district councils to prohibit caravans on commons

23.—(1) This section applies to any land in the area of a [district council] which is or forms part of a common, not being land falling within any of the following descriptions, that is to say—

(*a*) land to which section one hundred and ninety-three of the Law of Property Act, 1925 (which relates to the rights of the public over certain commons and waste lands), for the time being applies;

(*b*) land which is subject to a scheme under Part I of the Commons Act, 1899 (under which schemes may be made for the regulation and management of certain commons);

(*c*) land as respects which a site licence is for the time being in force.

(2) The council of a [district] may make with respect to any land in their area to which this section applies an order prohibiting, either absolutely or except in such circumstances as may be specified in the order, the stationing of caravans on the land for the purposes of human habitation.

(3) Without prejudice to the provisions of section one of this Act, any person who stations a caravan on any land in contravention of an order under this section for the time being in force with respect to the land shall be guilty of an offence and liable on summary conviction to a fine not exceeding [level 1 on the standard scale.]

(4) It shall be the duty of a [district council] to take all reasonable steps to secure that copies of any order under this section which is for the time being in force with respect to any land in their area are so displayed on the land as to give to persons entering thereon adequate warning of the existence of the order, and the council shall have the right to place on the land such notices as they consider necessary for the performance of their duty under this subsection.

(5) An order under this section may be revoked at any time by a subsequent order made thereunder by the [district council], or may be so varied either so as to exclude any land from the operation of the order or so as to introduce any exception, or further exception, from the prohibition imposed by the order.

(6) Where the whole or a part of any land with respect to which an order under this section is in force ceases to be land to which this section applies, the said order shall thereupon cease to have effect with respect to the said land or part; and where an order ceases under this subsection to have effect with respect to a part only of any land, the [district council] shall cause any copy of the order which is displayed on that part of the land with respect to which the order continues in force to be amended accordingly.

(7) The provisions of the Second Schedule to this Act shall, subject as therein provided, have effect with respect to orders under this section.

(8) In this section the word "common" includes any land subject to be enclosed under the Inclosure Acts, 1845 to 1882, and any town or village green.

146

AMENDMENTS
"district council" was substituted for "rural district council" by Local Government Act 1972, Sched. 29, para. 14 and "the council of a district" for "the council of a rural district" by the Local Authorities etc. (Miscellaneous Provisions) (No. 3) Order 1975 (S.I. No. 1636, art. 4(3)).

The maximum fine in subs. (3) was increased to the current amount at level 1 on the standard scale by the Criminal Justice Act 1982, s.38, and a reference to that level substituted for the original reference to £10 by s.46 of that Act, with effect from April 11, 1983 (S.I. 1982 No. 1857).

*Provision of caravan sites by local authorities*

### Power of local authorities to provide sites for caravans

24.—(1) A local authority shall have power within their area to provide sites where caravans may be brought, whether for holidays or other temporary purposes or for use as permanent residences, and to manage the sites or lease them to some other person.

(2) Subject to the provisions of this section, a local authority shall have power to do anything appearing to them desirable in connection with the provision of such sites, and in particular—

(a) to acquire land which is in use as a caravan site, or which has been laid out as a caravan site, or

(b) to provide for the use of those occupying caravan sites any services or facilities for their health or convenience;

and in exercising their powers under this section the local authority shall have regard to any standards which may have been specified by the Minister under subsection (6) of section five of this Act.

[(2A) Before exercising the power to provide a site conferred on them by subsection (1) of this section the local authority shall consult the fire authority, if they are not themselves the fire authority,—

(a) as to measures to be taken for preventing and detecting the outbreak of fire on the site; and

(b) as to the provision and maintenance of means of fighting fire on it.]

(3) The local authority shall make in respect of the use of sites managed by them, and of any services or facilities provided or made available under this section, such reasonable charges as they may determine.

(4) A local authority may make available the services and facilities provided under this section for those who do not normally reside in the area of the local authority as freely as for those who do.

(5) A local authority shall, in the performance of their functions under this section, have power, where it appears to them that a caravan site or an additional caravan site is needed in their area, or that land which is in use as a caravan site should in the interests of the users of caravans be taken over by the local authority, to acquire land, or any interest in land, compulsorily.

(6) The power of a local authority under the last foregoing subsection to acquire land, or any interest in land, compulsorily shall be exercisable in any particular case on their being authorised to do so by the Minister, and [the Acquisition of Land Act 1981], shall have effect in relation to the acquisition of land, or any interest in land, under the said subsection [*as if this Act had been in force immediately before the commencement of that Act.*]

(7) A local authority shall not have power under this section to provide caravans.

147

(8) In this section the expression "local authority" includes the council of a county and a joint planning board constituted under [section 1 of the Act of 1971] for an area which consists of or includes a National Park as defined by subsection (3) of section five of the National Parks and Access to the Countryside Act 1949, or any part of such a National Park.

(9) [*Repealed.*]

AMENDMENTS

Subs. (2A) was inserted by the Local Government (Miscellaneous Provisions) Act 1982, s.8.

Subs. (9) was repealed by the London Government Act 1962 (c. 33), s.93, Sched. XVIII.

The words in italics in subs. (6) were repealed, and the words in square brackets substituted, by the Acquisition of Land Act 1981, Sched. 4, para. 1, and Sched. 6, Pt. I.

## Miscellaneous and supplemental

### Registers of site licences

25.—(1) Every local authority shall keep a register of site licences issued in respect of land situated in their area, and every such register shall be open for inspection by the public at all reasonable times.

(2) Where under subsection (2) or subsection (4) of section ten of this Act a local authority endorse on a site licence the name of any person in the circumstances described in those subsections, they shall record his name, and the date entered in the licence, in the register of site licences.

### Power of entry of officers of local authorities

26.—(1) Subject to the provisions of this section, any authorised officer of a local authority shall, on producing, if so required, some duly authenticated document showing his authority, have a right at all reasonable hours to enter any land which is used as a caravan site or in respect of which an application for a site licence has been made,—

(a) for the purpose of enabling the local authority to determine what conditions should be attached to a site licence or whether conditions attached to a site licence should be altered;

(b) for the purpose of ascertaining whether there is, or has been, on or in connection with the land any contravention of the provisions of this Part of this Act;

(c) for the purpose of ascertaining whether or not circumstances exist which would authorise the local authority to take any action, or execute any work under this Part of this Act;

(d) for the purpose of taking any action, or executing any work, authorised by this Part of this Act to be taken or executed by the local authority:

Provided that admission to any land shall not be demanded as of right unless twenty-four hours' notice of the intended entry has been given to the occupier.

(2) If it is shown to the satisfaction of a justice of the peace—

(a) that admission to any land has been refused, or that refusal is apprehended, or that the occupier of the land is temporarily absent and the case is one of urgency, or that an application for admission would defeat the object of the entry; and

(b) that there is reasonable ground for entering on the land for any such purpose as is mentioned in subsection (1) of this section,

the justice may by warrant under his hand authorise the local authority by any authorised officer to enter the land, if need be by force:

Provided that such a warrant shall not be issued unless the justice is satisfied either that notice of the intention to apply for the warrant has been given to the occupier, or that the occupier is temporarily absent and the case is one of urgency, or that the giving of such notice would defeat the object of the entry.

(3) An authorised officer entering any land by virtue of this section, or of a warrant issued thereunder, may take with him such other persons as may be necessary.

(4) Every warrant granted under this section shall continue in force until the purpose for which the entry is necessary has been satisfied.

(5) A person who wilfully obstructs any person acting in the execution of this section, or of a warrant under this section, shall be liable on summary conviction to a fine not exceeding [level 1 on the standard scale.]

AMENDMENT

The maximum fine in subs. (5) was increased to the current amount at level 1 on the standard scale by the Criminal Justice Act 1982, s.38, and a reference to that level substituted for the original reference to £5 by s.46 of that Act, with effect from April 11, 1983 (S.I. 1982 No. 1857).

*     *     *

## Crown land

28. The provisions of this Part of this Act relating to site licences shall apply to land the occupier of which is not the Crown notwithstanding that an interest in the land belongs to Her Majesty in right of the Crown or of the Duchy of Lancaster, or to the Duchy of Cornwall, or belongs to a government department or is held in trust for Her Majesty for the purposes of a government department.

## Interpretation of Part I

29.—(1) In this Part of this Act, unless the context otherwise requires—

"caravan" means any structure designed or adapted for human habitation which is capable of being moved from one place to another (whether by being towed, or by being transported on a motor vehicle or trailer) and any motor vehicle so designed or adapted, but does not include—

(a) any railway rolling-stock which is for the time being on rails forming part of a railway system, or

(b) any tent;

"caravan site" has the meaning assigned to it by subsection (4) of section one of this Act;

"development order" means an order made under section [24] of the Act of [1971] (under which orders may be made which, in some cases, themselves grant permission for development and, in other cases, provide that permission shall be granted on an application in that behalf);

"existing site" has the meaning assigned to it by section thirteen of this Act;

"fire authority", in relation to any land, means the authority discharging in the area in which the land is situated the functions of fire authority under the Fire Services Act 1947;

"local authority" means a council of a [London borough or a] [borough or urban or rural] district [the Common Council of the City of London] and the Council of the Isles of Scilly;

"occupier" has the meaning assigned to it by subsection (3) of section one of this Act and "occupied" and "occupation" shall be construed accordingly;

"site licence" has the meaning assigned to it by subsection (1) of section one of this Act;

"the Minister" means [the Secretary of State].

(2) Any reference in this Part of this Act to the carrying out of works shall include a reference to the planting of trees and shrubs and the carrying out of other operations for preserving or enhancing the amenity of land.

(3) For the purposes of any provision of this Part of this Act relating to the expiration of permission granted under Part III of the Act of [1971] for any use of land, permission granted for the use of land for intermittent periods shall not be regarded as expiring at any time so long as the permission authorises the use of the land for further intermittent periods.

(4) Any reference in this Part of this Act to permission granted under Part III of the Act of [1971] for the use of land as a caravan site shall be taken as a reference to such permission whether or not restricted in any way or subject to any condition or limitation, and any reference in this Part of this Act to such permission shall include a reference to permission deemed to be granted under the said Part III.

(5) In this Part of this Act references to the local planning authority shall, were appropriate, be taken as references to any local authority to whom any of the functions of the local planning authority under Part III of the Act of [1971] have been delegated.

AMENDMENTS

The reference to the Common Council of the City of London in the definition of "local authority" was inserted as from April 1, 1965, by the London Government Act 1963 (c. 33), Sched. XVII, para. 21(1)(b). The words in italics were repealed by the Local Government Act 1972 (c. 70), Sched. 30. The reference to a London borough was inserted with retrospective effect from April 1, 1974, by the Greater London Council (General Powers) Act 1976, s.11. The definition of "fire authority" was inserted by the Local Government (Miscellaneous Provisions) Act 1982, s.8.

## Part repeal of s.269, Public Health Act 1936

30.—(1) Section two hundred and sixty-nine of the Public Health Act, 1936 (which empowers local authorities in England and Wales, excluding London, to control by means of licences the use of movable dwellings within their areas) shall cease to have effect in relation to caravans; and in subsection (5) of that section, paragraph (ii) thereof (which exempts from the provisions of the said section a movable dwelling belonging to and regularly used by a travelling showman in the course of travelling for the purposes of his business) shall be omitted.

(2) Any condition contained in a licence which, at the commencement of

this Act, is held by the occupier of any land under the said section two hundred and sixty-nine shall, until such time as a site licence is issued in respect of that land, continue to have effect as if subsection (1) of this section had not been enacted; and, subsection (7) of the said section two hundred and sixty-nine (which imposes penalties for failure to comply with a condition attached to a licence granted under that section) shall apply to any failure on the part of an occupier of land to comply with any condition having effect by virtue of this subsection, not being a condition limiting the number of caravans which may be stationed on the land.

\* \* \*

## FIRST SCHEDULE

### CASES WHERE A CARAVAN SITE LICENCE IS NOT REQUIRED

*Use within curtilage of a dwelling-house*

1. A site licence shall not be required for the use of land as a caravan site if the use is incidental to the enjoyment as such of a dwelling-house within the curtilage of which the land is situated.

*Use by a person travelling with a caravan for one or two nights*

2. Subject to the provisions of paragraph 13 of this Schedule, a site licence shall not be required for the use of land as a caravan site by a person travelling with a caravan who brings the caravan on to the land for a period which includes not more than two nights—

(a) if during that period no other caravan is stationed for the purposes of human habitation on that land or any adjoining land in the same occupation, and

(b) if, in the period of twelve months ending with the day on which the caravan is brought on to the land, the number of days on which a caravan was stationed anywhere on that land or the said adjoining land for the purposes of human habitation did not exceed twenty-eight.

*Use of holdings of five acres or more in certain circumstances*

3.—(1) Subject to the provisions of paragraph 13 of this Schedule, a site licence shall not be required for the use as a caravan site of land which comprises, together with any adjoining land which is in the same occupation and has not been built on, not less than five acres—

(a) if in the period of twelve months ending with the day on which the land is used as a caravan site the number of days on which a caravan was stationed anywhere on that land or on the said adjoining land for the purposes of human habitation did not exceed twenty-eight, and

(b) if in the said period of twelve months not more than three caravans were so stationed at any one time.

(2) The Minister may by order contained in a statutory instrument provide that in any such area as may be specified in the order this paragraph shall have effect subject to the modification—

(a) that for the reference in the foregoing sub-paragraph to five acres

151

there shall be substituted a reference to such smaller acreage as may be specified in the order, or

(b) that for the condition specified in head (a) of that sub-paragraph there shall be substituted a condition that the use in question falls between such dates in any year as may be specified in the order,

or subject to modification in both such respects.

(3) The Minister may make different orders under this paragraph as respects different areas, and an order under this paragraph may be varied by a subsequent order made thereunder.

(4) An order under this paragraph shall come into force on such date as may be specified in the order, being a date not less than three months after the order is made; and the Minister shall publish notice of the order in a local newspaper circulating in the locality affected by the order and in such other ways as appear to him to be expedient for the purpose of drawing the attention of the public to the order.

### Sites occupied and supervised by exempted organisations

4. Subject to the provisions of paragraph 13 of this Schedule, a site licence shall not be required for the use as a caravan site of land which is occupied by an organisation which holds for the time being a certificate of exemption granted under paragraph 12 of this Schedule (hereinafter referred to as an exempted organisation) if the use is for purposes of recreation and is under the supervision of the organisation.

### Sites approved by exempted organisations

5.—(1) Subject to the provisions of paragraph 13 of this Schedule, a site licence shall not be required for the use as a caravan site of land as respects which there is in force a certificate issued under this paragraph by an exempted organisation if not more than five caravans are at the time stationed for the purposes of human habitation on the land to which the certificate relates.

(2) For the purposes of this paragraph an exempted organisation may issue as respects any land a certificate stating that the land has been approved by the exempted organisation for use by its members for the purposes of recreation.

(3) The certificate shall be issued to the occupier of the land to which it relates, and the organisation shall send particulars to the Minister of all certificates issued by the organisation under this paragraph.

(4) A certificate issued by an exempted organisation under this paragraph shall specify the date on which it is to come into force and the period for which it is to continue in force, being a period not exceeding one year.

### Meetings organised by exempted organisations

6. Subject to the provisions of paragraph 13 of this Schedule, a site licence shall not be required for the use of land as a caravan site if the use is under the supervision of an exempted organisation and is in pursuance of arrangements made by that organisation for a meeting for its members lasting not more than five days.

*Agricultural and forestry workers*

7. Subject to the provisions of paragraph 13 of this Schedule, a site licence shall not be required for the use as a caravan site of agricultural land for the accommodation during a particular season of a person or persons employed in farming operations on land in the same occupation.

8. Subject to the provisions of paragraph 13 of this Schedule, a site licence shall not be required for the use of land as a caravan site for the accommodation during a particular season of a person or persons employed on land in the same occupation, being land used for the purposes of forestry (including afforestation).

*Building and engineering sites*

9. Subject to the provisions of paragraph 13 of this Schedule, a site licence shall not be required for the use as a caravan site of land which forms part of, or adjoins, land on which building or engineering operations are being carried out (being operations for the carrying out of which permission under Part III of the Act of 1947 has, if required, been granted) if that use is for the accommodation of a person or persons employed in connection with the said operations.

*Travelling showmen*

10.—(1) Subject to the provisions of paragraph 13 of this Schedule, a site licence shall not be required for the use of land as a caravan site by a travelling showman who is a member of an organisation of travelling showmen which holds for the time being a certificate granted under this paragraph and who is, at the time, travelling for the purposes of his business or who has taken up winter quarters on the land with his equipment for some period falling between the beginning of October in any year and the end of March in the following year.

(2) For the purposes of this paragraph the Minister may grant a certificate to any organisation recognised by him as confining its membership to bona fide travelling showmen; and a certificate so granted may be withdrawn by the Minister at any time.

*Sites occupied by licensing authority*

11. A site licence shall not be required for the use as a caravan site of land occupied by the local authority in whose area the land is situated.

[*Gipsy sites occupied by county councils or regional councils*

11A. A site licence shall not be required for the use of land occupied by a county council, or in Scotland by a regional council as a caravan site providing accommodation for gipsies.]

AMENDMENT
Para. 11(A) was inserted by the Local Government, Planning and Land Act 1980, s.176.

*Certification of exempted organisations*

12.—(1) For the purposes of paragraphs 4, 5 and 6 of this Schedule the Minister may grant a certificate of exemption to any organisation as to which he is satisfied that its objects include the encouragement or promotion of recreational activities.

(2) A certificate granted under this paragraph may be withdrawn by the Minister at any time.

*Power to withdraw certain exemptions*

13.—(1) The Minister may on the application of a local authority by order provide that, in relation to such land situated in their area as may be specified in the order, this Schedule shall have effect as if paragraphs 2 to 10, or such one or more of those paragraphs as may be so specified, were omitted from this Schedule.

(2) An order under this paragraph—

(a) shall come into force on such date as may be specified therein, and

(b) may, on the application of the local authority on whose application it was made, be varied or revoked by a subsequent order made thereunder,

and, except in the case of an order the sole effect of which is to revoke in whole or part a previous order, the local authority shall, not less than three months before the order comes into force, cause a notice setting out the effect of the order and the date on which it comes into force to be published in the London Gazette or, if the land is in Scotland, in the Edinburgh Gazette and in a local newspaper circulating in the locality in which the land to which the order relates is situated.

# Caravan Sites Act 1968 (1968 c. 52)

Act to restrict the eviction from caravan sites of occupiers of caravans and make other provision for the benefit of such occupiers; to secure the establishment of such sites by local authorities for the use of gipsies and other persons of nomadic habit, and control in certain areas the unauthorised occupation of land by such persons; to amend the definition of "caravan" in Part I of the Caravan Sites and Control of Development Act 1960; and for purposes connected with the matters aforesaid.

[26th July 1968]

## Part I

### Provisions for Protection of Residential Occupiers

**Application of Part I**

1.—(1) This Part of this Act applies in relation to any licence or contract (whether made before or after the passing of this Act) under which a person is entitled to station a caravan on a protected site (as defined by subsection (2) below) and occupy it as his residence, or to occupy as his residence a caravan stationed on any such site; and any such licence or contract is in this Part referred to as a residential contract, and the person so entitled as the occupier.

(2) For the purposes of this Part of this Act a protected site is any land in respect of which a site licence is required under Part I of the Caravan Sites and Control of Development Act 1960 or would be so required if paragraph 11 of Schedule 1 to that Act (exemption of land occupied by local authorities) were omitted, not being land in respect of which the relevant planning permission or site licence—

(a) is expressed to be granted for holiday use only; or
(b) is otherwise so expressed or subject to such conditions that there are times of the year when no caravan may be stationed on the land for human habitation.

(3) References in this Part of this Act to the owner of a protected site are references to the person who is or would apart from any residential contract be entitled to possession of the land.

## Minimum length of notice

2. In any case where a residential contract is determinable by notice given by either party to the other, a notice so given shall be of no effect unless it is given not less than four weeks before the date on which it is to take effect.

## Protection of occupiers against eviction and harassment

3.—(1) Subject to the provisions of this section, a person shall be guilty of an offence under this section—

(a) if, during the subsistence of a residential contract, he unlawfully deprives the occupier of his occupation on the protected site of any caravan which the occupier is entitled by the contract to station and occupy, or to occupy, as his residence thereon;
(b) if, after the expiration or determination of a residential contract, he enforces, otherwise than by proceedings in the court, any right to exclude the occupier from the protected site or from any such caravan, or to remove or exclude any such caravan from the site;
(c) if, whether during the subsistence or after the expiration or determination of a residental contract, with intent to cause the occupier—
    (i) to abandon the occupation of the caravan or remove it from the site, or
    (ii) to refrain from exercising any right or pursuing any remedy in respect thereof,
    he does acts calculated to interfere with the peace or comfort of the occupier or persons residing with him, or persistently withdraws or withholds services or facilities reasonably required for the occupation of the caravan as a residence on the site.

(2) References in this section to the occupier include references to the person who was the occupier under a residential contract which has expired or been determined and, in the case of the death of the occupier (whether during the subsistence or after the expiration or determination of the contract), to any person then residing with the occupier being—

(a) the widow or widower of the occupier; or
(b) in default of a widow or widower so residing, any member of the occupier's family.

(3) A person guilty of an offence under this section shall, without prejudice to any liability or remedy to which he may be subject in civil proceedings, be liable on summary conviction—

155

(a) [ . . . ]

(b) [ . . . ] to a fine not exceeding [level 5 on the standard scale] or to imprisonment for a term not exceeding six months, or to both.

(4) In proceedings for an offence under paragraph (a) or (b) of subsection (1) of this section it shall be a defence to prove that the accused believed, and had reasonable cause to believe, that the occupier of the caravan had ceased to reside on the site.

(5) Nothing in this section applies to the exercise by any person of a right to take possession of a caravan of which he is the owner, other than a right conferred by or arising on the expiration or determination of a residential contract, or to anything done pursuant to the order of any court.

AMENDMENTS
The words substituted in and deleted from subs. (3) were added or deleted by the Criminal Justice Act 1982, ss.35, 38 and 46.

**Provision for suspension of eviction orders**

4.—(1) If in proceedings by the owner of a protected site the court makes an order for enforcing in relation thereto any such right as is mentioned in paragraph (b) of subsection (1) of section 3 of this Act, the court may (without prejudice to any power apart from this section to postpone the operation or suspend the execution of an order, and subject to the following provisions of this section) suspend the enforcement of the order for such period not exceeding twelve months from the date of the order as the court thinks reasonable.

(2) Where the court by virtue of this section suspends the enforcement of an order, it may impose such terms and conditions, including conditions as to the payment of rent or other periodical payments or of arrears of such rent or payments, as the court thinks reasonable.

(3) The court may from time to time, on the application of either party, extend, reduce or terminate the period of suspension ordered by virtue of this section, or vary any terms or conditions imposed thereunder, but shall not extend the period of suspension for more than twelve months at a time.

(4) In considering whether or how to exercise its powers under this section, the court shall have regard to all the circumstances, and in particular to the questions—

(a) whether the occupier of the caravan has failed, whether before or after the expiration or determination of the relevant residential contract, to observe any terms or conditions of that contract, any conditions of the site licence, or any reasonable rules made by the owner for the management and conduct of the site or the maintenance of caravans thereon;

(b) whether the occupier has unreasonably refused an offer by the owner to renew the residential contract or make another such contract for a reasonable period and on reasonable terms;

(c) whether the occupier has failed to make reasonable efforts to obtain elsewhere other suitable accommodation for his caravan (or, as the case may be, another suitable caravan and accommodation for it).

(5) Where the court makes such an order as is mentioned in subsection (1) of this section but suspends the enforcement of that order by virtue of this section, the court shall make no order for costs unless it appears to the

court, having regard to the conduct of the owner or of the occupier, that there are special reasons for making such an order.

(6) The court shall not suspend the enforcement of an order by virtue of this section in the following cases, namely—

(a) where the proceedings are taken by a local authority within the meaning of section 24 of the Caravan Sites and Control of Development Act 1960;

(b) where no site licence under Part I of that Act is in force in respect of the site;

and where a site licence in respect of the site is expressed to expire at the end of a specified period, the period for which enforcement may be suspended by virtue of this section shall not extend beyond the expiration of the licence.

## Supplementary

5.—(1) In this Part of this Act "the court" means the county court; and any powers of a county court in such proceedings as are mentioned in subsection (1) of section 4 of this Act may be exercised with the leave of the judge by any registrar of the court, except in so far as rules of court otherwise provide.

(2) The power of the court under section 4 of this Act to suspend the enforcement of an order shall extend to any order made but not executed before the commencement of this Part of this Act.

(3) Nothing in this Part of this Act shall affect the operation of section 13 of the Compulsory Purchase Act 1965.

(4) Subsection (1) of section 12 of the Caravan Sites and Control of Development Act 1960 (power of site occupier to take possession and terminate a licence or tenancy in case of contravention of section 1 of that Act) shall have effect subject to the foregoing provisions of this Part of this Act.

(5) [The Protection from Eviction Act 1977] (protection against harassment and eviction without due process of law) shall not apply to any premises being a caravan stationed on a protected site.

AMENDMENT
The words in square brackets in subs. (5) were substituted by the Protection from Eviction Act 1977, Sched. 1.

## PART II

### GIPSY ENCAMPMENTS

*Provision of sites by local authorities*

### Duty of local authorities to provide sites for gipsies

6.—(1) Subject to the provisions of this and the next following section, it shall be the duty of every local authority being [the council of a county, metropolitan district or London borough] to exercise their powers under section 24 of the Caravan Sites and Control of Development Act 1960 (provision of caravan sites) so far as may be necessary to provide adequate accommodation for gipsies residing in or resorting to their area.

(2) The council of a [metropolitan district] or London borough shall not in any case be required under subsection (1) of this section to provide accom-

modation for more than fifteen caravans at a time, in the [metropolitan district] or, as the case may be, in the London borough] [ . . . ]

(3) Any local authority may defray or contribute towards expenditure incurred or to be incurred under this Part of this Act by any other authority.

(4) The powers of a local authority under the said section 24 shall include power to provide, in or in connection with sites for the accommodation of gipsies, working space and facilities for the carrying on of such activities as are normally carried on by them; but subsection (1) of this section shall not apply to the powers conferred by this subsection.

AMENDMENTS
The words in square brackets in subss. (1) and (2) were substituted by the L.G.A. 1985, s.16 and Sched. 8, para. 11. (The subsections had been earlier amended by the Local Government Act 1972, s.190(1) and Sched. 30).

The words omitted from subs. (2) were repealed by the Local Government, Planning and Land Act 1980, s.172 and Sched. 30.

## Functions of district councils

7.—(1) The duty imposed by section 6(1) of this Act on the council of a county shall extend only to determining what sites are to be provided and acquiring or appropriating the necessary land; and it shall be the duty of the council of the district in which any such site is located to exercise all other powers under section 24 of the Caravan Sites and Control of Development Act 1960 in relation to the site.

(2) The charges to be made by the council of a county district pursuant to subsection (3) of the said section 24 in respect of any such site shall be such as may be determined by the council of the county; and the council of the county shall pay to the council of the district sums equal to their expenditure reasonably incurred under this section (including the proper proportion of the remuneration and expenses of their officers and other administrative expenditure) so far as it exceeds their receipts thereunder.

(3) The council of any county district may, with the approval of the council of the county concerned, agree with the council of any other such district for the discharge by one of those councils, as agent for the other, of such of the functions under this section of the latter council as may be specified in the agreement.

(4) [Repealed.]

AMENDMENT
Subs. (4) was repealed by the Local Government Act 1972, Sched. 30.

## Location of sites in counties

8.—(1) Before adopting a proposal to acquire or appropriate land for a site pursuant to this Part of this Act, the council of a county shall consult the council of the county district in which the land is situated and such other authorities and persons as they consider appropriate.

(2) If objection is made to any such proposal by the council of a county district in or adjacent to which the land is situated and is not disposed of in consultation with the council of the county, the council of the county district may give notice of the objection to the Minister.

(3) After considering any such objection the Minister may, as appears to him proper, give directions to the council of the county—

(a) to abandon the proposal;

(b) to proceed with the proposal; or

(c) to make an application for planning permission in respect of the proposed use of the land;

and any application for planning permission made pursuant to such directions shall be deemed to be referred to the Minister under [section 35 of the Town and Country Planning Act 1971].

AMENDMENT

The words in square brackets in subs. (3) were substituted by the Town and Country Planning Act 1971, Sched. 23, Pt. II.

### Power of Secretary of State to direct local authorities to provide site

[9. The Secretary of State may, if at any time it appears to him to be necessary so to do, give directions to any local authority to which subsection (1) of section 6 of this Act applies requiring them to provide, pursuant to that section, such sites or additional sites, for the accommodation of such numbers of caravans, as may be specified in the directions; and any such directions shall be enforceable, on the application of the Secretary of State, by mandamus.]

AMENDMENT

This section was substituted for the original by the Local Government, Planning and Land Act 1980, Sched. 3, para. 13.

*Control of unauthorised encampments*

### Prohibition of unauthorised camping in designated areas

10.—(1) In any area designated under the following provisions of this Act as an area to which this section applies it shall be an offence for any person being a gipsy to station a caravan for the purpose of residing for any period—

(a) on any land situated within the boundaries of a highway; or

(b) on any other unoccupied land; or

(c) on any occupied land without the consent of the occupier.

(2) In proceedings against any person for an offence under this section it shall be a defence to prove that the caravan was stationed on the land in consequence of illness, mechanical breakdown or other immediate emergency and that he removed it (or intended to remove it) as soon as reasonably practicable.

(3) A person guilty of an offence under this section shall be liable on summary conviction to a fine not exceeding [level 1 on the standard scale]; and if the offence of which he is convicted is continued after the conviction he shall be guilty of a further offence and shall be liable in respect thereof to a fine not exceeding £5 for every day on which the offence is so continued.

AMENDMENT

The maximum fine in subs. (3) was increased to the current amount at level 1 on the standard scale by the Criminal Justice Act 1982, s.38, and a reference to that level substituted for the original reference to £20 by s.46 of that Act, with effect from April 11, 1983 (S.I. 1982 No. 1857).

### Orders for removal of unlawfully parked caravans and their occupants

[11.—(1) In any area to which section 10 of this Act applies, a magistrates' court may, on a complaint made by a local authority, and if satisfied that a caravan is stationed on land within that authority's area in contravention of that section, make an order requiring any caravan (whether or not identified in the order) which is so stationed on the land to be removed together with any person residing in it.

(2) An order under this section may authorise the local authority to take such steps as are reasonably necessary to ensure that the order is complied with and in particular, may authorise the authority, by its officers and servants—

(a) to enter upon the land specified in the order; and

(b) to take, in relation to any caravan to be removed pursuant to the order, such steps for securing entry and rendering it suitable for removal as may be so specified.

(3) The local authority shall not enter upon any occupied land unless they have given to the owner and occupier at least 24 hours notice of their intention to do so, or unless after reasonable inquiries they are unable to ascertain their names and addresses.

(4) A person who intentionally obstructs any person acting in the exercise of any power conferred on him by an order under this section shall be guilty of an offence and liable on summary conviction to a fine not exceeding [level 3 on the standard scale.]

(5) A constable in uniform may arrest without warrant anyone whom he reasonably suspects to be guilty of an offence under this section.

(6) Where a complaint is made under this section, a summons issued by the court requiring the person or persons to whom it is directed to appear before the court to answer to the complaint may be directed—

(a) to the occupant of a particular caravan stationed on the land in question; or

(b) to all occupants of caravans stationed there, without naming him or them.

(7) Where it is impracticable to serve such a summons on a person named in it, it shall be treated as duly served on him if a copy of it is fixed in a prominent place to the caravan concerned; and where such a summons is directed to the unnamed occupants of caravans, it shall be treated as duly served on those occupants if a copy of it is fixed in a prominent place to every caravan stationed on the land in question at the time when service is thus effected.

(8) The local authority shall take such steps as may be reasonably practicable to secure that a copy of any such summons is displayed on the land in question (otherwise than by being fixed to a caravan) in a manner designed to ensure that it is likely to be seen by any person camping on the land.

(9) Notice of any such summons shall be given by the local authority to the owner of the land in question and to any occupier of that land unless, after reasonable inquiries, the authority is unable to ascertain the name and address of the owner or occupier; and the owner of any such land and any occupier of any such land shall be entitled to appear and to be heard in the proceedings.

(10) Section 55(2) of the Magistrates' Courts Act 1980 (warrant for arrest

of defendant failing to appear) does not apply to proceedings on a complaint made under this section.]

AMENDMENTS

This section was substituted by the Local Government, Planning and Land Act 1980, s.174, as from February 13, 1981 (s.178 of that Act).

The reference in subs. (4) to level 3 on the standard scale was substituted for the original fine of £200 by the Criminal Justice Act 1982, s.46 with effect from April 11, 1982 (S.I. 1982 No. 1857).

### Designation of areas

[12.—(1) Subject to subsection (3) below, the Minister may by order made on the application of [the council of a county, metropolitan district or London borough] designate the area of that council as an area to which section 10 of this Act applies.

(2) Subject to subsection (3) below, the Minister may by order made on the joint application of a county council and one or more councils of districts within that county designate the area of the district or, as the case may be, the combined areas of the districts, as an area to which section 10 of this Act applies.

[(2A) Subject to subsection (3) below, the Minister may by order made on the joint application of two or more metropolitan district councils designate the area of those councils as an area to which section 10 of this Act applies.]

(3) The Minister shall not make an order under [subsection (1), (2) or (2A)] above in respect of any area unless it appears to him either that adequate provision is made in the area for the accommodation of gipsies residing in or resorting to the area, or that in all the circumstances it is not necessary or expedient to make any such provision.

(4) An order under this section may be revoked by an order made by the Minister, either on the application of the authority or authorities which made the original application or without such an application.

(5) The power of the Minister to make orders under this section shall be exercisable by statutory instrument; and any statutory instrument made by virtue of this section shall be subject to annulment in pursuance of a resolution of either House of Parliament.

(6) Where an order under this section is made in respect of any area it shall be the duty of the county council for that area or, as the case may be, [the metropolitan district council or councils or the London borough council] concerned to take such steps as are reasonably practicable to inform gipsies within the area of the making and effect of the order.]

AMENDMENTS

This section was substituted by the Local Government, Planning and Land Act 1980, s.175, as from December 13, 1981.

Subsection (2A) and the words in square brackets in subss.(1), (3) and (6) were inserted by the Local Government Act 1985, Sched. 8, para. 11.

PART III

MISCELLANEOUS

### Twin-unit caravans

13.—(1) A structure designed or adapted for human habitation which—

(a) is composed of not more than two sections separately constructed and designed to be assembled on a site by means of bolts, clamps or other devices; and

(b) is, when assembled, physically capable of being moved by road from one place to another (whether by being towed, or by being transported on a motor vehicle or trailer),

shall not be treated as not being (or as not having been) a caravan within the meaning of Part I of the Caravan Sites and Control of Development Act 1960 by reason only that it cannot lawfully be so moved on a highway when assembled.

(2) For the purposes of Part I of the Caravan Sites and Control of Development Act 1960, the expression "caravan" shall not include a structure designed or adapted for human habitation which falls within paragraphs (a) and (b) of the foregoing subsection if its dimensions when assembled exceed any of the following limits, namely—

(a) length (exclusive of any drawbar): 60 feet (18.288 metres);

(b) width: 20 feet (6.096 metres);

(c) overall height of living accommodation (measured internally from the floor at the lowest level to the ceiling at the highest level): 10 feet (3.048 metres).

(3) The Minister may by order made by statutory instrument after consultation with such persons or bodies as appear to him to be concerned substitute for any figure mentioned in subsection (2) of this section such other figure as may be specified in the order.

(4) Any statutory instrument made by virtue of subsection (3) of this section shall be subject to annulment in pursuance of a resolution of either House of Parliament.

### Offences

14.—(1) Where an offence under this Act committed by a body corporate is proved to have been committed with the consent or connivance of or to be attributable to any neglect on the part of, any director, manager, secretary or other similar officer of the body corporate or any person who is purporting to act in any such capacity, he as well as the body corporate shall be guilty of that offence and shall be liable to be proceeded against and punished accordingly.

(2) Proceedings for an offence under this Act may be instituted by any local authority.

### Financial provision

15. There shall be defrayed out of moneys provided by Parliament any increase which may arise in consequence of this Act in the sums payable out of moneys so provided in respect of rate support grant under the Local Government Act 1966.

### Interpretation

16. In this Act the following expressions have the following meanings that is to say—

"caravan" has the same meaning as in Part I of the Caravan Sites and Control of Development Act 1960, as amended by this Act;

"gipsies" means persons of nomadic habit of life, whatever their race or
origin, but does not include members of an organised group of travelling
showmen, or of persons engaged in travelling circuses, travelling
together as such;

"local authority" has the same meaning as in section 24 of the Caravan
Sites and Control of Development Act 1960;

"the Minister" means, in England other than Monmouthshire, [the Secretary of State] and in Wales and Monmouthshire the Secretary of State;

"planning permission" means permission under [Part III of the Town and
Country Planning Act 1971].

AMENDMENTS

The definition of "planning permission" was amended by the Town and Country
Planning Act 1971, s.291, Sched. 23.

Reference to the Secretary of State was substituted by virtue of S.I. 1970 No. 1681,
arts. 2(1) and 6(3).

### Short title, commencement and extent

17.—(1) This Act may be cited as the Caravan Sites Act 1968.

(2) This Act, except Part II, shall come into force at the expiration of the
period of one month beginning with the day on which it is passed, and Part
II shall come into force on such date as the Minister may by order made by
statutory instrument appoint.

(3) This Act does not extend to Scotland or Northern Ireland.

# Mobile Homes Act 1975 (1975 c. 49)

An Act to amend the law in respect of mobile homes and residential caravan
sites; and for purposes connected therewith.

[1st August 1975]

\*　　　\*　　　\*

### Power to prescribe minimum standards

7.—(1) Without prejudice to his powers under section 5(6) of the Act of
1960, the Secretary of State may by order prescribe minimum standards with
respect of the layout of, and the provision of facilities, services and equipment for protected sites within the meaning of Part I of the Act of 1968 on
which there are mobile homes occupied as an only or main residence.

(2) An order made under subsection (1) above may apply generally or to a
particular area, or to protected sites in a particular category and may prescribe different minimum standards in relation to protected sites in different categories.

(3) The power of the Secretary of State to make orders under this section
shall be exercisable by statutory instrument.

(4) An order under subsection (1) above shall be subject to annulment in
pursuance of a resolution of either House of Parliament.

(5) Any power of the Secretary of State to make an order under any provision of this section shall include a power to make an order varying or
revoking any order previously made under that provision.

### Interpretation

9.—(1) In this Act the following expressions have the following meanings, that is to say—

"the Act of 1960" means the Caravan Sites and Control of Development Act 1960;

"the Act of 1968" means the Caravan Sites Act 1968;

[ . . . ]

"mobile home" has the same meaning as "caravan" in Part I of the Act of 1960 as amended by the Act of 1968;

[ . . . ]

AMENDMENT

Definitions of "the court," "occupier," "owner," "planning permission," "protected site" and "site licence" in subs. (1), and the whole of subs. (2), were deleted by the Mobile Homes Act 1983, Sched. 2.

### Short title, commencement and extent

10.—(1) This Act may be cited as the Mobile Homes Act 1975.

(2) This Act shall come into force at the expiration of the period of two months beginning with the day on which it is passed.

(3) This Act does not extend to Northern Ireland.

# Rent Act 1977 (1977 c. 42)

An Act to consolidate the Rent Act 1968, Parts III, IV and VIII of the Housing Finance Act 1972, the Rent Act 1974, sections 7 to 10 of the Housing Rents and Subsidies Act 1975, and certain related enactments, with amendments to give effect to recommendations of the Law Commission.

[29th July 1977]

\*　　　\*　　　\*

## SCHEDULE 15

### GROUNDS FOR POSSESSION OF DWELLING-HOUSES LET ON OR SUBJECT TO PROTECTED OR STATUTORY TENANCIES

#### PART I

#### CASES IN WHICH COURT MAY ORDER POSSESSION

*Case 1*

Where any rent lawfully due from the tenant has not been paid, or any obligation of the protected or statutory tenancy which arises under this Act, or—

(a) in the case of a protected tenancy, any other obligation of the tenancy, in so far as is consistent with the provisions of Part VII of this Act, or

(b) in the case of a statutory tenancy, any other obligation of the previous protected tenancy which is applicable to the statutory tenancy,

has been broken or not performed.

### Case 2

Where the tenant or any person residing or lodging with him or any sub-tenant of his has been guilty of conduct which is a nuisance or annoyance to adjoining occupiers, or has been convicted of using the dwelling-house or allowing the dwelling-house to be used for immoral or illegal purposes.

### Case 3

Where the condition of the dwelling-house has, in the opinion of the court, deteriorated owing to acts of waste by, or the neglect or default of, the tenant or any person residing or lodging with him or any sub-tenant of his and, in the case of any act of waste by, or the neglect or default of, a person lodging with the tenant or a sub-tenant of his, where the court is satisfied that the tenant has not, before the making of the order in question, taken such steps as he ought reasonably to have taken for the removal of the lodger or sub-tenant, as the case may be.

### Case 4

Where the condition of any furniture provided for use under the tenancy has, in the opinion of the court, deteriorated owing to ill-treatment by the tenant or any person residing or lodging with him or any sub-tenant of his and, in the case of any ill-treatment by a person lodging with the tenant or a sub-tenant of his, where the court is satisfied that the tenant has not, before the making of the order in question, taken such steps as he ought reasonably to have taken for the removal of the lodger or sub-tenant, as the case may be.

### Case 5

Where the tenant has given notice to quit and, in consequence of that notice, the landlord has contracted to sell or let the dwelling-house or has taken any other steps as the result of which he would, in the opinion of the court, be seriously prejudiced if he could not obtain possession.

### Case 6

Where, without the consent of the landlord, the tenant has, at any time after—

(a) [ . . . ]

(b) 22nd March 1973, in the case of a tenancy which became a regulated tenancy by virtue of section 14 of the Counter-Inflation Act 1973;

[(bb) the commencement of section 73 of the Housing Act 1980, in the case of a tenancy which became a regulated tenancy by virtue of that section.]

(c) 14th August 1974, in the case of a regulated furnished tenancy; or

(d) 8th December 1965, in the case of any other tenancy,

assigned or sublet the whole of the dwelling-house or sublet part of the dwelling-house, the remainder being already sublet.

*Case 7*

[ . . . ]

*Case 8*

Where the dwelling-house is reasonably required by the landlord for occupation as a residence for some person engaged in his whole-time employment, or in the whole-time employment of some tenant from him or with whom, conditional on housing being provided, a contract for such employment has been entered into, and the tenant was in the employment of the landlord or a former landlord, and the dwelling-house was let to him in consequence of that employment and he has ceased to be in that employment.

*Case 9*

Where the dwelling-house is reasonably required by the landlord for occupation as a residence for—

(a) himself, or

(b) any son or daughter of his over 18 years of age, or

(c) his father or mother, or

(d) if the dwelling-house is let on or subject to a regulated tenancy, the father or mother of his wife or husband,

and the landlord did not become landlord by purchasing the dwelling-house or any interest therein after—

(i) 7th November 1956, in the case of a [tenancy which was then a controlled tenancy];

(ii) 8th March 1973, in the case of a tenancy which became a regulated tenancy by virtue of section 14 of the Counter-Inflation Act 1973;

(iii) 24th May 1974, in the case of a regulated furnished tenancy; or

(iv) 23rd March 1965, in the case of any other tenancy.

*Case 10*

Where the court is satisfied that the rent charged by the tenant—

(a) for any sublet part of the dwelling-house which is a dwelling-house let on a protected tenancy or subject to a statutory tenancy is or was in excess of the maximum rent for the time being recoverable for that part, having regard to [ . . . ] Part III of this Act, or

(b) for any sublet part of the dwelling-house which is subject to a restricted contract is or was in excess of the maximum (if any) which it is lawful for the lessor, within the meaning of Part V of this Act to require or receive having regard to the provisions of that Part.

## PART II

### CASES IN WHICH COURT MUST ORDER POSSESSION WHERE DWELLING-HOUSE SUBJECT TO REGULATED TENANCY

#### Case 11

[Where a person (in this Case referred to as "the owner-occupier") who let the dwelling-house on a regulated tenancy had, at any time before the letting, occupied it as his residence] and—

(a) not later than the relevant date the landlord gave notice in writing to the tenant that possession might be recovered under this Case, and

(b) the dwelling-house has not, since—

(i) 22nd March 1973, in the case of a tenancy which became a regulated tenancy by virtue of section 14 of the Counter-Inflation Act 1973;

(ii) 14th August 1974, in the case of a regulated furnished tenancy; or

(iii) 8th December 1965, in the case of any other tenancy,

been let by the owner-occupier on a protected tenancy with respect to which the condition mentioned in paragraph (a) above was not satisfied, and

[(c) the court is of the opinion that of the conditions set out in Part V of this Schedule one of those in paragraphs (a) and (c) to (f) is satisfied.]

If the court is of the opinion that, notwithstanding that the condition in paragraph (a) or (b) above is not complied with, it is just and equitable to make an order for possession of the dwelling-house, the court may dispense with the requirements of either or both of those paragraphs, as the case may require.

The giving of a notice before 14th August 1974 under section 79 of the Rent Act 1968 shall be treated, in the case of a regulated furnished tenancy, as compliance with paragraph (a) of this Case.

[Where the dwelling-house has been let by the owner-occupier on a protected tenancy (in this paragraph referred to as "the earlier tenancy") granted on or after 16th November 1984 but not later than the end of the period of two months beginning with the commencement of the Rent (Amendment) Act 1985 and either—

(i) the earlier tenancy was granted for a term certain (whether or not to be followed by a further term or to continue thereafter from year to year or some other period) and was during that term a protected shorthold tenancy as defined in section 52 of the Housing Act 1980, or

(ii) the conditions mentioned in paragraphs (a) to (c) of Case 20 were satisfied with respect to the dwelling-house and the earlier tenancy,

then for the purposes of paragraph (b) above the condition in paragraph (a) above is to be treated as having been satisfied with respect to the earlier tenancy.]

167

## Case 12

[Where the landlord (in this Case referred to as "the owner") intends to occupy the dwelling-house as his residence at such time as he might retire from regular employment and has let] it on a regulated tenancy before he has so retired and—

(a) not later than the relevant date the landlord gave notice in writing to the tenant that possession might be recovered under this Case; and

(b) the dwelling-house has not, since 14th August 1974, been let by the owner on a protected tenancy with respect to which the condition mentioned in paragraph (a) above was not satisfied; and

(c) the court is of the opinion that of the conditions set out in Part V of this Schedule one of those in paragraphs (b) to (e) is satisfied.]

If the court is of the opinion that, notwithstanding that the condition in paragraph (a) or (b) above is not complied with, it is just and equitable to make an order for possession of the dwelling-house, the court may dispense with the requirements of either or both of those paragraphs, as the case may require.

## Case 13

Where the dwelling-house is let under a tenancy for a term of years certain not exceeding 8 months and—

(a) not later than the relevant date the landlord gave notice in writing to the tenant that possession might be recovered under this Case; and

(b) that dwelling-house was, at some time within the period of 12 months ending on the relevant date, occupied under a right to occupy it for a holiday.

For the purposes of this Case a tenancy shall be treated as being for a term of years certain notwithstanding that it is liable to determination by re-entry or on the happening of any event other than the giving of notice by the landlord to determine the term.

## Case 14

Where the dwelling-house is let under a tenancy for a term of years certain not exceeding 12 months and—

(a) not later than the relevant date the landlord gave notice in writing to the tenant that possession might be recovered under this Case; and

(b) at some time within the period of 12 months ending on the relevant date, the dwelling-house was subject to such a tenancy as is referred to in section 8(1) of this Act.

For the purposes of this Case a tenancy shall be treated as being for a term of years certain notwithstanding that it is liable to determination by re-entry or on the happening of any event other than the giving of notice by the landlord to determine the term.

## Case 15

Where the dwelling-house is held for the purpose of being available for occupation by a minister of religion as a residence from which to perform the duties of his office and—

(a) not later than the relevant date the tenant was given notice in writing that possession might be recovered under this Case, and

(b) the court is satisfied that the dwelling-house is required for occupation by a minister of religion as such a residence.

### Case 16

Where the dwelling-house was at any time occupied by a person under the terms of his employment as a person employed in agriculture, and

(a) the tenant neither is nor at any time was so employed by the landlord and is not the widow of a person who was so employed, and

(b) not later than the relevant date, the tenant was given notice in writing that possession might be recovered under this Case, and

(c) the court is satisfied that the dwelling-house is required for occupation by a person employed, or to be employed, by the landlord in agriculture.

For the purposes of this Case "employed," and "employment" and "agriculture" have the same meanings as in the Agricultural Wages Act 1948.

### Case 17

Where proposals for amalgamation, approved for the purposes of a scheme under section 26 of the Agriculture Act 1967, have been carried out and, at the time when the proposals were submitted, the dwelling-house was occupied by a person responsible (whether as owner, tenant, or servant or agent of another) for the control of the farming of any part of the land comprised in the amalgamation and

(a) after the carrying out of the proposals, the dwelling-house was let on a regulated tenancy otherwise than to, or to the widow of, either a person ceasing to be so responsible as part of the amalgamation or a person who is, or at any time was, employed by the landlord in agriculture, and

(b) not later than the relevant date the tenant was given notice in writing that possession might be recovered under this Case, and

(c) the court is satisfied that the dwelling-house is required for occupation by a person employed, or to be employed, by the landlord in agriculture, and

(d) the proceedings for possession are commenced by the landlord at any time during the period of 5 years beginning with the date of which the proposals for the amalgamation continued in, or was first taken by, a person ceasing to be responsible as mentioned in paragraph (a) above or his widow, during a period expiring 3 years after the date on which the dwelling-house next became unoccupied.

For the purposes of this Case "employed" and "agriculture" have the same meanings as in the Agricultural Wages Act 1948 and "amalgamation" has the same meaning as in Part II of the Agriculture Act 1967.

### Case 18

Where—

(a) the last occupier of the dwelling-house before the relevant date was a person, or the widow of a person, who was at some time during his occupation responsible (whether as owner, tenant, or servant or agent or another) for the control of the farming of land which formed, together with the dwelling-house, an agricultural unit within the meaning of the Agriculture Act 1947, and

(b) the tenant is neither—

(i) a person, or the widow of a person, who is or has at any time been responsible for the control of the farming of any part of the said land, nor

(ii) a person, or the widow of a person, who is or at any time was employed by the landlord in agriculture, and

(c) the creation of the tenancy was not preceded by the carrying out in connection with any of the said land of an amalgamation approved for the purposes of a scheme under section 26 of the Agriculture Act 1967, and

(d) not later than the relevant date the tenant was given notice in writing that possession might be recovered under this Case, and

(e) the court is satisfied that the dwelling-house is required for occupation either by a person responsible or to be responsible (whether as owner, tenant, or servant or agent of another) for the control of the farming of any part of the said land or by a person employed or to be employed by the landlord in agriculture, and

(f) in a case where the relevant date was before 9th August 1972, the proceedings for possession are commenced by the landlord before the expiry of 5 years from the date on which the occupier referred to in paragraph (a) above went out of occupation.

For the purposes of this Case "employed" and "agriculture" have the same meanings as in the Agricultural Wages Act 1948 and "amalgamation" has the same meaning as in Part II of the Agriculture Act 1967.

## [Case 19

Where the dwelling-house was let under a protected shorthold tenancy (or is treated under section 55 of the Housing Act 1980 as having been so let) and—

(a) there either has been no grant of a further tenancy of the dwelling-house since the end of the protected shorthold tenancy or, if there was such a grant, it was to a person who immediately before the grant was in possession of the dwelling-house as a protected or statutory tenant; and

(b) the proceedings for possession were commenced after appropriate notice by the landlord to the tenant and not later than 3 months after the expiry of the notice.

A notice is appropriate for this Case if—

(i) it is in writing and states that proceedings for possession under this Case may be brought after its expiry; and

(ii) it expires not earlier than 3 months after it is served nor, if, when it is served, the tenancy is a periodic tenancy, before that periodic tenancy could be brought to an end by a notice to quit served by the landlord on the same day;

(iii) it is served—

(a) in the period of 3 months immediately preceding the date on which the protected shorthold tenancy comes to an end; or

(b) if that date has passed, in the period of 3 months immediately preceding any anniversary of that date; and

(iv) in a case where a previous notice has been served by the landlord on the tenant in respect of the dwelling-house, and that notice was an appropriate notice, it is served not earlier than 3 months after the expiry of the previous notice.]

## [*Case* 20

Where the dwelling-house was let by a person (in this Case referred to as "the owner") at any time after the commencement of section 67 of the Housing Act 1980 and—

(*a*) at the time when the owner acquired the dwelling-house he was a member of the regular armed forces of the Crown;

(*b*) at the relevant date the owner was a member of the regular armed forces of the Crown;

(*c*) not later than the relevant date the owner gave notice in writing to the tenant that possession might be recovered under this Case;

(*d*) the dwelling-house has not, since the commencement of section 67 of the Act of 1980 been let by the owner on a protected tenancy with respect to which the condition mentioned in paragraph (*c*) above was not satisfied; and

(*e*) the court is of the opinion that—

(i) the dwelling-house is required as a residence for the owner; or

(ii) of the conditions set out in Part V of this Schedule one of those in paragraphs (*c*) to (*f*) is satisfied.

If the court is of the opinion that, notwithstanding that the condition in paragraph (*c*) or (*d*) above is not complied with, it is just and equitable to make an order for possession of the dwelling-house, the court may dispense with the requirements of either or both of these paragraphs, as the case may require.

For the purposes of this Case "regular armed forces of the Crown" has the same meaning as in section 1 of the House of Commons Disqualification Act 1975.]

## PART III

### PROVISIONS APPLICABLE TO CASE 9 AND PART II OF THIS SCHEDULE

#### *Provision for Case* 9

1. A court shall not make an order for possession of a dwelling-house by reason only that the circumstances of the case fall within Case 9 in Part I of this Schedule if the court is satisfied that, having regard to all the circumstances of the case, including the question whether other accommodation is available for the landlord or the tenant, greater hardship would be caused by granting the order than by refusing to grant it.

#### *Provision for Part II*

2. Any reference in Part II of this Schedule to the relevant date shall be construed as follows:—

(*a*) except in a case falling within paragraph (*b*) or (*c*) below, if the protected tenancy, or, in the case of a statutory tenancy, the previous contractual tenancy, was created before 8th December 1965, the relevant date means 7th June 1966; and

(b) except in a case falling within paragraph (c) below, if the tenancy became a regulated tenancy by virtue of section 14 of the Counter-Inflation Act 1973 and the tenancy or, in the case of a statutory tenancy, the previous contractual tenancy, was created before 22nd March 1973, the relevant date means 22nd September 1973; and

(c) in the case of a regulated furnished tenancy, if the tenancy, or, in the case of a statutory furnished tenancy, the previous contractual tenancy was created before 14th August 1974, the relevant date means 13th February 1975; and

(d) in any other case, the relevant date means the date of the commencement of the regulated tenancy in question.

## Part IV

### Suitable Alternative Accommodation

3. For the purposes of section 98(1)(a) of this Act, a certificate of the [local] housing authority for the district in which the dwelling-house in question is situated, certifying that the authority will provide suitable alternative accommodation for the tenant by a date specified in the certificate, shall be conclusive evidence that suitable alternative accommodation will be available for him by that date.

4. Where no such certificate as is mentioned in [paragraph 3] above is produced to the court, accommodation shall be deemed to be suitable for the purposes of section 98(1)(a) of this Act if it consists of either—

(a) premises which are to be let as a separate dwelling such that they will then be let on a protected tenancy, [(other than one under which the landlord might recover possession of the dwelling-house under one of the Cases in Part II of this Schedule)] or

(b) premises to be let as a separate dwelling on terms which will, in the opinion of the court, afford to the tenant security of tenure reasonably equivalent to the security afforded by Part VII of this Act in the case of a protected tenancy [of a kind mentioned in paragraph (a) above],

and, in the opinion of the court, the accommodation fulfils the relevant conditions as defined in paragraph 5 below.

5.—(1) For the purposes of paragraph 4 above, the relevant conditions are that the accommodation is reasonably suitable to the needs of the tenant and his family as regards proximity to place of work, and either—

(a) similar as regards rental and extent to the accommodation afforded by dwelling-houses provided in the neighbourhood by any [local] housing authority for persons whose needs as regards extent are, in the opinion of the court, similar to those of the tenant and of his family; or

(b) reasonably suitable to the means of the tenant and to the needs of the tenant and his family as regards extent and character; and

that if any furniture was provided for use under the protected or statutory tenancy in question, furniture is provided for use in the accommodation which is either similar to that so provided or is reasonably suitable to the needs of the tenant and his family.

(2) For the purposes of sub-paragraph (1)(*a*) above, a certificate of a [local] housing authority stating—

(*a*) the extent of the accommodation afforded by dwelling-houses provided by the authority to meet the needs of tenants with families of such number as may be specified in the certificate, and

(*b*) the amount of the rent charged by the authority for dwelling-houses affording accommodation of that extent,

shall be conclusive evidence of the facts so stated.

6. Accommodation shall not be deemed to be suitable to the needs of the tenant and his family if the result of their occupation of the accommodation would be that it would be an overcrowded dwelling-house for the purpose of Part X of the Housing Act 1985.

7. Any document purporting to be a certificate of a [local] housing authority named therein issued for the purposes of this Schedule and to be signed by the proper officer of that authority shall be received in evidence and, unless the contrary is shown, shall be deemed to be such a certificate without further proof.

8. [In this Part "local housing authority" and "district" in relation to such an authority, have the same meaning as in the Housing Act 1985.]

[PART V

*Provisions applying to Cases* 11, 12 *and* 20

1. In this Part of this Schedule—

"mortgage" includes a charge and "mortgagee" shall be construed accordingly;

"owner" means, in relation to Case 11, the owner-occupier; and

"successor in title" means any person deriving title from the owner, other than a purchaser for value or a person deriving title from a purchaser for value.

2. The conditions referred to in paragraph (*c*) in each of Cases 11 and 12 and in paragraph (*e*)(ii) of Case 20 are that—

(*a*) the dwelling-house is required as a residence for the owner or any member of his family who resided with the owner when he last occupied the dwelling-house as a residence;

(*b*) the owner has retired from regular employment and requires the dwelling-house as a residence;

(*c*) the owner has died and the dwelling-house is required as a residence for a member of his family who was residing with him at the time of his death;

(*d*) the owner has died and the dwelling-house is required by a successor in title as his residence or for the purpose of disposing of it with vacant possession;

(*e*) the dwelling-house is subject to a mortgage, made by deed and granted before the tenancy, and the mortgagee—

(i) is entitled to exercise a power of sale conferred on him by the mortgage or by section 101 of the Law of Property Act 1925; and

(ii) requires the dwelling-house for the purpose of disposing of it with vacant possession in exercise of that power; and

(f) the dwelling-house is not reasonably suitable to the needs of the owner, having regard to his place of work and he requires it for the purposes of disposing of it with vacant possession and of using the proceeds of that disposal in acquiring, as his residence, a dwelling-house which is more suitable to those needs.]

AMENDMENTS

The words in square brackets in Case 9 were substituted and those in Part IV, para. 4, substituted or added by the Housing Act 1980, s.152 and Sched. 25, paras. 57 and 58. Other amendments to Part IV, paras. 3, 5, 6, 7 and 8 were effected by the Housing (Consequential Provisions) Act 1985, s.3 and Sched. 2, para. 35.

The first and last set of words in square brackets in Case 11 were added by Rent (Amendment) Act 1985, s.1, and the middle words in square brackets in Case 11, and those in Case 12, Cases 19 and 20 and Part V, added by Housing Act 1980, ss.55, 66, 67 and Sched. 7.

Case 7 and the words omitted in Cases 6 and 10 were repealed by *ibid.*, s.152 and Sched. 26.

Case 6, para. (bb) was added to *ibid.*, Sched. 8, para. 2.

# Mobile Homes Act 1983 (1983 c. 34)

An Act to make new provision in place of sections 1 to 6 of the Mobile Homes Act 1975.

[13th May 1983]

**Particulars of agreements**

1.—(1) This Act applies to any agreement under which a person ("the occupier") is entitled—

(a) to station a mobile home on land forming part of a protected site; and

(b) to occupy the mobile home as his only or main residence.

(2) Within three months of the making of an agreement to which this Act applies, the owner of the protected site ("the owner") shall give to the occupier a written statement which—

(a) specifies the names and addresses of the parties and the date of commencement of the agreement;

(b) includes particulars of the land on which the occupier is entitled to station the mobile home sufficient to identify it;

(c) sets out the express terms of the agreement;

(d) sets out the terms implied by section 2(1) below; and

(e) complies with such other requirements as may be prescribed by regulations made by the Secretary of State.

(3) If the agreement was made before the day on which this Act comes

into force, the written statement shall be given within six months of that day.

(4) Any reference in subsection (2) or (3) above to the making of an agreement to which this Act applies includes a reference to any variation of an agreement by virtue of which the agreement becomes one to which this Act applies.

(5) If the owner fails to comply with this section, the occupier may apply to the court for an order requiring the owner so to comply.

(6) Regulations under this section—

(a) shall be made by statutory instrument; and

(b) may make different provision with respect of different cases or descriptions of case, including different provision for different areas.

### Terms of agreements

2.—(1) In any agreement to which this Act applies there shall be implied the terms set out in Part I of Schedule 1 to this Act; and this subsection shall have effect notwithstanding any express term of the agreement.

(2) The court may, on the application of either party made within six months of the giving of the statement under section 1(2) above, order that there shall be implied in the agreement terms concerning the matters mentioned in Part II of Schedule 1 to this Act.

(3) The court may, on the application of either party made within the said period of six months, by order vary or delete any express term of the agreement.

(4) On an application under this section, the court shall make such provision as the court considers just and equitable in the circumstances.

### Successors in title

3.—(1) An agreement to which this Act applies shall be binding on and enure for the benefit of any successor in title of the owner and any person claiming through or under the owner or any such successor.

(2) Where an agreement to which this Act applies is lawfully assigned to any person, the agreement shall enure for the benefit of and be binding on that person.

(3) Where a person entitled to the benefit of and bound by an agreement to which this Act applies dies at a time when he is occupying the mobile home as his only or main residence, the agreement shall enure for the benefit of and be binding on—

(a) any person residing with that person ("the deceased") at that time being—

(i) the widow or widower of the deceased; or

(ii) in default of a widow or widower so residing, any member of the deceased's family; or

(b) in default of any such person so residing, the person entitled to the mobile home by virtue of the deceased's will or under the law relating to intestacy but subject to subsection (4) below.

(4) An agreement to which this Act applies shall not enure for the benefit of or be binding on a person by virtue of subsection (3)(b) above in so far as—

175

(a) it would, but for this subsection, enable or require that person to occupy the mobile home; or

(b) it includes terms implied by virtue of paragraph 5 or 9 of Part I of Schedule 1 to this Act.

### Jurisdiction of the court

4. The court shall have jurisdiction to determine any question arising under this Act or any agreement to which it applies, and to entertain any proceedings brought under this Act or any such agreement.

### Interpretation

5.—(1) In this Act, unless the context otherwise requires—
"the court" means—

(a) in relation to England and Wales, the county court for the district in which the protected site is situated or, where the parties have agreed in writing to submit any question arising under this Act or, as the case may be, any agreement to which it applies to arbitration, the arbitrator;

(b) in relation to Scotland, the sheriff having jurisdiction where the protected site is situated or, where the parties have so agreed, the arbiter;

"local authority" has the same meaning as in Part I of the Caravan Sites and Control of Development Act 1960;

"mobile home" has the same meaning as "caravan" has in that Part of that Act;

"owner," in relation to a protected site, means the person who, by virtue of an estate or interest held by him, is entitled to possession of the site or would be so entitled but for the rights of any persons to station mobile homes on land forming part of the site;

"planning permission" means permission under Part III of the Town and Country Planning Act 1971 or Part III of the Town and Country Planning (Scotland) Act 1972;

"protected site" does not include any land occupied by a local authority as a caravan site providing accommodation for gipsies or, in Scotland, for persons to whom section 24(8A) of the Caravan Sites and Control of Development Act 1960 applies but, subject to that, has the same meaning as in Part I of the Caravan Sites Act 1968.

(2) In relation to an agreement to which this Act applies—

(a) any reference in this Act to the owner includes a reference to any person who is bound by and entitled to the benefit of the agreement by virtue of subsection (1) of section 3 above; and

(b) subject to subsection (4) of that section, any reference in this Act to the occupier includes a reference to any person who is entitled to the benefit of and bound by the agreement by virtue of subsection (2) or (3) of that section.

(3) A person is a member of another's family within the meaning of this Act if he is his spouse, parent, grandparent, child, grandchild, brother, sister, uncle, aunt, nephew or niece; treating—

(a) any relationship by marriage as a relationship by blood, any relationship of the half blood as a relationship of the whole blood and the stepchild of any person as his child; and

(b) an illegitimate person as the legitimate child of his mother and
    reputed father;
or if they live together as husband and wife.

### Short title, repeals, commencement and extent

6.—(1) This Act may be cited as the Mobile Homes Act 1983.

(2) The enactments mentioned in Schedule 2 to this Act are hereby
repealed to the extent specified in the third column of that Schedule.

(3) This Act shall come into force on the expiry of the period of one week
beginning with the day on which it is passed.

(4) This Act does not extend to Northern Ireland.

## SCHEDULE 1

### AGREEMENTS UNDER ACT

### PART I

### TERMS IMPLIED BY ACT

#### *Duration of agreement*

1. Subject to paragraph 2 below, the right to station the mobile home on
land forming part of the protected site shall subsist until the agreement is
determined under paragraph 3, 4, 5 or 6 below.

2.—(1) If the owner's estate or interest is insufficient to enable him to
grant the right for an indefinite period, the period for which the right subsists shall not extend beyond the date when the owner's estate or interest
determines.

(2) If planning permission for the use of the protected site as a site for
mobile homes has been granted in terms such that it will expire at the end
of a specified period, the period for which the right subsists shall not extend
beyond the date when the planning permission expires.

(3) If before the end of a period determined by this paragraph there is a
change in circumstances which allows a longer period, account shall be
taken of that change.

#### *Termination by occupier*

3. The occupier shall be entitled to terminate the agreement by notice in
writing given to the owner not less than four weeks before the date on
which it is to take effect.

#### *Termination by owner*

4. The owner shall be entitled to terminate the agreement forthwith if, on
the application of the owner, the court—
    (a) is satisfied that the occupier has breached a term of the agreement

177

and, after service of a notice to remedy the breach, has not complied with the notice within a reasonable time; and

(b) considers it reasonable for the agreement to be terminated.

5. The owner shall be entitled to terminate the agreement forthwith if, on the application of the owner, the court is satisfied that the occupier is not occupying the mobile home as his only or main residence.

6.—(1) The owner shall be entitled to terminate the agreement at the end of a relevant period if, on the application of the owner, the court is satisfied that, having regard to its age and condition, the mobile home—

(a) is having a detrimental effect on the amenity of the site; or

(b) is likely to have such an effect before the end of the next relevant period.

(2) In sub-paragraph (1) above "relevant period" means the period of five years beginning with the commencement of the agreement and each succeeding period of five years.

### Recovery of overpayments by occupier

7. Where the agreement is terminated as mentioned in paragraph 3, 4, 5 or 6 above, the occupier shall be entitled to recover from the owner so much of any payment made by him in pursuance of the agreement as is attributable to a period beginning after the termination.

### Sale of mobile home

8.—(1) The occupier shall be entitled to sell the mobile home, and to assign the agreement, to a person approved of by the owner, whose approval shall not be unreasonably withheld.

(2) Where the occupier sells the mobile home, and assigns the agreement, as mentioned in sub-paragraph (1) above, the owner shall be entitled to receive a commission on the sale at a rate not exceeding such rate as may be specified by an order made by the Secretary of State.

(3) An order under this paragraph—

(a) shall be made by statutory instrument which shall be subject to annulment in pursuance of a resolution of either House of Parliament; and

(b) may make different provision for different areas or for sales at different prices.

### Gift of mobile home

9. The occupier shall be entitled to give the mobile home, and to assign the agreement, to a member of his family approved by the owner, whose approval shall not be unreasonably withheld.

### Re-siting of mobile home

10. If the owner is entitled to require that the occupier's right to station the mobile home shall be exercisable for any period in relation to other land forming part of the protected site—

(a) that other land shall be broadly comparable to the land on which the occupier was originally entitled to station the mobile home; and

(b) all costs and expenses incurred in consequence of the requirement shall be paid by the owner.

## Part II

### Matters Concerning Which Terms May be Implied by Court

1. The right of the occupier to quiet enjoyment or, in Scotland, undisturbed possession of the mobile home.

2. The sums payable by the occupier in pursuance of the agreement and the times at which they are to be paid.

3. The review at yearly intervals of the sums so payable.

4. The provision or improvement of services available on the protected site, and the use by the occupier of such services.

5. The preservation of the amenity of the protected site.

6. The maintenance and repair of the protected site by the owner, and the maintenance and repair of the mobile home by the occupier.

7. Access by the owner to the land on which the occupier is entitled to station the mobile home.

# Appendix II: Statutory Instruments

## Caravan Sites (Licence Applications) Order 1960 (S.I. 1960 No. 1474)

*Dated August, 17, 1960, made by the Minister of Housing and Local Government under the Caravan Sites and Control of Development Act 1960, s.3.*

1.—(1) This order may be cited as the Caravan Sites (Licence Applications) Order, 1960, and shall come into operation on the 29th day of August 1960.

(2) The Interpretation Act, 1889, shall apply to the interpretation of this order as it applies to the interpretation of an Act of Parliament.

2. The particulars to be given by an applicant for a site licence under Part I of the Caravan Sites and Control of Development Act, 1960, shall be those required by the schedule to this order and shall be set out in the form substantially to the like effect.

### SCHEDULE

FORM OF PARTICULARS TO BE SUPPLIED BY APPLICANT FOR SITE LICENCE

1. Name and address of applicant;  .............................................................
.............................................................
.............................................................

2. Applicant's interest in the land. (Give particulars of lease or tenancy, if any):  .............................................................
.............................................................
.............................................................

3. Address or description of site for which site licence is required:  .............................................................
.............................................................
.............................................................

4. Acreage of site:  .............................................................

5. Has the applicant held a site licence which has been revoked at any time in the last three years?  .............................................................

6. State type of caravan site for which licence is required:

   * Permanent residential:  .............................................................

180

\* Seasonal, between the following dates each year: ...............................

\* For touring caravans only, between the following dates in each year: ........................................................................................................

7. State maximum number of caravans proposed to be stationed on the site at any one time for the purposes of human habitation: ........................

---

8. A lay-out plan of the site to a scale of not less than 1:500 should be attached showing the boundaries of the site, the positions of caravan standings, and (where appropriate)—

Roads and footpaths,
Toilet blocks, stores and other buildings,
Foul and surface water drainage,
Water supply,
Recreation spaces,
Fire points,
Parking spaces.

The plan should distinguish between facilities already provided and facilities proposed.

---

9. Give details of the arrangements for refuse disposal and for sewage and waste water disposal: ..............................................................................
10. Has planning permission for the site been obtained from the local planning authority?

    \* If so, state   (i) Date of permission:        .........................................

                (ii) Issuing authority:       .........................................

                                        .........................................

                (iii) Date (if any) on which
                      permission will expire:   .........................................

\* If not, has permission been applied for? .......................................................

---

FOR CARAVAN SITES ALREADY IN USE ON OR BEFORE 9TH MARCH, 1960, WITHOUT PLANNING PERMISSION FROM THE LOCAL PLANNING AUTHORITY

11. Is it claimed that the site has "existing use rights" and does not require permission?

If so, state the facts on which the claim is based.

12. Was the site in use as a caravan site for the purposes of human habitation?—

(a) on 9th March, 1960 ...........................................................................

(b) on 29th August 1960 ........................................................................

(c) at any other time since 9th March, 1958, if so when .........................

---

* Delete as appropriate.

Signature of applicant ...................................

Date ...................................

# Town and Country Planning General Development Order 1977 (S.I. 1977 No. 289)

*Dated February 22, 1977, made by the Secretary of State for the Environment under the Town and Country Planning Act 1971 and Local Government Act 1972.*

## SCHEDULE 1

The following development is permitted under article 3 of this order subject to the limitations contained in the description of that development in column (1) and subject to the conditions set out opposite that description in column (2).

| Column (1) Description of Development | Column (2) Conditions |
|---|---|
| *  *  * | * |
| *Class IV.—Temporary buildings and uses* | |
| *  *  *  * | |
| 2. The use of land (other than a building or the curtilage of a building) for any purpose or purposes except as a caravan site on not more than 28 days in total in any calendar year (of which not more than 14 days in total may be devoted to use for the purpose of motor car or motor-cycle racing or for the purpose of the holding of markets), and the erection or placing of moveable structures on the land for the purposes of that use; | Such buildings, works, plant or machinery shall be removed at the expiration of the period of such operations and where they were sited on any such adjoining land, that land shall be forthwith reinstated. |

182

| Column (1)<br>Description of Development | Column (2)<br>Conditions |
|---|---|
| Provided that for the purposes of the limitation imposed on the number of days on which land may be used for motor car or motor-cycle racing, account shall be taken only of those days on which races are held or practising takes place. | |
| *Class V.—Uses by members of recreational organisations* | |
| The use of land, other than buildings and not within the curtilage of a dwellinghouse, for the purposes of recreation or instruction by members of an organisation which holds a certificate of exemption granted under section 269 of the Public Health Act 1936, and the erection or placing of tents on the land for the purposes of that use. | |
| * * * | * |
| *Class XXII.—Use as a caravan site*<br>The use of land, other than a building, as a caravan site in any of the circumstances specified in paragraphs 2 to 9 (inclusive) of Schedule 1 to the Caravan Sites and Control of Development Act 1960 or in the circumstances (other than those relating to winter quarters) specified in paragraph 10 of the said Schedule. | The use shall be discontinued when the said circumstances cease to exist, and all caravans on the site shall then be removed. |
| *Class XXIII.—Development on licensed caravan sites*<br>Development required by the conditions of a site licence for the time being in force under Part I of the Caravan Sites and Control of Development Act 1960. | |

# Mobile Homes (Commissions) Order 1983 (S.I. 1983 No. 748)

*Dated May 16, 1983, and made by the Secretary of State, in exercise of the powers conferred upon him by paragraph 8 of Part I of Schedule 1 to the Mobile Homes Act 1983 and of all other powers enabling him in that behalf.*

1.—This order may be cited as the Mobile Homes (Commissions) Order 1983 and shall come into operation on 20th May 1983.

2.—The maximum rate of commission to which an owner shall be entitled, under the provisions of paragraph 8 of Part I of Schedule 1 to the Mobile Homes Act 1983, on the sale by an occupier of a mobile home shall be 10 per cent.

## EXPLANATORY NOTE

(THIS NOTE IS NOT PART OF THE ORDER.)

The Mobile Homes Act 1983 provides for certain terms to be implied into any agreement under which a mobile home occupier is entitled to station a mobile home on land forming part of a protected site. These terms are set out in Part I of Schedule I to the Act. Paragraph 8 of Part I deals with the sale of the mobile home by the occupier and the assignment of the agreement. Under paragraph 8(2) the owner of the site is entitled to receive a commission on such a sale at a rate not exceeding that specified by order. This order fixes the maximum rate of commission at 10 per cent.

# Mobile Homes (Written Statement) Regulations 1983 (S.I. 1983 No. 749)

*Dated May 16, 1983 and made by the Secretary of State in exercise of the powers conferred upon him by section 1(2)(e) and (6) of the Mobile Homes Act 1983 and of all other powers enabling him in that behalf.*

1.—These regulations may be cited as the Mobile Homes (Written Statement) Regulations 1983 and shall come into operation on 20th May 1983.

2.—The requirements with which a written statement has to comply for the purposes of section 1(2)(e) of the Mobile Homes Act 1983 are that it shall be in the form prescribed in the Schedule to these regulations or a form substantially to the like effect.

## SCHEDULE

WRITTEN STATEMENT UNDER MOBILE HOMES ACT 1983

> IMPORTANT—PLEASE READ THIS STATEMENT CAREFULLY AND KEEP IT IN A SAFE PLACE. IT SETS OUT THE TERMS ON WHICH YOU ARE ENTITLED TO KEEP YOUR MOBILE HOME ON SITE AND TELLS YOU ABOUT THE RIGHTS GIVEN YOU BY LAW. IF THERE IS ANYTHING YOU DO NOT UNDERSTAND YOU SHOULD GET ADVICE (FOR EXAMPLE FROM A SOLICITOR OR A CITIZENS ADVICE BUREAU).

PART I

1. You have an agreement to which the Mobile Homes Act 1983 applies.

2. The parties to the agreement are—

......................................................................................................

......................................................................................................

*(name and address of mobile home occupier)*

......................................................................................................

*(name and address of site owner)*

3. The agreement commenced on ....................................................................

*(fill in date)*

4. The particulars of the land on which you are entitled to station your mobile home are .................................................................................

......................................................................................................

[5. The site owner's estate or interest in the land will end on .......................

...................................................................................................... ; or

*(fill in date)*

The site owner's planning permission for the site will end on ......................

......................................................................................................

*(fill in date)*

*This means that your right to stay on the site will not continue after that date unless the site owner's interest or planning permission is extended.]* Cross out words in square brackets if they do not apply.

PART II

INFORMATION

1. Because you have an agreement with a site owner which entitles you to keep your mobile home on his site and live in it as your home, the Mobile Homes Act 1983 gives you certain rights, affecting in particular your security of tenure and the sale of your mobile home.

2. These rights, which are contained in the implied terms set out in Part III of this statement, apply automatically and cannot be overriden, so long as your agreement continues to be one to which this Act applies.

3. A full explanation of your rights can be find in the booklet "Mobile Homes" produced jointly by the Department of the Environment, the Welsh Office and the Scottish Development Department. From 1st August 1983 the booklet is available free from Council offices and housing aid centres and you are advised to read it.

4. If you are not sure what any of the terms of your agreement mean or how they will work in future, you should get advice at once from a solicitor or citizens advice bureau.

5. If you are not happy with any of the express terms of your agreement (as

185

set out in Part IV of this statement) you should discuss them with the site owner, who may agree to change them. But if you are still not satisfied you can challenge the agreement in two ways, as explained in paragraphs 6 to 9 below, provided you do so within 6 months of the time you are given this statement.

6. A challenge can be made either in the county court (in Scotland, the sheriff court) or before an arbitrator (in Scotland, an arbiter). You can:—

(a) ask for any of the express terms of the agreement (those set out in Part IV of this statement) to be changed or deleted;

(b) ask for further terms to be included in the agreement concerning the matters set out in Part II of Schedule 1 to the Act (see paragraph 9 below).

The site owner can also go to court or to an arbitrator to ask for the agreement to be changed in these two ways.

7. The appointment of an arbitrator may be provided for in one of the express terms of the agreement. If not, you and the site owner can still agree in writing to appoint an arbitrator to settle a dispute between you.

8. The court or the arbitrator must make an order on terms they consider just and equitable in the circumstances. If you wish to challenge your agreement, you should get advice from a solicitor or citizens advice bureau.

9. The matters set out in Part II of Schedule 1 to the Act are as follows:—

(a) the right of the occupier to quiet enjoyment, or in Scotland, undisturbed possession of the mobile home;

(b) the sums payable by the occupier in pursuance of the agreement and the times at which they are to be paid;

(c) the review at yearly intervals of the sums so payable;

(d) the provision or improvement of services available on the protected site, and the use by the occupier of such services;

(e) the preservation of the amenity of the protected site;

(f) the maintenance and repair of the protected site by the owner, and the maintenance and repair of the mobile home by the occupier;

(g) access by the owner to the land on which the occupier is entitled to station the mobile home.

10. If no application to court or an arbitrator is made within the six months time limit, both you and the site owner will be bound by the terms of the agreement and will not be able to change them unless both parties agree.

## Part III

### Implied terms

*Under the Act, certain terms must be contained in your agreement. This part of the statement sets out those terms.*

*Duration of agreement*

1. Subject to paragraph 2 below, the right to station the mobile home on land forming part of the protected site shall subsist until the agreement is determined under paragraph 3, 4, 5 or 6 below.

2.—(1) If the owner's estate or interest is insufficient to enable him to grant the right for an indefinite period, the period for which the right subsists shall not extend beyond the date when the owner's estate or interest determines.

(2) If planning permission for the use of the protected site as a site for mobile homes has been granted in terms such that it will expire at the end of a specified period, the period for which the right subsists shall not extend beyond the date when the planning permission expires.

(3) If before the end of a period determined by this paragraph there is a change in circumstances which allows a longer period, account shall be taken of that change.

*Termination by occupier*

3. The occupier shall be entitled to terminate the agreement by notice in writing given to the owner not less than four weeks before the date on which it is to take effect.

*Termination by owner*

4. The owner shall be entitled to terminate the agreement forthwith, if, on the application of the owner, the court—
  (a) is satisfied that the occupier has breached a term of the agreement and, after service of a notice to remedy the breach, has not complied with the notice within a reasonable time, and
  (b) considers it reasonable for the agreement to be terminated.
5. The owner shall be entitled to terminate the agreement forthwith if, on the application of the owner, the court is satisfied that the occupier is not occupying the mobile home as his only or main residence.
6.—(1) The owner shall be entitled to terminate the agreement at the end of a relevant period if, on the application of the owner, the court is satisfied that, having regard to its age and condition, the mobile home—
  (a) is having a detrimental effect on the amenity of the site; or
  (b) is likely to have such an effect before the end of the next relevant period.
(2) In sub-paragraph (1) above, the "relevant period" means the period of five years beginning with the commencement of the agreement and each succeeding period of five years.

*Recovery of overpayments by occupier*

7. Where the agreement is terminated as mentioned in paragraph 3, 4, 5 or 6 above, the occupier shall be entitled to recover from the owner so much of any payment made by him in pursuance of the agreement as is attributable to a period beginning after the termination.

*Sale of mobile home*

8.—(1) The occupier shall be entitled to sell the mobile home and to assign the agreement to a person approved of by the owner, whose approval shall not be unreasonably withheld.

(2) Where the occupier sells the mobile home, and assigns the agreement, as mentioned in sub-paragraph (1) above, the owner shall be entitled to receive a commission on the sale at a rate not exceeding such rate as may be specified by an order made by the Secretary of State.

*The maximum rate is presently fixed at 10 per cent. by the Mobile Homes (Commissions) Order 1983 (S.I. 1983/748).*

### Gift of mobile home

9. The occupier shall be entitled to give the mobile home, and to assign the agreement, to a member of his family approved by the owner, whose approval shall not be unreasonably withheld.

### Re-siting of mobile home

10. If the owner is entitled to require that the occupier's right to station the mobile home shall be exercisable for any period in relation to other land forming part of the protected site—

(a) that other land shall be broadly comparable to the land on which the occupier was originally entitled to station the mobile home; and

(b) all costs and expenses incurred in consequence of the requirement shall be paid by the owner.

## PART IV

### EXPRESS TERMS OF THE AGREEMENT

*This part of the statement sets out the terms of the agreement settled between you and the site owner in addition to the implied terms.*
*Terms to be filled in by site owner.*

## EXPLANATORY NOTE

### (THIS NOTE IS NOT PART OF THE REGULATIONS.)

Under section 1 of the Mobile Homes Act 1983, the owner of a mobile home site must give a written statement under the Act to any person who has a right to station his mobile home on the site as a residence. Section 1(2) of the Act provides that this written statement must contain certain information and comply with such other requirements as the Secretary of State may prescribe.

These regulations require such a statement to be in the form set out in the Schedule or a form substantially similar.

# Appendix III: Ministerial Communications

## Caravan Sites and Control of Development Act 1960

**Model Standards** (Revised 1977)

I. *Section* 5(6) of the Act provides that the Secretary of State may from time to time specify Model Standards with respect to the lay-out of, and the provision of facilities, services and equipment for, caravan sites or particular types of caravan site; and that in deciding what (if any) conditions to attach to a site licence the local authority shall have regard to any standards so specified.

*Section* 7(1) provides that on an appeal against any condition of a site licence a magistrates' court, if satisfied (having regard amongst other things to any standards specified by the Secretary of State under section 5(6)) that a condition is unduly burdensome, may vary or cancel the condition.

*Section* 24, which empowers local authorities to provide caravan sites, provides, in subsection (2), that in exercising their powers under the section the local authority shall have regard to any standards that may have been specified by the Secretary of State under section 5(6) of the Act.

II. In pursuance of his powers under section 5(6) of the Act, the Secretary of State hereby specifies the following standards. They are Model Standards: they represent the standards normally to be expected, as a matter of good practice, on sites which are used regularly by residential or holiday caravans. They are not intended to apply to any other type of caravan site. They should be applied with due regard to the particular circumstances of each case, including the physical character of the site, any services or facilities that may already be available within convenient reach, and other local conditions.

### I. PERMANENT RESIDENTIAL CARAVAN SITES

**Density and space between caravans**

1. Every caravan should be not less than 6 metres from any other caravan in a separate occupation, and not less than 3 metres from a carriageway.

2. The gross density should not exceed 50 caravans to the hectare.

**Roads and footpaths**

3. Roads of suitable material should be provided so that no caravan standing or toilet block is more than 45 metres from a road. Each standing and toilet block should be connected to a carriageway by a footpath with a hard

189

surface. Carriageways should be not less than 3.65 metres wide, or, if they form part of a one way traffic system, 2.75 metres wide. Footpaths should not be less than 0.75 metres wide.

## Hard standings

4. Every caravan should stand on a hard-standing of a suitable material which should extend over the whole area occupied by the caravan placed upon it, and should project not less than 1 metre outwards from the entrance or entrances of the caravan.

## Fire fighting appliances

*Fire Points*

5. These should be established so that no caravan or site building is more than 30 metres from a fire point. They should be easily accessible and clearly and conspicuously marked "FIRE POINT."

*Fire Fighting Equipment*

6. Where water standpipes are provided and there is a water supply of sufficient pressure and flow to project a jet of water approximately 5 metres from the nozzle, such water standpipes should be situated at each fire point together with a reel for small diameter hose of not less than 30 metres in length, having a means of connection to a water standpipe (preferably a screw thread connection) and terminating in a small hand control nozzle. Hoses should be housed in a box painted red and marked "HOSE REEL."

7. Where standpipes are not provided or the water pressure or flow is not sufficient, each fire point should be provided with either water extinguishers (2 × 9 litre) or a water tank of at least 500 litres capacity fitted with a hinged cover, 2 buckets and 1 hand pump or bucket pump.

*Fire Warning*

8. A means of raising the alarm in the event of a fire should be provided at each fire point. This could be by means of a manually operated sounder, *e.g.* metal triangle with a striker, gong or hand operated siren.

*Maintenance*

9. All alarm and fire fighting equipment should be maintained in working order and available for inspection by or on behalf of the licensing authority.

10. All equipment susceptible to damage by frost should be suitably protected.

*Fire Notices*

11. A clearly written and conspicuous notice should be provided and maintained at each fire point to indicate the action to be taken in case of fire and the location of the nearest telephone. This notice should include the following:
"On discovering a fire
    i. ensure the caravan or site building involved is evacuated

    ii. raise the alarm

    iii. call the fire brigade (the nearest telephone is sited . . . . . . . . . . . .
       . . . )

    iv. attack the fire using the fire fighting equipment provided.

It is in the interest of all occupiers of this site to be familiar with the above routine and the method of operating the fire alarm and fire fighting equipment.''

*Fire Hazards*

12. Long grass and vegetation should be cut at frequent and regular intervals to prevent it becoming a fire hazard. Any such cuttings should be removed from the vicinity of caravans.

13. Provision should be made for the storage of liquefied petroleum gas and regard should be had to the Health and Safety Executive Code of Practice for the keeping of Liquefied Petroleum Gas in Cylinders and Similar Containers.

*Telephones*

14. A telephone should be available on the site for calling the police, fire brigade, ambulance or other services in an emergency.

*Note on Fire Hydrants*

Where there is a water supply of sufficient pressure and flow, there may be a requirement to install a fire hydrant to conform with BSS 750 within 100 metres of every caravan standing.

**Electrical Installations**

15. Sites should be provided with an electricity supply sufficient in all respects to meet all reasonable demands of the caravans situated thereon.

16. Such electrical installation other than Electricity Board works and circuits subject to regulations made by the Secretary of State for Energy, under Section 60 of the Electricity Act 1947, should be installed and maintained in accordance with the requirements of the Institution of Electrical Engineers Regulations for the Electrical Equipment of Buildings (the IEE Wiring Regulations) for the time being in force, and where appropriate to the standard which would be acceptable for the purposes of the Electricity (Overhead Lines) Regulations 1970, S.I. 1970 No. 1355.

17. The installation should be inspected not less than once in every 12 months, (in the case of underground installations 3 years) or in such longer period as may be recommended by a person who should be one of the following:—

A professionally qualified electrical engineer;

A member of the Electrical Contractors' Association;

A member of the Electrical Contractors' Association of Scotland;

A certificate holder of the National Inspection Council for Electrical Installation Contracting; or

A qualified person acting on behalf of one of these (in which case it should be stated for whom he is acting).

Such person should within 1 month of such an inspection issue an inspection certificate in the form prescribed in the IEE Wiring Regulations which should be retained by the site operator and displayed with the site licence. The cost of the inspection and report should be met by the site operator.

## Water supply

18. All sites should be provided with a water supply complying with British Standard Code of Practice C.P. 310 (1952).

19. Each caravan standing should be provided with a piped water supply. Alternatively, water standpipes with an adequate supply of water should be situated not more than 18 metres from any standing.

## Drainage, sanitation and washing facilities

20. Satisfactory provision should be made for foul drainage, either by connection to a public sewer or by discharge to a properly constructed septic tank or cesspool.

21. For caravans having their own water supply and water closets, each caravan standing should be provided with a connection to the foul drainage system; the connection should be capable of being made air-tight when not in use.

For caravans without such facilities, communal toilet blocks should be provided, with adequate supplies of water, on at least the following scales:

Men: 1 W.C. and 1 urinal per 15 caravans.

Women: 2 W.C.s per 15 caravans.

1 wash basin for each W.C. or group of W.C.s.

1 shower or bath (with hot and cold water) for each sex per 20 caravans.

22. Laundry facilities should be provided, in a separate room, on the scale of not less than one deep sink with running hot and cold water per 15 caravans.

23. Properly designed disposal points for the contents of chemical closets should be provided, with an adequate supply of water for cleaning the containers.

24. There should be adequate surface water drainage for carriageways, footways and paved areas, and for the site generally.

## Refuse disposal

25. Every caravan standing should have a refuse bin with a close fitting lid, and arrangements should be made for the bins to be emptied regularly.

## Storage space

26. At least 2.75 square metres of covered storage space should be provided for each caravan standing. The structures should be separate from the caravans they serve, and not less than 5 metres from any other caravan. They should be capable of being locked.

## Car parking

27. Suitably surfaced parking places should be provided, with space for at least one car for every three caravan standings. Additional space should be set aside to accommodate further cars, up to 1 car per caravan, to be surfaced as required.

**Recreation space**

28. Space equivalent to about one-tenth of the total area should be allocated for children's games and other recreational purposes.

## II. HOLIDAY CARAVAN SITES

*(Sites in regular use, except during the winter)*

The foregoing standards should apply subject to the following modifications:

(1) The gross density should not exceed sixty-two caravans to the hectare.

(2) Water supply and drainage connections to individual caravan standings, paved footpaths, and the provision of storage space may be dispensed with.

(3) Hard standings may be dispensed with if the caravans are removed during the winter.

(4) Wash basins should be provided on a scale of not less than one for men and one for women per fifteen caravans.

(5) Laundry facilities should be provided on a scale of not less than one deep sink with running hot and cold water per thirty caravans.

(6) Where gross densities are thirty to the hectare or less, no caravan standing should be more than 55 metres from a water standpipe.


# Development Control Policy Note No. 8 (1969): Caravan Sites

*(This note, which is Crown copyright, is reproduced by kind permission of the Controller of Her Majesty's Stationery Office.)*

These Notes set out current Ministerial policy and their purpose is to give general guidance to intending developers. Policies are not rigid and from time to time new Notes will be issued in this series taking account of changes in emphasis in policy or of new policy decisions.

Each application or appeal is treated on its merits and the application of a general policy to the particular case must always be a matter calling for judgment.

Any legal views stated in these Notes have no statutory force and should not be relied upon as authoritative interpretations of the law.

A list of other current Notes in this series can be obtained free from the Ministry of Housing and Local Government or the Welsh Office.

1. *Caravans as homes.* Many people live permanently in caravans. They do so, as an inquiry a few years ago showed, because they have not been able to find houses in the right places or on the right terms; or because caravans meet their needs for convenience or mobility, or simply because they like caravan life.

2. Planning policy recognises the demand for sites. The main objects of policy are, first, to enable the demand to be met in the right places, while preventing sites from springing up in the wrong places; and, second, to allow caravan sites, where permitted, to be established on a permanent or long-term basis, in order to facilitate the provision of proper services and equipment and to allow the occupants reasonable security of tenure.

3. Residential caravan sites need the same services—water, sewerage and electricity—as ordinary houses, and they require ancillary development such as roads and hard-standings. They should also be within easy each of schools, shops and health services. For these reasons they cannot normally be sited in green belts or in open country, but should be close to existing development. Caravans may, however, be out of place in the middle of ordinary housing development, so that the best place will usually be on the edge of a residential area, within reach of the necessary services but not far out in the country. Caravans are more adaptable than houses: being light and moveable, they can sometimes be accommodated satisfactorily on irregular or uneven sites unsuitable for building. But this is not to suggest that they may be relegated to unwanted corners among railway lines and factories, for a decent environment is just as important for caravans as for orthodox houses.

4. Sites are now being established entirely for "mobile homes"—the name commonly given to the larger single and twin-unit caravans which have inside bathrooms and lavatories and are connected to main water and drains. In appearance they are much like bungalows (some have pitched roofs), the wheels being removed and the chassis usually screened in some way. Because these caravans are large and have their own built-in facilities the "living outside" element is much reduced. Lavatory blocks are unnecessary on these "Mobile Home Parks," and with good layout and landscaping they can look pleasant and not out of place near traditional residential development. (Some "mobile homes" are constructed in two parts, designed to be assembled on site by bolts and clamps. The Caravan Sites Act 1968 makes it clear that such a structure is a "caravan" if, when assembled, it is physically capable of being moved by road and does not exceed the dimensions of 60 feet long, 20 feet wide and 10 feet high. Any twin-unit structure bigger than that is not a caravan for the purposes of the Caravan Sites Acts.)

5. For caravan sites of all kinds the access arrangements are important. Accesses should be carefully planned and should be designed to allow safe movement for cars and caravans to and from the sites. Caravan sites with direct access to trunk and principal roads will not normally be permitted.

6. Planning permission will normally be required for the change of use of the land involved in stationing caravans upon it, rather than the site works and services. Caravan sites (with certain exceptions) also have to be licensed under the Caravan Sites and Control of Development Act 1960, and such matters as services, equipment and living conditions on the site are regulated by the terms of the site licence. Any ancillary development required by the site licence has a general permission under the Town and Country Planning General Development Order 1963, so that any conditions attached to the planning permission will normally be concerned with the land use aspects and not with matters that can more properly be dealt with by the site licence. The distinction is broadly between the external effects of the

project, *i.e.*, the impact of the site on its surroundings, and the internal conditions or matters which affect only the caravanners. There may, however, be circumstances in which it would be right for the planning permission to regulate a matter which is normally left to the site licence. For example, it may sometimes be necessary for amenity reasons to limit the number of caravans on a site or to control the layout, design or siting of ancillary buildings more strictly than would be necessary for licensing purposes.

7. *Caravans for holidays.* In addition to the caravans used as homes, a much larger number are used by holidaymakers. Thousands of people now spend their holidays touring with caravans, and an even larger number go and stay on "static" caravan sites, where the caravans stay and the people come and go. Planning policy is concerned to see that there are adequate facilities for both these purposes—that the touring caravanner has reasonable freedom to wander and explore and the static caravanner a reasonable choice of sites to visit; but without spoiling the countryside and coast or amenities which other people enjoy.

8. The General Development Order and the exemptions from licensing in the Caravan Sites and Control of Development Act allow a wide measure of freedom for the individual touring caravanner who moves from place to place (see Sched. 1 to the Caravan Sites and Control of Development Act 1960). Development control is concerned chiefly with sites which are to be regularly used by numbers of caravans. The siting requirements for these are the same as for residential sites, in so far as they need the same services—water, sewerage, electricity and road access; but the fact that the demand is concentrated largely on the most popular holiday areas, particularly on the coast, creates special problems. Not only are caravans particularly conspicuous on open moorland and hillsides by the sea, but small seaside places are liable to be saturated by the sheer numbers of caravans if they are allowed in unchecked. Many parts of the coast have already been spoilt by uncontrolled development of this kind. The establishment of new sites on the coast and in popular holiday areas is now strictly controlled. Sites will not as a rule be allowed immediately by the sea, but should be set back a short distance inland. Conspicuous sites and well known beauty spots must be avoided and places found where the caravans will be screened by trees or shrubs. Old orchards or parkland attached to large houses are sometimes suitable, where the houses are no longer inhabited and can be used for restaurants and club rooms. Again, the access arrangements will be important (see paragraph 5 above).

9. As a general rule, planning control aims to steer holiday caravan development to a limited number of areas, usually those in which caravans are already established, rather than allow them to be scattered more widely. No further expansion will, however, be allowed in places where the number of caravans has already reached saturation point. All proposals will, of course, be considered in the light of any published statements of policy by the local planning authority about holiday development or the protection of the coast.

10. What is said in paragraph 6 above about the conditions that may be attached to planning permissions also applies to holiday caravan sites, since they are also subject to licensing. To ensure that a site is used for holidays only and not for all-the-year residence, the permission may include a condition limiting the use of the site to the holiday season. If the circumstances

warrant it conditions may also be imposed to require the caravans to be removed at the end of each season or to require a number of pitches on the site to be reserved for touring caravans.

11. *Caravan sites for gipsies.* Special considerations apply to the provision of caravan sites for "gipsies" (meaning people of nomadic habit of life, whatever their race or origin). The dominant factor here is the need for such sites. A census carried out by the Ministry of Housing and Local Government in 1965 showed that the gipsy population of England and Wales was then about 15,000, or some 3,400 families. Only a small proportion of these lived on proper sites; the rest were camping haphazardly on farm land, woodlands, commons, roadside verges, quarries, refuse tips and waste land. Only a third of all the families had access to mains water, and fewer to lavatories. The majority had no sanitary or other facilities whatever. The families included some 6,000 children under 16, few of whom got any regular schooling. Many had none and were growing up illiterate. At the same time unauthorised gipsy encampments on road verges and waste land were frequently insanitary and unsightly and the cause of justified complaints by people living near by.

12. The Government has emphasised that this situation cannot be allowed to continue and that the first need is to provide an adequate number of properly equipped sites on which the gipsies can live in decent conditions and where they can be encouraged to settle down and send their children to school. The main responsibility for ensuring that such sites are provided rests with the local authorities, who are already responsible for the associated planning, welfare and education problems. Part II of the Caravan Sites Act 1968, when it becomes operative, (the date of operation is to be fixed by the Minister under s.17(2) of the Act) will place a duty on the council of every county to provide adequate sites for gipsies residing in or resorting to its area. County district councils will have the duty to equip and run the sites. County borough and London borough councils will have a duty to provide up to 15 pitches, unless exempted by a direction by the Minister. The Minister may, if necessary, direct a council to provide a site or sites. When enough sites are provided in an area he will be able to designate it as one where special powers will be applied to prevent unauthorised camping by gipsies.

13. In choosing a site a county council must consult the district council concerned. The choice, however, should not be governed solely by the numbers of gipsies habitually visiting the particular district since it may be desirable to distribute the sites about the county in order to avoid a large concentration in one place. The availability of houses in the area is not a relevant consideration. Although the true Romany population is now small and "gipsies" embrace various sorts of nomadic people, many of whom earn their living by scrap metal dealing, very few of them have ever been house dwellers. Their need, unlike that of the settled population, is for caravan sites, not houses. Eventually, of course, they may move into houses, but the majority are not yet fitted or willing to do so. The availability of schools in proximity to the proposed site is an important consideration. Most gipsy parents, however, have some form of transport (car or lorry) and arrangements can sometimes be made by the local authority to take the children to school. So "proximity" could reasonably be anything up to two miles. A site should not be next to a substantial area of residential development nor too

196

far from a settled community. Few sites will, however, be entirely suitable and most will give rise to objections of one kind or another. These will often have to be faced. Local objections to a proposal are likely to prove to be unfounded when a well laid out and well run site is established and the people have settled down. Conditions on a properly equipped and supervised site are very different from those on an unauthorised, uncontrolled gipsy encampment with no facilities whatever. The need, which is urgent, and the evils arising from the lack of proper sites, may be the decisive considerations.

14. Gipsy sites will sometimes contain working areas on which the gipsies will store or sort their scrap metal or other material. Alternatively, these activities may be confined to their lorries. Neither of these uses (including the stationing of the lorries, unless they are to be used entirely for towing the caravans) are normally ancillary to the use of the land as a caravan site and must be specifically covered by the terms of the planning permission.

Further information on the subject-matter of this Note can be found in the following publications:

*Caravans as Homes* (HMSO 1959).
*Caravan Parks* (HMSO 1962).
MHLG Circular No. 42/60 *Caravan Sites and Control of Development Act 1960*.
MHLG Circular No. 49/68 *Caravan Sites Act* 1968.
MHLG Circulars Nos. 6/62, 26/66 and 49/68 *Gipsies*.

*Note:* Certain changes have occurred since the 1968 Act became law. In particular, the duty to provide sites now rests on county councils, metropolitan district councils (as from April 1, 1986) and London borough councils. There is no longer any power to be exempted from this duty. The limitation of the duty to provide sites for up to 15 caravans applies to London borough councils and (as from April 1986) metropolitan district councils.

# Circular No. 119/77
# Welsh Office Circular No. 42/77

*Dated December 29, 1977, and issued jointly by the Department of the Environment and the Welsh Office.*

# Caravan Sites and Control of Development Act 1960—Model Standards

1. We are directed by the Secretary of State for the Environment and the Secretary of State for Wales to refer to the model standards for licensed caravan sites in England and Wales specified under the Caravan Sites and Control of Development Act 1960.

### Amendment to the model standards

2. The Secretary of State for the Environment in agreement with the Secretary of State for Wales has now specified a revised model standard on fire precautions in accordance with recommendations of the Joint Fire Prevention Committee of the Central Fire Brigades Advisory Council for England and Wales and for Scotland, and a new standard on electrical installations. Local authorities should have regard to these amended model standards which apply to permanent residential caravan sites and to holiday caravan sites, in deciding what, if any, conditions to attach to a caravan site licence.

### Implementation of the amended model standards

3. Local authorities are reminded that the model standards represent the standards normally to be expected as a matter of good practice on sites which are regularly used by residential or holiday caravans. They are not intended to apply to any other type of caravan site. They should be applied with due regard to the particular circumstances of each case including the physical character of the site, any services or facilities that may already be available within convenient reach and other local conditions.

4. Local authorities should review the conditions attached to existing site licences to determine which, if any, of the amended model standards should apply. Consideration should be given to a carefully phased introduction of any new standard, after consultation with the site owner, the caravan occupiers and the fire authority as appropriate.

### Consultation with fire authorities

5. Where the licensing authority is not also the fire authority, it is most desirable that the latter should be consulted both on the site licence conditions and on arrangements for inspection. Local fire officers should also be given the opportunity to consider whether site entrances and access roads are adequate for their fire fighting appliances.

6. When emergency services are called to a caravan site, valuable time can be saved if the site is readily identifiable. Local authorities may therefore wish to ensure that site owners erect suitable name boards at site entrances.

### Awnings and storage buildings

7. Local authorities should have regard to the effect which canvas awnings and storage buildings may have in reducing the space between caravans, specified in paragraph 1 of the model standards. Any such reduction could increase the risk of a more rapid spread of fire.

# Circular No. 23/83
# Welsh Office Circular No. 32/83

*Dated September 19, 1983, issued jointly by the Department of the Environment and the Welsh Office.*

# Caravan Sites and Control of Development Act 1960

*     *     *

## ANNEX

### Caravan Sites and Control of Development Act 1960, Section 5 Model Standards for Touring Caravan Sites

I. Section 5(6) of the Act provides that the Secretary of State may from time to time specify Model Standards with respect to the lay-out of, and the provision of facilities, services and equipment for, caravan sites or particular types of caravan site; and that in deciding what (if any) conditions to attach to a site licence the local authority shall have regard to any standards so specified. Under Section 5(1)(c) such conditions may regulate the positions in which caravans are stationed for the purposes of human habitation, and the placing or erection at any time when caravans are so stationed, of structures and vehicles of any description whatsoever and of tents.

II. Section 7(1) of the Act provides that on an appeal against any condition of a site licence a magistrates' court, if satisfied (having regard amongst other things to any standards specified by the Secretary of State under Section 5(6)) that a condition is unduly burdensome, may vary or cancel the condition.

III. Section 24, which empowers local authorities to provide caravan sites, provides, in subsection (2), that in exercising their powers under the section the local authority shall have regard to any standards they may have been specified by the Secretary of State under Section 5(6) of the Act.

IV. Section 8(2) of the Local Government (Miscellaneous Provisions) Act, 1982 inserted provisions into Section 5, 8 and 24 of the Caravan Sites and Control of Development Act 1960 requiring local authorities to consult fire authorities when exercising their powers under that Act in relation to the issuing of site licences for caravan sites and the provision of local authority caravan sites. The local authority is now required to consult the fire authority as to the extent to which any model standards relating to fire precautions are appropriate in relation to the site. If the fire authority considers that the standards specified are inappropriate in relation to the site, the local authority is required to consult them as to what conditions relating to fire precautions ought to be attached to the site licence. The local authority is also required to consult the fire authority before altering any condition in a site licence that relates to fire precautions or before themselves providing a caravan site.

V. In pursuance of his powers under Section 5(6) of the Act, the Secretary of State now specifies Model Standards for sites for touring caravans. Although these represent the standards normally to be expected, as a matter of good practice, the Secretary of State does not wish them to be applied to all sites, regardless of the economic and other implications for the site operators, people using the site and public amenity. They should be applied with due regard to the particular circumstances of each case, including the physical character of the site, any services or facilities that may already be available within convenient reach, and other local conditions including the kind of holidays which the site is designed to offer. Where usage is restricted to caravans equipped with their own toilet and washing facilities, communal toilet and washing facilities may not be necessary and lower standards than

199

specified may be desirable in some locations for the avoidance of visually intrusive structures or installations.

VI. These Model Standards are for sites used by touring caravans, by which is meant caravans which are not permanently placed on the site throughout the year or the holiday season. Where a site is used both for touring caravans and for static caravans, the local authority should judge whether to refer to the Revised 1977 Model Standards or to the following Standards according to the predominant use of the site. For example, where static caravans predominate, application of the Revised Model Standards of 1977 will be appropriate. Account should, however, be taken of the fact that significant changes in the nature of the use might warrant the alteration of site licence conditions.

### Caravan Sites and Control of Development Act 1960 Section 5 Model Standards for Touring Caravan Sites 1983

*Density*

1. Site density should not exceed 75 units (caravans or motor caravans) per hectare (30 units per acre) calculated on the basis of the useable area rather than the total site area (*i.e.* excluding crags, lakes, roads, communal services etc.), provided that, where tent camping is also permitted, the maximum number of units stationed on the site at any one time should be reduced by the number of pitches occupied by main tents stationed for human habitation.

2. Where the number of units on the site is to be limited by condition, it may be appropriate to prescribe maxima by references to specified periods so as to permit up to 10 more units during such peak holiday periods as may be agreed between the site licensing authority and the licence holder without the provision of additional facilities, provided that:

(i) the provisions of paragraph 1 above are complied with; and

(ii) the standards relating to spacing, as set out in paragraphs 3–5 below, are complied with.

*Spacing*

3. Every unit should be not less than 6 metres from any other unit in separate family occupation and not less than 3 metres should be permitted between units in any circumstances.

4. Vehicles and other ancillary equipment should be permitted within the 6 metres space between units in separate family occupation but, in order to restrict the spread of fire, there should always be 3 metres clear space within the 6 metres separation.

5. Emergency vehicles should be able to secure access at all times to within 90 metres of any unit on the site.

*Drinking water supply and waste water disposal*

6. There should be an adequate supply of drinking water. Each pitch on a site should be no further than 90 metres from a water tap. At each tap there should be a soakaway or gulley.

7. Waste water disposal points should be provided so that each pitch is no further than 90 metres from a waste water disposal point. The appropriate Water Authority should be consulted about the arrangements for disposal of water likely to be contaminated.

*Toilets: WCs and chemical closets*

8. The scale of provision should be 1 WC and 1 urinal for men and 2 WCs for women per 30 pitches and their location should be to the satisfaction of the licensing authority. The pro rata scale can be reduced where sites have over 120 pitches (see also paragraph 9 below). Toilets may not be justified where sites have less than 10 pitches but on sites with between 10 and 30 pitches at least one WC and 1 urinal for men and 2 WCs for women should be provided.

9. Where the provision of WCs is not feasible or justified entry should be confined to units with their own toilets or chemical closets should be provided.

*Disposal point for chemical closets*

10. Whether or not WCs are provided, a properly designed disposal point for the contents of chemical closets should be provided together with an adjacent adequate supply of water for cleansing containers. The method of disposal will need to be considered in the light of the particular circumstances and should be to the satisfaction of the local authority and the appropriate Water Authority. Where appropriate, the water supply should be clearly labelled as non-potable.

*Washing points*

11. There should be a minimum of 4 wash basins supplied with water per 30 units; 2 each for men and women. They should be adjacent to the toilets.

*Hot water: Showers*

12. Showers should not be obligatory on sites with less than 70 pitches. If showers are required, provision should be on the basis of 1 shower per 25 pitches and hot water should be available.

*Disabled persons*

13. Particular consideration should be given to the needs of the disabled in the provision made for water points, toilets, washing points and showers.

*Electrical installations*

14. Where there is an electrical installation other than Electricity Board works and circuits subject to Regulations under Section 60 of the Electricity Act 1947, it should be installed to the requirements of the Institution of Electrical Engineers' Regulations for Electrical Installations (the IEE Wiring Regulations) for the time being in force and, where appropriate, to the standard acceptable for the Electricity (Overhead Lines) Regulations 1970, S.I. 1970 No. 1355. Any installation should be maintained in such a way as to prevent danger as far as reasonably practicable and should be periodically

inspected and tested by a competent person in accordance with the IEE Wiring Regulations.

*Refuse disposal*

15. Adequate provision should be made for the storage, collection and disposal of refuse. (It is expected that site operators should normally be able to meet their responsibilities by making arrangements with the local authority.)

*Fire precautions*

16. No unit should be further than 90 metres from a fire point. At each point there should be two water (gas expelled) extinguishers each of 10 litres capacity and complying with British Standard 5423:1980 together with a means of raising the alarm in the event of fire (*e.g.* a manually operated sounder, gong or hand operated siren). All fire fighting equipment susceptible to damage by frost should be suitably protected.

17. Wherever there is a likelihood of fire spreading due to vegetation catching fire, suitable beaters, of the type used by the Forestry Commission, should also be provided at each fire point.

18. The fire points should be clearly marked and easily accessible. All firefighting equipment should be maintained in working order and kept available for use and for inspection by the licensing authority.

19. Each fire point should exhibit a conspicuous notice indicating the action to be taken in case of fire and the location of the nearest telephone. The notice should include the following:

On discovering fire
1. Raise the alarm
2. Ensure the affected unit is evacuated
3. Call the Fire Brigade (the nearest telephone is sited . . . )
4. If practicable, attack the fire using the firefighting equipment provided.

*Liquefied Petroleum Gas*

20. Arrangements for the storage of Liquefied Petroleum Gas (LPG) on the site should be in accordance with the current national Code of Practice and regulations.

*Site notices*

21. A sign indicating the name of the site should be displayed at the site entrance.

22. Notices should be displayed prominently on the site indicating the action to be taken in the event of an emergency and shown where the police, fire brigade, ambulance, and local doctors can be contacted, and the location of the nearest public telephone. Where practicable a telephone should be provided on the site and the full address of the site should be displayed near the telephone.

23. At sites subject to flood risk, warning notices should be displayed giving advice about the operation of the flood warning system.

24. At sites with overhead electric lines, warning notices should be dis-

played on the supports for the lines and at the site entrance. Where appropriate, these should warn against the danger of contact between the lines and the masts of yachts or dinghies.

25. A copy of the site licence with its conditions should be displayed prominently on the site.

# Index